Misunderstanding Freud

Misunderstanding Freud

Arnold Goldberg

Edited by Fred Busch
A JAPA Book

OTHER

Other Press
New York

Permission to reprint previously published chapters is gratefully acknowledged:
Chapter 2, "Gaps, Barriers, and Splits," © 2000 *Journal of NeuroPsychoanalysis* 2(1).
Chapter 5, "Enactment as Understanding and as Misunderstanding," © 2003 *Journal of the American Psychoanalytic Association* 50(3):869–883.
Chapter 11, "Postmodern Psychoanalysis," © 2000 Institute of Psychoanalysis, London, UK.
Chapter 12, "Me and Max," © 2001 *The Psychoanalytic Quarterly* 70(1):117–130.

Production Editor: Robert D. Hack

This book was set in 11 pt. Goudy by Alpha Graphics of Pittsfield, NH.

10 9 8 7 6 5 4 3 2 1

Library of Congress Cataloging-in-Publication Data

Goldberg, Arnold, 1929-
    Misunderstanding Freud / by Arnold Goldberg.
        p. cm.
    Includes bibliographical references and index.
    ISBN 1-59051-112-3 (alk. paper)
    1. Psychoanalysis. 2. Freud, Sigmund, 1856–1939. 3. Self psychology.
4. Kohut, Heinz. I. Title.

    BF173 .G59 2004
    150.19'52—dc22

                                                                            2003023132

To Sarah and Andrew

Contents

Part III: From Interpretation to a Place for the Mind

Part IV: No Single Answer

Appendix

Acknowledgments

I owe special thanks to Drs. Arnold Richards and Bonnie Litowitz for the encouragement and advice that they offered to pursue and complete this book. Of course I owe them as well for much, much more. My debt to my family is equally broad and deep. Ms. Chris Susman has given her usual and unusual help in seeing this book to its final form. Dr. Fred Busch is the perfect editor who is always positive and supportive. My year at the University of Chicago was arranged by Dr. Susan Fisher and Dr. Herman Sinaiko, and gave me the opportunity to read some of the books that inspired me to grapple with the ideas offered here.

Introduction

Psychoanalysis is not so simple. That simple fact has not stopped men and women from trying to simplify it, and those efforts regularly and fortunately reveal the fault lines that result from any oversimplification. One such effort is that of reducing psychoanalysis to neuroscience and so, rather conveniently, eliminating it entirely. Things can't get much simpler than that. Another effort at simplification is the redescribing of psychoanalysis as primarily a study of relationships, a sort of complicated inquiry into the ways people either do or do not get along with one another. The appeal of that pursuit is to common sense and so it is of a quite different nature than the reduction to neurophysiology, inasmuch as it seems more akin to everyday living. The focus on relationships may not be quite as simple, but it surely is much more familiar than that of brain studies. However, that familiarity may come at the cost of losing some significant parts of psychoanalysis.

Psychoanalysis seems to defy these and other efforts to package it neatly. Its inherent complexity causes some to abandon it entirely, others to focus on one or another aspect of psychoanalysis while claiming it to be the whole story, and still others to embrace its fundamental inexhaustibility. This book belongs to the ranks of the last. The claim being advanced here, however, *is* a simple one: it is that psychoanalysis is the in-depth study of understanding and its intellectual partner, misunderstanding. And more often than not things cannot get much more complex than that.

This book is an outgrowth of my personal worry about the complex state of psychoanalysis that for me was initiated by the opening up of analysis offered by Heinz Kohut and self psychology. From the start, I knew that self psychology was important and fruitful and, from the start, it seemed to make things more complicated for some people and paradoxically much simpler for others. If one takes a step back from this observation and asks about this state, or merely worries about it, it soon appears to take its place as being among the regular and expectable repetitive themes in the history of the entire field. Every new idea upsets the apple cart and leads to a tendency to move in two directions for a solution, so that, it is all much too diverse to encompass in a single uniformity *or* it all boils down to just this (or that) particular aspect. This dual development inevitably results in another sort of problem in which semi-isolated arenas of theory and practice appear. These insulated islands occasionally endorse efforts at unity or at least a sharing of information at conferences devoted to ecumenical efforts, or else regularly burst out into depreciation and hostility to other points of view. So I watched as self psychology was either elevated to its place as the single answer to all maladies or else was trashed as a hokey form of love-thy-neighbor indulgence. Both extremes manage to cheapen the field while also drawing it into discussions that are more political than scientific. I wondered why.

One answer to this personal bewilderment of mine came with the recognition that all of us want some single answer that would cover a multitude of problems—a sort of all-purpose theory. Another answer seemed to lie in observing the many dualities that we live by, and that seem to haunt our field. These are the familiar ones of mind versus brain, speech versus action, internal versus external, and form versus content. Once we have accepted either the search for a unified theory or those inevitable and unshakable dualisms, we become locked into a process of inquiry that may turn out to be a straitjacket of confusion. Nevertheless, answers to these problems are available, and they make up the core of this book. The first has to do with pluralism and will be one theme in this book. The second has to do with ridding or relieving ourselves of these dualisms. This resolution is not the familiar "both-and" that is so often given as a response to such oppositions as mind versus brain, or verbal versus nonverbal, and many others. Rather it is an activity that subsumes them both. It is interpretation that leads to understanding. That last word was the common thread that allowed for a unification, one that corresponded to our search for a way out of this sea of competing voices all claiming different eternal truths while deaf to the claims of others of equal supposed merit.

The single and most salient fact about self psychology that for me joined it with all of psychoanalysis was its helpfulness in the understanding of others. But since this could well be true of Kleinian or Lacanian or any other brand-name analysis, it seemed fair to see them all as aids to understanding, and so one had to move to investigate that human phenomenon. During the course of such an inquiry, I was fortunate enough to take a course on Heidegger and psychoanalysis given by Irad Kimhi, a scholar who practiced the very sort of teaching that both Kohut and Heidegger seemed to offer, that is, one that opened up more of the world to one's eyes. I refer the interested reader to my Appendix about Heidegger and Kohut to understand more about the affinity of these two men and what the connection of their ideas meant to me. Suffice it to say that this book has allowed me to pursue my worry about the reception of new ideas by way of my own focus on the single issue: misunderstanding and understanding as the core of human connectivity. I make no attempt here to explain either of these two men, only their common vision and what it led to for me. And surely I am guilty of introducing a new dualism while I proceed to discount or dismiss so many that are dear to psychoanalysis.

The first chapter has to do with our misunderstanding of Sigmund Freud, the founder of psychoanalysis and perhaps the most outstanding example of a person simultaneously adored and abhorred. I take this as paradigmatic of what the extremes of understanding and misunderstanding may do to us. Misunderstanding can be a shock to the system only relieved by the peace of understanding. What Freud did was essentially to increase the valence of each of these points. He insisted that we regularly misunderstand the common facets of human life that cleverly conceal the unconscious, while he showed us how to overcome this and come to understanding by way of deciphering the unconscious. Alas, he is regularly misunderstood, and perhaps no more so than by those who would relegate him to the dualist trash-heap by reducing analysis to a sort of monist study that replaces the mind with the brain.

Chapter 2 directly confronts this misdirection of psychoanalysis into the area of neurophysiology by insisting that the two fields of depth psychology and brain studies are conceptually distinct. The reduction of one to the other is thus not a matter requiring time and effort. Rather it is an uncrossable divide. The pursuit of the eventual elimination of depth psychology exemplifies today's latest and best-accepted exercise of the misunderstanding of Freud. This chapter also illustrates the misconception of considering that our thinking operates in linear terms, and thus takes up our unrealizable hope to one day cross that uncrossable divide in order to arrive at a final answer. We soon realize that the problem may be in that very search for epistemic unification, for the one-size-fits-all resolution (Hanig and Stark 2001). Discussing the effort to cross the divide and to unite domains that cannot and should not be joined serves to highlight a host of problems that plague our field.

Once the claims of neuroscience are put to rest, we reach the central concept of the book, essentially set forth in Chapter 3, which posits psychoanalysis as best seen as a psychology that is devoted to understanding. The struggle in the scientific community over the optimal position for psychoanalysis is as old as the field itself and is a topic much more actively debated in the years before the advent of neurobiological popularity. In those bygone years, one of the basic texts demonstrating the controversy was that of Heinz Hartmann (1927) who urged us, in his essay "Understanding and Explanation," *not* to be seduced into getting unscientific about psychoanalysis or to let it be diminished as an understanding psychology and so be led astray. This chapter takes up just that warned-against position and claims that understanding restores, retains, and advances psychoanalysis. It announces a hope for understanding as the linchpin of psychoanalysis.

Once the centerpiece of the book is clear, the next section, in Part II, seeks to explain more precisely just how understanding is achieved, as well as why it often fails. In Chapter 4 I demonstrate the limited value of the contributions of brain studies to the operation of understanding. Some cases are illustrated here, and they are those that allow us to see the limits of one person's capacity to understand another, limits that are imposed not solely by the existence of psychological barriers but also by neurobiological ones. This should not be seen as contradicting my insistence upon nonreductionism, but rather as a proper border or boundary making the extent and area of our psychological inquiry; that is, the limits of our competence as psychoanalysts. Neurophysiology can be a partner to the pursuit of understanding but cannot replace it. Partners need not marry.

The following Chapter 5 on enactment is designed to move us away from the usual practice of concentrating on verbal exchanges and on to a realization that a much wider net must be cast for us to begin to consider all manner of signs, here employing the science of semiotics as the underpinning for understanding. Analysts have routinely sought to segregate and even denigrate action as a lesser or more primitive form of communication and have tried to bring everything back to the language of words. However, action in analysis is but another form of communication that needs to be understood. One result of this perspective is to open us up to the limitless possibilities of understanding.

In analysis, the actions that occur between patient and analyst can also be considered in a purely psychoeconomic sense. Chapter 6 on form and content is primarily clinical, and focuses on a special kind of communication that occurs in treatment. This is one based on the overall pattern of conduct that is revealed in the particular manner or pattern of behavior elicited by the patient. These forms or patterns demand interpretations that are different from the usual ones intended to reveal unconscious content, and offer counterexamples to another claim, one that sometimes aims to reduce treatment to the construction of a narrative—yet another attempt at reduction. The uniqueness of the interpretations considered in this chapter creates an apt preface to Part III, which introduces interpretation as the bridge between misunderstanding and understanding.

There is another, or perhaps companion, core element of this book, that of interpretation. I have tried throughout the book to emphasize some of the fundamentals of hermeneutics and the hermeneutic circle. I am indebted to Martin Heidegger for this particular treatment of hermeneutics, and here merely wish to emphasize that there need be no more controversy about its place in psychoanalysis than in all of science. The inexhaustibility of interpretation is the key to the multiplicity of theoretical positions in psychoanalysis, and it needs to be seen as both valuable and inevitable. If this is accepted, we can come to recognize that there is no need to aim for a single theoretical approach that will be the definitive one, and that pluralism may well be the proper state in which analysis will flourish.

Interpretation leads to meaning, and "the opening to the world" (a phrase borrowed from Heidegger) allows us to see meaning as not residing in the brain or within the skull, but as a construction of a mind that includes others in its scope. Once we move away from the idea of self-contained minds or persons, we are able to visualize a different sort of connection between persons or selves, and to see us all as partially formed and maintained by others. This movement is best seen in the plea expressed here to rid ourselves of the representational theory of the mind. Perhaps no other basic tenet of psychoanalysis has been more casually adopted than the idea that the world we live in is somehow transposed to one that lives within us. The resulting theoretical doctrine has lulled generations of analysts into thinking that they are explaining something. In fact what is more likely is that such explanations lead to an unfortunate disengagement of the person from the world. It makes us spectators rather than actors. Representation as a theory of internal objects costs us far more than it offers.

Part IV offers the conclusion, which is contained within the concept of the inexhaustibility of interpretation. Rather than this or that interpretation leading us to one or more definitive answers, the inexhaustibility of interpretation opens us to a plethora of possibilities. Just as there are many ways to gain understanding, and each such way is a product of individuals with different histories living at different times, so too must psychoanalysis itself become inexhaustible and open to multitudes of meanings. We have all been participants in an indoctrination, one that claims that there is something fundamental about the unconscious and that Freud showed us what that was. Another viewpoint is that there are endless possibilities in the unconscious, and Freud merely opened a door to them.

There is little doubt that many people have become disenchanted with Freud and psychoanalysis. The fault may lie with our original enchantment, one that seemed to promise us final and definitive answers. For awhile, we did seem to achieve that, and psychoanalysis flourished with that achievement. But we soon came upon questions that we could not readily and easily answer, and there arose a series of alternative possibilities, leading everywhere, from those who claimed fidelity to Freud to those who allowed for deviations from Freud, and on to those who dispensed with him for the most part while claiming a new psychoanalysis. This is as it should be. We need to allow ourselves to be persuaded, to change our minds, to try out a new interpretation. We do not understand things once and for all. Understanding is endless. It is the essence of living.

One must continually struggle to make a brief for pluralism, for allowing multiple truths or multiple renditions of what surely seems to be a single world. But history has taught us that we must be prepared to recognize today's truth as tomorrow's folly. If we accept the possibility that what Freud discovered in the unconscious was not a static and fixed reservoir called the psyche but was more like a field of unknown and unrealized potentialities, we may be better equipped to see and explain the misunderstanding that accompanies Freud. In a sense, that does make it sound rather simple.

PART ONE

From Misunderstanding to Understanding

Misunderstanding Freud

INTRODUCTION

The title may be misleading. Perhaps it should have been "The Misunderstanding of Freud," so that one reader might see it as a misunderstanding that belonged to Freud; or, quite differently, that another might see it as a chance to learn more about how others misunderstand Freud. Or both. There can be little doubt that a case could be made for each of these possibilities, but it seems that the two cannot be separated from one another. If Freud did not understand something, that would surely impact upon the reader. If, on the other hand, something that Freud said could be seen as valid and true to some of us, it could well be true that others would either misunderstand or disagree. Indeed, misunderstanding could exist on either or even on both sides of the exchange. The defenders of Freud often claim that he is misunderstood. The critics of Freud regularly make the case that he just got things wrong—or, perhaps more kindly, that he did not understand. In truth, not only has that to-and-fro argument been exhausted, but also, for many, it is by now quite exhausting.

A new conversation is in order, one that concerns itself with the nature of our understanding and misunderstanding. We may never be able to resolve the differences that have grown up around what Freud may have said and may have believed, differences that have managed to stir up a century of study and worry, of excitement as well as despair. But resolution may happily elude us, and so lead us to a more proper investigation into the rewards of maintaining an ever-present unsettled state of inquiry.

Everyone misunderstands Freud. I am no exception. Misunderstanding has this inherent wonderful capacity, providing it does not become too severe, of allowing one to stop and to wonder. For some, the emotion of wonder is essential to an aesthetic experience, but it may also go beyond that to be "the hospitality of the mind to newness," and so it becomes the spark of mental activity (Fisher 1999). But just as misunderstanding may be filled with wonder, it regularly and unfortunately eases over into anger and/or dismissal. The ideal setting for misunderstanding, in which it can live and thrive, is within the realm of curiosity: only if one remains there, living and breathing the requisite uncertainty, can one profit from misunderstanding—especially of and about Freud. Whenever you feel that the good doctor is now as clear as a bell, the odds are good that you have shut the door and probably have it wrong as well. However, if you are of a mind to claim either that he is too opaque or simply has nothing to say, you are equally mistaken and have also lost an opportunity. Slipping into certainty and escaping into smugness are the regular routes to places of error. Freud is too meaningful to be dismissed and too complex to be easily grasped. He is best understood and misunderstood in small, digestible, and metabolized doses on the way to a somewhat less severe misunderstanding: a modicum of understanding.

The misunderstandings of Freud range from determining the *what* of his study, that is, the particular area that he talked and wrote about, to the *why* of his work, including the reasons that are employed to explain its significance, and on to the *how* of it, which has to do with the sequences of causes that he offered to make sense of it. At some time or other, everyone gets it a bit wrong. This is as it should be; if the field of inquiry that Freud outlined is of value it must be one where the effort to grow and to change is a constant struggle. Making sense of it all can only be a sometime thing, a momentary resting place until one point or other seems to not quite fit; otherwise one finds an almost automatic and ready explanation that can be applied to everything. The latter can be seen when we claim, for example, that everything psychological is a compromise formation, a resolution of sorts between id, ego, and superego. Here we may be able to be uncompromising for a time and so see clinical material in a certain light, for example, as a struggle of opposing forces or opinions. But that word "certain" may carry a dangerous meaning that leads to one knowing things for certain as well. Our once-open eyes gradually become closed to catching sight of other phenomena, and soon this particular view loses its value, as the idea of compromise formation becomes obvious and so needs no more attention. If it is everywhere and boundless, it is nowhere to be independently found. A similar loss of utility can be seen whether one claims that the analyst must operate from a possible position of neutrality or from one that says that all analysis involves some sort of enactment. When we scrutinize the analytic exchange as a series of enactments we are able to notice a host of subtle behaviors that go on between patient and analyst and we see, once more, with a new set of lenses. The ensuing excitement soon turns to routine and the routine loses meaning. Compromise formation and enactment can be argued over or may be categorized into good or bad, minimum or meaningful, and so on. Soon the argument wanes, and these certainties take a back seat. The theory moves on. The crucial point has to do with usefulness, not certitude. *YES*

Complacency about Freud and psychoanalysis comes from a quite natural antipathy toward vagueness and uncertainty. There are also a number of opportunities and occasions within the writing and teaching of psychoanalysts that allow one to settle upon one or another bit of firmament. It is not at all difficult to conclude that all of one's patients are suffering from a single problem; nor is it especially worrisome to see them all as having a multitude of maladies. Since psychoanalysis does not have the good fortune of dealing with the objective reading of numbers or pictures, inasmuch as the neurons of the brain are truly silent (Munz 1999), we are unfortunately both able and willing to settle upon truths that may seem to fly suspiciously close to mere matters of opinion. The claim of certainty is often but a case of successful persuasion. *But now do. Theories Grow?*

And Freud is of no help here. He changed his mind and his models. He flirted with biology and fairy tales and himself realized that his ideas sounded more like the latter than the former. Efforts to make him the one—a biologist (Sulloway)—or the other, a writer of literary tales (Lear)—are fine examples of a pigeonholing that comes from misunderstanding. It is not so much that it is irrelevant whether Freud was scientist or poet as it is dangerous to have to decide. The philosopher Ludwig Wittgenstein claimed that the teachings of Freud made people drunk, and so they did not know how to use them soberly (Bouveresse 1995, p. 11). However, Wittgenstein said the same for his own teaching and he worried over the possibility that it too would one day be as noxious as that of Freud (p. 12). Indeed Bouveresse concludes that Wittgenstein felt that a person who thinks that there is one correct explanation and one correct reason for "the sort of phenomena treated by psychoanalysis" is not someone who is adopting a scientific attitude, but is instead one who is already on the road to producing a mythology. Wittgenstein did believe that all philosophical difficulties *originated* in a sense of conviction, but he argued that one could never rest easily with such certainty. For this great philosopher, all philosophy is "essentially work against oneself" (Wittgenstein 1978). Science, for Wittgenstein, in contrast to philosophy, is an activity subject to empirical control, while mythology is an effort at persuasion that rejects disagreement. Like mythology, psychoanalysis is all-encompassing and imperious and rejects in advance all possibilities of disagreement. Wittgenstein, along with Freud, felt that psychoanalysis could only be rescued from the vagaries of mythology by becoming truly scientific, that is, it could not simply work against itself. Rather it must open itself to outside argument.

PSYCHOANALYSIS AS SCIENCE

Psychoanalysis, as it is understood and practiced today in the United States, is a much different phenomenon than it was fifty or even twenty years ago. It is also equally distinct from what is identified by the same name outside the states, say in Europe and South America. Although many of its adherents study, teach, and claim psychoanalysis to be a monolithic set of ideas and procedures, in truth it is a diverse and heterogeneous bundle of claims and techniques held together by a somewhat vague allegiance to the seminal ideas of Sigmund Freud.

Indeed, periodically even that line of tradition to its founder is given little more than a nod, as to an association that is more historical than ideological. The sometimes futile efforts to draw borders around the field by giving it a definition and a set of established technical procedures more often than not end in acrimony and discord with a resultant further separation and estrangement of one set of beliefs from another. Every thought-provoking issue, ranging from the niceties of the setting such as the frequency, the use of the couch, and the duration of the analyst–patient contact to the more hallowed principles of technique such as free association, the sharing of personal information about the analyst, and even the way to interpret dream material has, at one time or another, come under scrutiny and attack, and either alteration or dismissal. The field is often seen either as a mess, or as a victim of bad science that stands in need of straightening out. All sorts of friends and enemies of psychoanalysis have jumped upon the bandwagon of "true" science and its link to Freudian thought. These fellow-travelers range from those who insist that it is a science (Shevrin 1995) to those that see it as becoming a science to those who feel it need not be a science (Lear 1998), to some who seem not to care very much one way or the other (Michels 1995). The hardiest group, composed of those who oppose all of the former, is composed of those critics of psychoanalysis who see it both as pseudoscience (Crews 1995) and incapable of ever achieving a status worthy of that category deemed a true science (Cioffi 1998, Grünbaum 1984). In perhaps a most telling and pithy statement Cioffi says: "Psychoanalysis is a testimonial science" (Roth 1988, p. 182), thus relegating it to a field only for those who are foolish enough to believe that its adherents and proponents are trustworthy. They are believers rather than investigators and so cannot themselves be believed.

In its struggles over admission to the true scientific community psychoanalysis still continues to bedevil those who are themselves able to feel confident about exactly what a science is supposed to be. In spite of the warning of the philosopher Hilary Putnam (1987), who tells us that the appeal to the scientific method is empty since there is no such thing as *the* scientific method, some still pursue the quest. Others claim that admission as a true science is futile. Some continue to hope (Opatow 1999).

After the expulsion of psychoanalysis from the arena of true science, its easy dismissal can be underscored by simply repositioning it and its

[handwritten margin note: But isn't this the process see p 4 #1]

supposed findings into one or another form of neuroscience. From the gentle wish of Oliver Sacks that the fields of psychoanalysis and neurobiology become congruent and mutually supportive (Roth 1998, p. 234) to Edelman's (1992) peremptory nod to Freud in his dedication, followed by his ultimate dismissal of Freud, on to the complete disregard of Freud by others in the latest efforts toward unifying the mind and the brain (Churchland 1986), we see a march that essentially encourages us simply to forget Freud. He was an historical figure who meant a lot and who certainly ought to be recognized and appreciated now that we are able to do so much more with the problems that preoccupied him. As such he surely has a place, an important place, in history, but he is no longer to be taken seriously inasmuch as we now know that the mind is the brain, and we are much better served focusing on that. It is this debate about psychoanalysis as science or art, along with the position that psychoanalysis is to be ultimately displaced by brain studies, that together encompass the misunderstanding of psychoanalysis. That this debate and this conclusion do not die and cannot be resolved speaks to the likelihood of a continual misunderstanding of just what psychoanalysis really is.

WHAT IT IS: THE UNCONSCIOUS

Freud told us that the unconscious was *what* we are to study. The why and the how of psychoanalysis, to be discussed later, direct our attention toward two areas: first, the reasons offered for claiming that what Freud had to say is important and worthy of consideration; and second, the causes advanced to explain what psychoanalysis is all about. I offer this particular (threefold) categorization of psychoanalysis not so much as a guide to its understanding but more as a map of its misunderstanding. Students of psychoanalysis are less than clear about the central place of the unconscious in our theory, and this fogginess often extends to our knowing and explaining just how it works.

Most of us from Freud on have worried not only over the status of psychoanalysis as a science, but equally as much over its concentration on the makeup or composition of the mind, and its recurrent efforts to join with neurology. In one way or another these worries have made for as much confusion as clarity. If everything that goes on in our mind is a product of rational intelligence and conscious deliberation, then there is no place for a study of the irrational and no reason to posit an unconscious—that is, it is all a matter of thinking straight. Consider the following: I go to my favorite coffee shop for my regular purchase of a morning cup only to find the premises closed because of some electrical problem. Disappointed but not discouraged, I proceed to a competing coffee purveyor, obtain a cup there, and find another regular patron of my own usual shop just ahead of me in line. On the way out he murmurs to me that this shop's coffee is not as good as what he and I are accustomed to. Everything in my day continues in its usual manner with my coffee intake joining in this everyday ordinary pattern until, for some totally inexplicable reason, a sudden movement of my elbow knocks the coffee over onto the floor. As I wipe up the spilled contents of this somewhat alien cup I am surprised to find that I have not much remorse or regret. Rather, I plan to use my next break as a time to try out a new and promising coffee shop down the street, one that I had been considering patronizing at some future date.

Now my knocking over the cup certainly ranks as an accident or a parapraxis of everyday life. One might say that my accident could qualify as belonging to that unfortunate group of never-to-be-explained events (Keller 1999). However, one can easily string together a workable explanation that begins with my disappointment, continues with the disparagement voiced by my fellow coffee consumer, and is further fueled by my wish to have an excuse for a more adventurous cup. It is conjecture, but it makes sense. Yet none of the accidents could qualify as conscious; I would, I believe, never be able to consciously want to knock over the cup. It—the accident—was irrational, defied common sense, and could only be classified as either accidental or crazy. The lure of our making some sense of it is the reason for postulating an unconscious. My irrational plan becomes logical and rational once we assign it to a place (not an area but rather a place of thought) that operates with a different set of ideas and principles. That need for making sense of the senseless is the reason for psychoanalysis. It is not a study of the normal, but rather it is inquiry into the inexplicable. The reasons of the unconscious are unreasonable and so insist upon a new way of approaching the "why."

AGAINST NEURO SCIENCE?

Most if not all of the puzzles and problems of any science that are solvable become slowly transformed by way of explanation into the sensible or the understandable. The unlocking of the manner in which, say, a virus attacks the body and evokes the resulting responses of the immune system is cast as a solution to a problem, one that begins as a mystery that can be made clear. Once solved it can be seen as rational, no matter how undesirable it may also be. Psychoanalysis is a bit different. Its explanations, which depend upon the unconscious, derive their meaning from what is ordinarily felt to be either nonsense or perhaps silly or even downright awful. We easily ascribe a motive to a virus when we feel it aims to replicate itself, and we consider the course of its activity and the accompanying illness as part and parcel of that explanation. The puzzle is solved when we comprehend the motive and the meaning. To apply the same effort to understand why I knocked over my coffee would lead to some sort of contradiction. I clearly had no conscious desire or motive to spill my coffee, while I would be assigned such a wish by a Freudian who could point to the supposed contents of my unconscious. If psychoanalysis is a science, then it appears to be one of contradictions or even of downright nonsense. Each sequence of understanding, my wanting or my not wanting to drink my coffee, individually merits a claim of correctness, but together they are contradictory. We should, however, recognize that the "irrational" intrusion of beliefs that make no sense can also describe those beliefs that spark conceptual revolutions. For Donald Davidson (1980) such mental or irrational causes, those that are not good reasons, explain deviant behavior but also allow for self-improvement and change. All in all, the offering of a reason makes the irrational reasonable and serves as a valid explanation.

Reading the case histories of Freud, one cannot help but see how he dealt with these contradictions, which he felt were an essential aspect of the human psyche. However, there often remains a sense of incompleteness for the reader, a persistent feeling that Freud did not fully understand these patients. For Freud, the inevitable and basic result of these psychic contradictions was an inner conflict. The conflict was categorized in different ways at different times, but it was best represented as a struggle between the psychic agencies he termed the id, ego, and superego. Although these titles were intended only as conveniences for discussion, they were considered to be agencies, inevitably came to be thought of as real, and were often even given personalities. Thus the ego was spoken of as the executive, and the superego was called harsh and punitive. Alas, the need for simplification and clarity became a force for oversimplification and emptiness. A certain mechanistic approach seemed to overtake the study of just what to attribute to the ego and what to the superego, just how to explain how drives became harnessed to action, and especially how knowing right from wrong did not necessarily lead to a proper morality. Whether one added energic qualities such as sexualization and neutralization, subtracted certain areas (as has been suggested with superego lacunae), or even invoked overall qualities to the total system to allow for ego depletion, these were all efforts to retain and maintain conflict as the soul of the theory.

The model of psychic conflict does make sense of some irrational behavior, and so one must respect its utility. However, the case histories of Freud have also been a fertile field for the debunking of the influence of conflicts, inasmuch as they leave a picture of mere clashing psychic forces too much unexplained. Many students of psychoanalysis have pointed to Freud's misunderstanding of these cases, and especially to that of Dora, which probably stands as a prime example of Freud's failure to understand his patient (Ornstein 1993). This case does not so much illustrate a failing of his (later) model about the effects of conflict, as it is representative of Freud at a loss, and yet it serves as a case to which one can return repeatedly in order to search for better and better explanations.

THE WHY: EXPLAINING THE IRRATIONAL

The Dora case is paradigmatic of the misunderstanding that persists in the study of reasons and causes: that is, *why* people do what they do and just what causes them to do so. For most readers there seem to be one or several crucial elements missing in the clinical narratives of Freud, and although this lack is made to order to explain the elaborations of a psyche in conflict, it has also led to the introduction of something else, such as adding a new element either to remedy the deficiency or to offer a new explanation. Each generation of analysts has sought to translate its case histories into "the language of today" (Glenn 1980) while remaining faithful to the fundamental struggle of the irrational unconscious at odds with the rational (in this case) ego. However, there does seem to be one inescapable fact about Dora, inasmuch as it is here that one sees the impact of Freud's presence upon his patient and what thereafter transpired. This crucial element, the transference and all of its variations and elaborations, becomes the underpinning for the *why* of psychoanalytic explanation. We must add to the *what* by giving it a reason for existence. One way that the unconscious is revealed is by way of the transference. In a sense, the unconscious can escape its confinement by way of parapraxes, transference, and dreams. Although my coffee mishap was a parapraxis accomplished in solitude, Freud demonstrated the power of transference in all of his clinical illustrations. It is in the examination of the significance of his presence that Freud illuminated the transference while simultaneously misunderstanding much of what he had found. He concentrated on the conflicts within the mind. And it is in the fuller explication of the unconscious and transference that psychic conflict, standing alone as explanation, appeared wanting. Freud claimed that his patients all contaminated their vision of him because of that insistent pressure of the unconscious, but that explanation always seemed insufficient, since his presence often was not without its own significance; that is, it added something, a something that went beyond mere distortion on the patient's part. Transference goes both ways.

Psychoanalysis since Freud has struggled with making sense of this added factor, inasmuch as the analyst seemed not only to be the receptacle of the patient's psychic products but also functioned as some sort of contributor, and not only the site of distortions but also as the one responsible for adding his or her own distortions. Thus not only does psychoanalysis remain problematic in its status as a science, but also the explanation of its significance routinely extends beyond the individual and his inner psyche to a larger arena: the role of others. Bringing other people into an explanation of psychological behavior allows us to expand beyond the core concept of the unconscious impulse, but it introduced a new sort of problem: that of the other. What to do with him or her while remaining faithful to the isolated psyche and its conflict introduces a problem with many solutions.

CAUSAL EXPLANATION AND THE HIDDEN PERSON

Once psychoanalysts recognized the enlarged scope of their study, that is, saw that it cast a wider net than simply referring to the unconscious, they began to think up new ways to explain what happened, and to ask what are the sequences of causes that best encompass the concerns of psychoanalysis—the *how* it happens. Causal explanation begins in the sciences from what is called the Covering-Law Model developed by Carl Hempel and proceeds to a sharp distinction between the social sciences and the natural sciences articulated by Habermas (1971), who elaborated the claim that causes are more relevant to the natural sciences while reasons are applicable to the social sciences. Miller (1987) goes even further, as he insists that reasons are a form of cause. There can be little doubt that a peculiar form of hybrid explanation has grown over the years to weave together reasons, causes, natural science, and the human sciences. "How" explanations tend to make for stories with characters.

INTERESTING

There have been a number of efforts to properly position the hidden person that Freud discovered. These range from making him or her into a part of the brain to the construction of a dramatic scenario. At the onset it is important for us to recognize these efforts as primarily being aids to understanding rather than as truths of depictions of reality. Sometimes they work, sometimes they seem reasonable, often they seduce us into thinking that they are more than the workable tools that they should be.

YES

The philosopher Owen Flanagan, in a book (2000) claimed on its cover to be a model of clarity, gives a nice example of this modern mix of metaphors as he writes, "During REM sleep, the cortex must, insofar as it can, work up a story that builds largely on the contents activated by the PGO (pons-geniculate body-occipital lobe) waves. Often these contents are not the building blocks [that] a teller of literal tales would start with. These contents will enter into the dream narrative, but it will be up to the cortex to determine where the image of, for example the Museum of Art, can be fit" (pp. 123–124). This sort of slippage between the activity of a complex brain structure and an act of intention and aim is now a common exercise employed by those who seem uncomfortable with remaining either in psychology or neuroscience. Thus a resolution of their uncertainty is achieved by the employment of a narrative, a story which allows the construction of a causal sequence, one in which mute bits of the brain are given human roles that become justified by reasons. So the cortex can then plan and determine in order to maintain one's scientific credentials. This explanation does follow a sequence of causes, albeit by using two kinds of language: one about theory and one involving personal intentions.

We soon see another extreme of explanation, one that lies outside a narrow vision of the mind and introduces the wider net of others. From the subtle slipping-in of a human force, as illustrated with Flanagan, analytic theory moves on to the person as the central actor in a story.

Mitchell (1988) describes the work of a relational-conflict model as follows: "The analyst discovers himself a coach in a passionate drama involving love and hate, sexuality and murder, intrusion and abandonment, victims and executioners. Whatever path he chooses, he falls into one of the patient's predesigned categories and is experienced by the patient in that way. The struggle is toward a new way of experiencing both himself and the patient, a different way of being with the analysand, in which neither is fused nor detached, seductive nor rejecting, victim nor executioner. The struggle is to find an authentic voice in which to speak to the analysand, a voice more fully one's own, less shaped by the configuration and limited options of the analysand's relational matrix and, in so doing, offering the analysand a chance to broaden and expand the matrix" (p. 295). In this perspective the field of concern has grown beyond the circuitry of the brain, and beyond the transference and its projection onto the analyst, to encompass what is essentially the social field. It now requires a language and vocabulary of relations. It has broken the bounds of pure neurology or pure psychology, and moved like the hybrid model of Flanagan to a sort of story, one of people relating to one another.

Flanagan seems able to make sense of the thought process only by the construction of an old-fashioned homunculus or miniature person who works up a story, while the relational perspective extends this to a drama between persons. Pure neuroscience inevitably misses out on what a person does and feels. Pure psychology flirts with Wittgenstein's worry—that it is merely a sense of conviction without objective proof. The hybrid mixture of brain and person always seems to lead to a secret person living amid all those circuits and synapses. The move to a relational standpoint worries some that the unconscious may be lost. None of these quite satisfies. What is one to do with the hidden person of the transference and his effect on others?

In an extensive and compelling discussion of anthropomorphism, in terms of putting the person into psychoanalysis, Grossman and Simon (1969) trace the history of its effect, from the Vienna Psychoanalytic Society in 1906 to the present day. They compare one position championed by Hartmann, which aimed to free analysis from the metaphor of anthropomorphism, to another that they themselves seem to promote: one that claims that it is unnecessary to purge clinical theory of this form of language. One must recognize that anthropomorphism is defined as the assigning of human qualities to nonhuman things that may range all the way from inanimate Coke machines to animals. Hartmann wished to make it clear that the ego was *not* a person but rather a psychic organization. Only a careful insistence on this sort of cleansing would allow psychoanalysis to ascend to a more scientific place. However, Grossman and Simon point out that introspective and experiential clinical data do seem to be served best with anthropomorphic language. They also feel that "higher-order" explanatory propositions need another language. Thus they seem to rather easily distinguish the experiences of humans who are being handled well with "human" talk, from the functions of the mind that instead require a lexicon of what they term wish, intention, and need. One cannot escape from concluding that the view of the mind offered by these authors is like Flanagan's view of the cortex—that is, it sounds like a person but it is surely not one. The Coke machine does not want to keep our money without giving us our drink—that is just a way of speaking. Yet surely Mitchell would not say that his persons were not persons. They certainly are not metaphors, since in no way is this talk of relations merely an exercise in ascribing human qualities to nonhumans. It is all about humans and, I guess, it is also about minds. We need a more scientific way of talking about the two.

The misunderstandings of Freud and psychoanalysis may be seen in the struggle over the status of psychoanalysis as science, as a cause of concern about the existence and place of the unconscious and transference, and as an ever-present preoccupation for those who would like a neat overarching model of the way things happen in the mind or brain. There is something both haunting and unsettling about the entire field. Enter the postmodern.

A POSTMODERN APPROACH TO MISUNDERSTANDING

Postmodern philosophy, by its very name, followed the modern, a philosophy that was characterized by an insistence on reason and

POSTMODERN:
REASON a
RATIONALITY — WHY a HOW?

rationality. Science was a field in which a rational person could see a logic and find order and so could join with other such rational minds in agreeing on the makeup of the world. The hope was to extend this rationality, one day to encompass and explain all of the mysteries of the world. Psychoanalysis was and is felt by many *not* to qualify as a science both because it insisted upon the irrational as a bona fide object of study and (mainly) because it failed the many requirements of science having to do with predictability and replication. The postmodern approach offered one convenient answer to the critics of the scientific status of psychoanalysis by challenging this insistence on a universal rationality and by claiming that there can be no unification of knowledge. The impossibility of defining what is postmodern (Cilliers 1998, p. 113) presents an opportunity to use it to justify a claim that almost anything goes. Since the postmodern essentially denies the existence of fixed external reference points or checks and balances, it would appear to allow an individual, any individual, to use herself as a reference point. This viewpoint, although popular, does a disservice to Lyotard, who first suggested the postmodern and defined it (Lyotard 1984) as an antidote to the consideration of science as representative of all true knowledge. Lyotard claimed that there are a plurality of explanations or narratives of science rather than one overarching one. The befuddlement of those who struggle over Freud's proper place and position is eliminated if a claim is made for "isolated discourses." There can therefore exist a multitude of correct descriptions of phenomena, and these need not articulate with one another. It seems at times that the many schools or theories that coexist in psychoanalysis illustrate this characteristic of multiplicity.

I LOVE THIS!

For all of psychoanalysis, we turn to pragmatism, which asks that we recognize that we are engaged in multiple conversations that aim to increase our capacities to better make our way in the world. Each of these conversations employs a favored vocabulary. Only the test of effectiveness should cause us to choose one over another. And effectiveness is always relevant to time, place, and consensus. *THERE MUST BE MORE? INTERESTING*

TODAY'S PSYCHOANALYSIS

Although there may be a good deal of disagreement, it does seem to be the case that the differing schools of psychoanalysis help many people, and they seem to do so in roughly equal numbers. To be sure, one particular patient may not profit at all from one approach while doing quite well in another, but no school of treatment that survives can either claim one hundred percent effectiveness or be a complete bust. They all work. None can trumpet its superiority over the other based on track records of cure or improvement or patient appreciation. We presently have no comparable statistics, so we rely on folklore. Therefore the question to be asked is why and how such diverse and even oppositional ways of practice can enjoy relatively equal effectiveness. Unfortunately that question either is not asked or is dismissed. The preferred question is usually how so many thoroughly erroneous or wrong-headed approaches have managed to fool so many people. A good deal of attention is also paid to issues of deviance or difference rather than to those of consensus. We tend to listen to others while marshaling an argument, rather than being open to what may be beneficial for the patient.

Coexisting correct descriptions may not necessarily be distinct, and the coexistence of correct descriptions need not imply complete isolation (Cilliers 1998, p. 115). These are not to be thought of as tiny kingdoms of true facts that exist as separate bastions of scientific study. They do influence one another. The answer to the problem of differing universes of discourse lies in the study of complexity, of the organization of complex, open systems. Complex organizations consist of a large number of elements that interact in nonlinear, nonpredictive ways that are framed under certain descriptions, which in turn are influenced by the position of the observer. Sometimes these different descriptions can be translated into one another, sometimes one can be reduced to another, and sometimes both can be subsumed under one more overarching theory. But not often and not necessarily. It is also true that some particular thing or state of affairs can be spoken about in more than one way. But we must remember that every description is a selection. The translation of a sentence from one language into another is offered as an example of this, but some insist that there is always some sort of compromise in translation, leaving open the possibility that a particular nuance or meaning runs the chance of being lost. Beyond the simplest case of translation there exist a number of more telling difficulties. Translation is a reformulation that is essentially an interpretation. At times the description focuses upon a different area or is initiated from a different perspective; one can describe my coffee incident from the viewpoint of the process of the purchase, or from a consideration of the quality of the coffee, or from my mishap. This difference in focus or perspective consists of more than saying the same thing in different words and so extends to saying different things about the same event. If we move beyond these differences, we often enter an area where the use of a different vocabulary is needed for a more accurate description. The view we have been describing then asks that we be clear as to whether this new set of words is doing more than merely substituting one set of words for another—and is also yielding a new meaning as well. We are regularly and mistakenly led to believe that alternative descriptions are revealing of fresh insights rather than recognizing that they are merely replacing tired language. Some, if not all, of these problems plague psychoanalysis, which at times seems to be saying the same things in different words, while at others seems to be talking about something else. "Human activity is complex and cannot be understood according to one paradigm or model" (Stroll 2000, p. 131). Pluralism may allow us to use many models to aid in understanding others as long as we take care not to lose sight of the essentials of psychoanalytic inquiry, a neglect that regularly visits many efforts toward alternate description. However, although there are many ways to explain how the unconscious manages to exact an influence upon us, the essentials of psychoanalysis must be retained. Our theories and models cannot lose sight of the what, why, and how of the field.

Misunderstanding occurs at crucial points. One theory may be felt to be capable of being reduced to another, or translated from one language into another, or have something to gain from a longed-for membership in a larger establishment of explanation. Often this sort of resolution is neither possible nor desirable. Neuroscience and depth psychology, as well as interpersonal and intersubjective psychology, along with many similar subject headings, all suffer from what has been called a nostalgia for full and complete explanation. However, complexity in a system always entails more possibilities than can be actualized (Cilliers 1998, p. 2) and more explanations than are necessary. When we look at a complex system we can study one or more individual elements, or the interactions between elements, or the overall structure of the organization. We regularly employ different languages for each of these inquiries, and we are naturally reluctant to move from one set of discourse to another. Thus our failure to understand is felt to be the result of a missing piece of knowledge, much like that elusive search for just how the brain produces consciousness. When the goal becomes one of resolving these misunderstandings, it has resulted in a variety of unhappy solutions.

Perhaps a cure to the misunderstanding will lie in freeing ourselves from the confines of the enclosed psyche of Freud and moving to the more open study of the person. Rather than focusing upon the three-fold set of agencies struggling within the mind, we can begin to look at the life of the person in action, all the while taking care not to lose what is essential about psychoanalysis. All the while remembering that there need be no one answer to cover all questions. Lacking one answer, however, need not mean that we lack a common goal. That goal embraces both complexity and pluralism. It is the pursuit of understanding.

PSYCHOANALYSIS AS THE SCIENTIFIC STUDY OF UNDERSTANDING

If you pick up a rock or a piece of wood and examine it carefully, you may be able to discern a number of things about it—mostly physical characteristics like weight and composition, or useful attributes such as holding a door open or being useful to throw at some annoying squirrel—but never would you be moved to say that you understand it. Understanding just does not fit for stones and pieces of wood. So, too, if you examined a mechanism such as a watch or even an automobile you could perhaps claim that you knew or "understood" how it worked, but never that you understood it as a watch or a car. Of course we routinely imbue our machines with human characteristics in an act called anthropomorphization, but essentially what we call understanding, along with its negative companion misunderstanding, is reserved for humans, both singly and in groups. And as much as the word is used and abused it does seem clear that it retains a special status as a connector of human beings.

Looking at the rock or the car also allows us to stand someplace, a locality away from and so neutral toward the examined object. Our position with respect to, let us say, vision is also apart from the object in that our looking does not in any way impact upon the object. Apart from the complications introduced by the Heisenberg principle in physics, most observation of visible objects seems to call for this element of objectivity, of keeping ourselves out of the picture. Once we enter into the picture, as in jiggling the watch or starting the car, we automatically include ourselves, for the moment, in the equation. In doing so, we also bracket the procedure so as to allow us to once again step to the side as a neutral observer.

This sort of objective observation is often attributed to Descartes (1993), who sketched a view of man as a conscious entity connected to material things, and so to others, by his perceptions and judgments. This view is carried forward by most scientific efforts. With the concept of understanding, it joins in the effort to understand how something works or why something does what it does—that is, its function. If we study the brain, for instance, we wish to know the role of some particular area or neuroreceptor and we aim to thereby understand it. However, even that use of the word falls a bit short of what we mean when we say that we understand how another person feels. Imagining the way a neuroreceptor works often involves making up a bit of a story involving humanization. Understanding how another person feels involves an act or fantasy of something akin to role-taking. We do put ourselves in place of another person in our effort to understand him, but that does seem different from our study of rocks and watches and even brains.

Ludwig Wittgenstein (1963) wrote of understanding another person as just that bit of an internal rehearsal of figuring out the action of someone else. He felt that we witnessed behavior and inferred the internal process from that overt behavior.

As a scientific investigator, Sigmund Freud is felt by many to follow in the tradition of Descartes. Yet Freud rather quickly realized the relative impossibility of objectivity and thereafter called attention to the inevitable interference the investigator's presence has upon the observed. His prescription for the solution of this problem was directed to efforts to free the investigator from his bias, which was to be achieved by attention to one's countertransference. The way was now open to the study of the *study*, to the study of the methods by which a person could examine another person with the hope of a purity of vision that might match that of the study of a rock or a watch. All the efforts that were directed to this study posited that the subject or observer investigating the object or the observed remain fully cognizant of the necessary and unavoidable influence of the subject upon the object.

With the introduction of these two entities, subject and object, one could develop a host of possible theoretical devices to better conceptualize and explain the nature of their connection, and to ask just how do we do it. Immanual Kant (1965) told us that our experience is made possible by certain basic conditions or categories or schema that allow us to understand. He thereby claimed an inherent organization or limitation of the mind, one that applied to both rocks and persons. He did, however, insist upon a distinction between an individual's mind and the rest of the world and, in following this basic premise, the psychoanalytic theories that were later developed dealt with the nature of the interaction between subject and object or between self and other. We quickly adopted this initial dualism.

One popular theoretical device of analysts had to do with a separation, the events of the world being seen as external and the events of the individual mind taken as internal. This led to the possibility of transposing aspects of the outside or social phenomena to an internal organization, or vice versa. Here we buy into another dualism. With this sharp distinction between inside and outside, there arose a need to explain how the stuff got back and forth, and so the mechanisms of projection and introjection were postulated. The gain in this portrayal of mental activities was that it permitted an explanation of the lasting influence of another person, an object, upon the subject, the self. The explanation suggested that the internalized object took up permanent residence inside the head of the self. The convenience of this setup allowed for all of the ramifications involving the concept of transference, which is no more than the persistent influence of an internalized presence.

This step away from a concentration upon the internal conditions of the mind of an individual introduces a picture of the interaction between the subject and the object. There are fundamentally two quite different theoretical devices employed here. The first or *interpersonal position* concerns itself more with the exchange of messages between persons. Some interpersonalists remain on this level, which is basically a perspective on social interaction, that is, interaction available to a neutral onlooker. Other interpersonalists join this view with the above-described activity of transposing external doings to the inside of the mind and essentially employ a two-step process of explanation.

In contrast to the interpersonal outlook is that of *intersubjectivity*, which suggests a focus upon the field shared or jointly formed between the two subjects. This field is co-constructed by the participants, and so one should focus upon the contributions of each as influenced by the other. The tendency here is to minimize the individuality of the participants, and the claim is made that it is an advance on the self-selfobject concept, which also effectively reduces or eliminates the sharp distinction between self and object. In fairness to both self psychology and intersubjectivity, it is probably best to see each as quite different.

The philosopher most responsible for the radical shift away from the subject–object dichotomy is Martin Heidegger, and his contribution best highlights the distinction between self psychology and all of the other theoretical tools, including those of intersubjectivity. To be very brief about a rather complex subject, the position Heidegger set out did away with the Cartesian point of view of the separate subject objectively viewing anything outside of itself. Thus, for Heidegger, there is no place for an interpersonal or intersubjective field, since one cannot be seen except as part of the world. Only self psychology joins with him in obliterating the divide between persons.

As we move from the dispassionate, objective stance attributed to Descartes, and to all of science, to a position that insists upon our becoming part of the context of study, we encounter a bevy of complaints along with a variety of suggestions. The complaints are various, with some leveling accusations of the fuzziness of the findings while others claim therapy is nothing more than loving care. The suggestions vary, too: from an insistence that psychoanalysis is an art form, to an assertion that it is some sort of storytelling. It seems we are locked in a dilemma, where we must choose between those who insist that there is a legitimate grounding for science, or be forced into the arms of those who claim that we write fiction.

Can we reconcile Freud's scientific stance, his devotion to objective observation, with a psychoanalysis that has moved to a new view of how we understand others? Can we bring our love affair with brain science and its emphasis on the way the brain works, which sounds very much like how a watch works, to a happier union with the study of human psychology? Is it possible that we have misunderstood Freud because he himself misunderstood how one might study the work of understanding itself? If psychoanalysis is devoted to the scientific study of understanding and misunderstanding, then we need to move away from the picture of an investigator objectively examining a subject and approach an inquiry that focuses upon how people connect with one another. To do so, we will turn to the status of the brain sciences and how they cause us to misunderstand psychoanalysis, as it is the first of the dualisms that plague our field, and is also representative of an effort to reach a unified theory to explain everything, an effort that may be doomed to futility (Hanig and Stark 2001).

2

Gaps, Barriers, and Splits: The Psychoanalytic Search for Connection

INTRODUCTION

It is my contention that psychoanalysis makes trouble for itself by assuming a number of problems that need not exist. One such problem is the mind–brain dualism, as seen in the never-ending effort to undo this "world knot." Beyond this dualism lie a host of others that have preoccupied analysts and have led to all sorts of complicated but needless solutions. This chapter introduces us to a present-day preoccupation that may really be an exercise in futility. How shall we think of and talk about the mind? If we join the legions of scholars (Searle 1992) who claim that "the mind is what the brain does," then we enter a problem area, one that questions whether our mind and our brain are one and the same, or are in some way connected, or are perhaps running parallel to one another with no intermediary traffic. Or perhaps mind and brain are brought together in a host of other solutions to that peculiar story and the struggle with sameness that for some reason seems to insist upon difference—if the mind really is nothing but the brain.

We begin the sad tale of the first of the impossible dualisms that beset psychoanalysis and the first of the impossible tasks of attempting a union.

Once we come to some, even temporary, answer to the supposed gap between brain and mind, how shall we then think of the barrier between the unconscious and the conscious and preconscious? Is there really a repression barrier, a sort of wall, that prevents certain forms of thinking from entering into awareness? Is it actually something composed of vectors of energy that serve like an honest-to-goodness police force? Or is it only a convenient metaphor that can be displayed on a blackboard just like that gap in which our neurophysiology becomes our psychology? The lifting of repression is then no more than a bit of magic employed to explain why and how a person feels differently or sees things differently, just as when an area of the brain can be said to contain the ingredients of (say) a social phobia. To be sure, many members of the above-noted scholarly legion would hardly agree with this nonscientific idea about magic. They need to know with more exactness just how a neuron or a bunch of neurons become transformed into a "thought."

And what of splits, of one person said to be halved like Jekyll and Hyde? Of course there is no real division, but how can one mind be two? How can I not know what I am doing? Is that split the same as the gap or the barrier, or is it all just a word game that has no standing in the real world? Is all this geometry merely spatial figures of speech or is it something more?

These questions come together in the now active and even frenzied pursuit aimed at either closing the gap or lifting the barrier or healing the split. Such efforts seem to range from a relatively solid commitment to the reality of these varied types of obstacles, to a connection with a much more romantic version of gaps and barriers and splits as mere imagery with no possible relevance to reality. However, no matter where one places one's hat, the pursuit seems to be a common and uniform one marked by connection and continuity. Psychoanalysis seems not much different from other sciences in its discontent with the lack of a straight line between point *a* and point *b*, and so maintains its own urgent search for the answer to just how *a* manages to become *b*. Where once the field worried mainly about *a* (the unconscious) becoming *b* (the conscious or preconscious), now it seems equally concerned with the gap between neurophysiology and psychology and, perhaps to a lesser extent, with the split between the "two minds" of a single person. One very appealing response to these discontinuities is that of reducing all those mental phenomena to the effects of brain or neuronal connectivity and thereby just erasing them all (Uttal 1998). Is that really a possibility (Sachdev 1999)? We shall start with the gap.

Not all dualisms are alike. Some, like internal–external, seem to have a somewhat peaceful coexistence and a freedom of exchange. Others, like mind–brain, have a more uneasy relationship, with each asserting regular efforts to reduce one to the other and, in this particular case, to proceed to vigorous attempts at elimination so that some (such as Churchland [1986]) would aim to one day be able to achieve "eliminative materialism" and to finally speak only of the brain. My own favorite dualism, misunderstanding and understanding, is different. Because no one champions misunderstanding, its existence creates a universal plea that it be transformed into understanding. It is a dualism that reflects only trouble. One problem for psychoanalysis is to distinguish those difficulties that aid us from those that beset us; and, among the latter, those we can do without. This chapter makes a case for the latter.

THE GAP

Just as throwing a stone against a window will cause it to break, so, too, do we say that the brain and/or its neurophysiological states cause, let us say for example, consciousness. Of course the fragility of the window and the strength of the boy who threw the stone are also able to join the ranks of causes, along with the other boy who dared the perpetrator of the deed and on and on. Most of us like to stop at some point in a list of causes while others of us prefer either a top-down or bottom-up approach. Starting from the brain, the bottommost cause seems to be today's focus on neurotransmitters, while for the mind the topmost would be some folk-psychological explanation. A problem begins to appear when one wishes to connect bottom to top, to form a straight line. Sometimes a connection is achieved by the device of a complex causal network, one that might be a convenient way of handling all of the causes of that broken window. However, such a method regularly involves a struggle over levels that is occasioned by the yearning to reach what is the most fundamental level or ultimate cause. This usually takes the form of what the *real* cause is claimed to be. Here we encounter the *how* question. Of course this is a different "how" question from that of how the unconscious effects consciousness, but this is where confusion often begins.

THE REAL CAUSE

When my television set broke down, the repairman studied the inner workings of the apparatus, while he took little note of the picture save to judge its presence and clarity. For myself I cared only for the contents of the picture, although I knew that it depended upon (was caused by, was a product of) the pixel arrangements broadcast to the screen of my tube. No matter how much I might join my repairman in peering at the pixels, I could not tell the score of the basketball game or the plot of the movie that captured my interest. My repairman, much like a psychopharmacologist, was intent upon fixing the set with no heed of the ongoing game, while I, as the viewer, was equally oblivious of the mystery of the mechanisms inside it, perhaps more like a psychotherapist.

Suddenly a fuse blew. The lights went out, and the TV set was dead. It was clear to both of us that the blackout was caused by an electrical failure, and we both knew that the real cause of the television's ability to operate was electricity. The repairman assured me that he, or someone, knew how this electrical current allowed the set to deliver a picture, that is, he had a neat picture of linear causality. However, I told him that I also could explain how a game of basketball or movie came to be placed on the schedule and how it was decided to play it and just what was happening on my screen. I might also be able to draw a similar line, although in no way could I fit the result of the *game* into any kind of law or set of regular predictive results. Clearly, the game or the news report or whatever it was that managed to be received by my set could not be reduced to those pixels and certainly not to a current of electricity.

At one point, the repairman reported that the red pixels did seem more prominent during a particular part of a game or show. He bet me that he could tell if it was an exciting game just by studying the pixel arrangement on the inside of the tube. This is not strictly realistic, but nevertheless comparable to neuro-imaging such as that seen in a PET (positron emission tomography) scan. However, it allows for a pause, which I will take to allow me to leave my TV analogy and return to the brain, with a promise to return to the problem of ultimate or real causes.

The study of the pixels does have a similarity and so a relevance to the study of our neurons. As noted in the work of Peter Munz (1999), our neurons are silent. Whenever an area of the brain is activated as revealed in a PET scan, it results in some sort of mood or feeling which, in human beings, is mute—it must have language attached to it in order for it to qualify as an expression of any specific quality such as curiosity, or for any specific pathology, such as social phobia. Since we regularly live in a community of like-language users, there is some consensus and agreement in terms of communicating our thoughts and feelings to one another. However the language that is clipped on to this mute mood comes from a different part of the brain. E. Tulving (1983) tells us that the neural engram connects to a verbal label by a process that he terms ecphorization, and that it, the engram, does not itself contain sufficient information to lead to a verbal label. As Munz says, "All PET scans reveal is that at certain times, certain parts of the brain are active and somebody glues words like 'anticipatory fear' to the tomographically identified brain event. The tomography does not contain an expression like 'anticipatory fear'" (p. 8). Indeed the neural events that Searle (1992) says produce mental events are actually biochemical events that do not contain the sort of information that can determine what words to employ (Munz 1999, p. 6). Psychology does consist of words, but the language comes from another part of the brain and, as Saussure (1916) and others have taught us, consists of arbitrary links, so that we have sliding signifiers, meaning that no part of the brain always means something specific. Indeed it is not a matter of information being obtained from the neurons, information that then leads to language; rather, information is added to the neuronal events.

The study of my brain, like the study of the inside of my television, cannot tell me the whole story unless and until I have the words and the language. For TV, this process may begin with the writer of the show. For the mind it begins with the world in which I live. To say that the mind *is* what the brain *does* is also to say that the show *is* what is on TV. Both are right, but both are also wrong, since there is also much more. That leads us back to our question about causes and to our effort to close the gap between the inside and the outside of the tube.

All the explanations we offer and claim as causal originate from our own particular purposes in providing such specific causal explanations. Thus the people at the electric company claim that their amperage is what fundamentally causes my TV to operate, while the writer of the dramatic show claims his or her own work as the initiator of the process. There is no show without the writer or creator, but the same is true for many other points along the process. It is surely a fact that electricity, a working TV, a signal being sent from the studio, and a script to be read by the actors are all necessary. These are all facts. The most significant point to recognize is that facts do not compete for causal space (Steward 1997). As Steward so aptly tells us,

> There is no problem about holding simultaneously both: (1) the fact that I believe it was raining was causally relevant to the fact that I picked up an umbrella as I left the house, and (2) the fact that neurons N1–N100 fired was causally relevant to that same fact; since it is true, presumably, both that I wouldn't have picked up the umbrella if I hadn't thought it was raining *and* that I wouldn't have picked it up if neurons N1–N100 hadn't fired. . . . It is just not true that there is no room for multiple layers of causally relevant facts in the causal explanation of a single effect. [p. 261]

Reducing everything to physics does not make other explanations superfluous. All of these facts rank as causes and none of them erases another. They live in different universes of discourse much as electricity and the story on the TV tube could be said to do.

There is no gap. The very necessary work in understanding neurophysiology will better ascertain the causes of the moods and feelings that become attached to the language created by another part of the brain. That language comes from one's personal life, but the verbal attachments are *not* a lawlike product of the brain. The mind is elusive. The gap is a will-o'-the-wisp. Or, better said, there is a gap but we have invented it in order to return the idea of a sequence of causes.

THE BARRIER

If the mind is so elusive, how can there be a psychology, especially one that posits an unconscious? The silence of the neurons allows one to make many claims for one or another meaning of a particular brain activity. This assignment of meaning, this fixing of words upon those moods and feelings is the beginning of the work of interpretation. The language utilized to say that one is happy or sad, perplexed or alert, is one that offers itself as something to be interpreted and understood. Of course the words that we attach to neuronal activity or serotonin levels are also able to be changed around, but we do feel, perhaps erroneously, that the arbitrariness stops at the brain, while it seems to live on in the mind. The PET scan can indicate what brain area is activated, but only *I* can say if it is the color brown or the feeling of joy. But if we enter this universe of mind talk, are we cut off from the solid base of neuroscience and cast into the vagueness of opinion?

Once let loose in a world of sliding signifiers, all psychology struggles to nail the words down through laws of regularity and prediction or, at least, rules of generality. This search for laws is reflected in the familiar preoccupation of psychoanalysis, and indeed of all psychology, as to whether it can honestly call itself a science. That question is now best sidestepped, since interpretation is true of all of our language, and Mary Hesse (1980) tells us that "all science is metaphorical and unformalizable, and . . . the logic of science is circular interpretation, reinterpretation and self-correction of data in terms of theory, theory in terms of data" (p. 173). Of course, there are all sorts of answers to what has created divisions between natural science and hermeneutics, between objective science and social science. And these naturally lead back to the question of whether the unconscious is real, whether it is a metaphor for handling some psychological material that seems inaccessible, or is simply an imaginary idea that should be eliminated. However, we must remember that we live in language and all language is interpretable.

The essence of hermeneutics, derived from the somewhat murky prose of Martin Heidegger, is clear on one point, and that is that one sees what one is looking for—or, as Heidegger (1946) says, "the interpretation has always already decided . . . upon a definite conceptuality:

it is grounded in a fore-conception" (p. 141). Thus, the analyst knows beforehand what is to be discovered in the unconscious and so searches for it with the aim of getting the patient to see it that way as well. However, once we leave the linear sequence that runs from neurons to language to consciousness, we can also leave the troubled search of Searle (1992) who wants the ontology (what Searle calls the "What it is?") of neurology to match the ontology of the unconscious (p. 172). That is a fruitless effort. Rather, we should focus on the contents of the mind, which range from the accessible to the relatively accessible to the inaccessible. For that we turn to the method of interpretation, and to the way one learns (as a patient) what somebody else (the analyst) knows is there all the time, or to put it a better way, to what the analyst anticipates will be discovered.

THE NEED FOR DISCOURSE

From Socrates to Freud we have seen demonstrations in which one person elicits information from another, information that this *other* would otherwise have insisted was clearly unavailable. In the *Meno*, Plato (1892) describes how Socrates demonstrates that an uneducated boy has a knowledge of geometry. Plato holds that all our knowledge is innate, and that experience is the occasion for the *recollection* of that knowledge. A reading of the *Meno* may suggest that Socrates could indeed be supplying the correct answers to the boy as in his question: "Tell me boy, do you know that a figure like this is a square?" Yet one may also be led to conclude that the boy did clearly seem to manage to know some things as well as struggle to know others. Socrates concludes that one does not require teaching but only needs someone to ask questions. Questioning releases the knowledge.

This position of Socrates bears a striking similarity to that of Freud (1909) who also recognizes the need for another person when he explains that

> In a psychoanalysis the physician always gives his patient . . . the conscious anticipatory ideas by the help of which he is put in a position to recognize and to grasp the unconscious material. For there are some patients who need more of such assistance and some who need less, but there

are none who get through without some of it. . . . Another person must be brought in, and in so far as that other person can be of assistance the neurosis will be curable. [p. 204]

This midwifery of ideas is not one involving the transformation of neurophysiology into psychology, a subject that besets Searle (1992) and other scholars, but rather is an activity that allows an idea to gain recognition. Here is a place for the presence of another, and one that seems not to be solely the transference as originally offered by Freud.

Our concern here is not with the existence of the unconscious or with the correctness of interpretations of the unconscious, or even with the exact contents of the unconscious, all of which are worthwhile issues with which to contend. It is rather a focus upon the idea of a barrier, one that acts to prevent the entrance of unconscious ideation to a state of conscious experience. Such a barrier is said to be composed of forces that prevent the conscious recognition of hidden fantasies and memories, usually those that are offensive and/or repugnant and must be kept locked away. This barrier may be a structure more fanciful than real, because the supposed lifting of repression seems closer to suggestion than to unearthing. No matter, since the person alone cannot undo the barrier.

In the case of the Rat Man, Freud (1909) announces: "At this point I told him that he had now produced the answer we were waiting for" (p. 182). Freud seems to be noting that this answer was lying in some state of hibernation, one that could be undone by way of psychoanalysis. This correct response now could emerge, just as Socrates aided such a breakthrough with his young protégé. However, without the learned assistance of their mentors, neither the Rat Man nor the young boy could ever hope to know if they had "got it right." This seems to qualify less as a barrier and more as a case of an absence of the aid of language. Socrates and Freud supply the language that they know is needed by their students and patients—a form of assistance that is in keeping with the principles of interpretation or of the hermeneutic approach. Heidegger (1946) tells us that the hermeneutic circle is not a vicious circle nor is it a circle where any random kinds of knowledge operate (p. 143). Rather, interpretation contains the three components, called fore-having or relevance, fore-sight or comprehensibility, and foreconception or a definite conception. Together they do not or should not lead to an acknowledgment of what is already known, but should lead to a state of developing possibilities. Indeed the effort of interpretation must be directed toward understanding, and Heidegger claims that interpretation *is* the development of understanding. Thus what Socrates and Freud are doing is enabling the boy to understand geometry and the Rat Man to understand his feelings and wishes about his father. It should be no surprise, then, when the work of one mentor sounds different or strange because a different language is employed. There is no single way in which one may understand oneself, but the supply of workable explanations is not unlimited. Although we may be unable to claim the existence of clear laws within this complex field of understanding, we are not therefore able to claim that all explanations are equal. Interpretation unearths and discloses and so allows understanding. Understanding is individual yet it is not capricious.

Although Socrates claimed that his student *really* knew, and Freud held to the conviction that the material of the unconscious is *really* there, it is clear that each offered something spoken in order to allow their subjects to claim complete knowledge. Freud cautions us that it is not ignorance that his patients suffer from (Freud 1910, p. 225), while Socrates says the same thing. The concept of a barrier seems a less useful possibility, while the act of interpretation as one of uncovering or opening seems more fitting. No matter the choice, the gap between neurons and ideation seems much like the force preventing unconscious ideas from recognition, in that both are equally unhelpful and erroneous. Continuity seems more a matter of connecting different ways of speaking than of building bridges or removing roadblocks. If one person interprets something for another person and thereby discloses to that person what is said to be hidden, this act of interpretation takes place by way of language or a statement. This statement or judgment can be seen either as a matter of fact or a "truth" *or* as a meaningful state for that person. Only the latter opens up a set of possibilities. The production of the "answer" of the Rat Man is really only a beginning to the exploration of what this means for this patient. The barrier of repression is best seen as an inability to understand, to experience. Heidegger (1946) says that there are many intermediary stages between statements of objective things or events and those of "heedful understanding" (p. 148), but these, that is, objective statements and understanding, are essentially opposites, and it is only through discourse that one comes to understanding. In a phrase very apt for all psychoanalysts Heidegger says: "Only he who already understands is able to listen" (p. 154). Thus the necessary ingredient for the disclosing of the unconscious is a relationship—one that enables one to experience—rather than an act of removing an obstacle. However, this is but one ingredient, since understanding requires more than the relationship.

Gadamer (1994) tells us that human beings are incapable of understanding themselves by themselves, and that all attempts to do so—as well as to understand themselves apart from the world—are ill-fated. For religion this added factor is revelation, but for psychoanalysis the way to understanding is that of interpretation or, as Heidegger might say, in interpretation understanding becomes itself. Every understanding is said always to be "underway" and so it never comes completely to a close. The fundamental axiom of hermeneutics is "there is much to say." A certain freedom comes about when one is able to say what one means and when another person is understood. To posit a barrier of repression is to make a static or one-dimensional image of a complex and unpredictable dialogue. Such an image diminishes the possibility of a fuller understanding, a process that is always multilayered.

Ways of speaking about the mind seem to reach their limit of practicality and usefulness when we study a different type of split, the situation in which one person behaves or acts differently at different times, or when a person is characterized as being like two people.

THE VERTICAL SPLIT

If one mind is elusive, then what of two or more of them? From Robert Louis Stevenson's story of Dr. Jekyll and Mr. Hyde, to the film *The Three Faces of Eve*, and on to even wilder tales of multiple personalities, there is a mystery and an intrigue to the idea of more than one person residing in one body as well as in a single brain. Such a lack of unity poses a question, the answer to which requires a description of the particular contexts in which these episodes of a division into two (for a start) come about.

If a perfectly respectable and responsible man tells you that he periodically engages in some behavior that he (and you) find offensive, and he then proceeds to claim that he feels that it is as if it were another person who was involved in that particularly vile business, he is offering you a picture of a person who is vertically split into two. If this person proceeds to say that such behavior is relatively unpredictable and beyond his control, he expands this image of two parallel persons, portraying the difference between them as significant and unbridgeable, perhaps even one of a different variety of gap. This difference is intensified by the abhorrence that this respectable man feels toward that periodically appearing other, inasmuch as he usually wishes to disown that person whenever he (or she) emerges.

The neurological answer to the question of how something unconscious manages to become conscious, and to pass that mythical barrier, is at present an unsettled issue, with responses ranging from a complete dismissal of the question to claims that such an answer can never be achieved (Chalmers 1996). No such mystery attends the problem of the split brain, however, and the preeminent authority, Michael Gazzaniga, claims that one-half of the brain contains "the interpreter"—that hemisphere, usually the left, whose job is to interpret our behavior and our responses—while the other concerns itself mainly with spatial relations (Gazzaniga 1998). He describes an experiment performed on a patient who had a surgical disconnect between the two hemispheres. He showed a picture of a chicken's claw to the left brain and a snow scene to the right. The patient was asked to choose from a set of pictures those that corresponded to the individual pictures shown to each hemisphere, and he chose a shovel with the left hand and a chicken with the right. When asked why, he responded, "Oh, that's simple. The chicken claw goes with the chicken and you need a shovel to clean out the chicken shed." Gazzaniga explains the response by saying that the explanation is entirely from the left hemisphere, which responds with its own sphere of knowledge while ignorant of the snow scene registered in the right hemisphere. He says that the left brain weaves a story to convince itself and others that it is in full control (p. 25). We are reminded here of Owen Flanagan and his own account of the little person in the cortex. Little men or women are regularly called upon to finish off these brain explanations.

The fascination of such stories of split brains is marred by the subtle slippage from brain talk, such as discussing the severed corpus callosum, to mind talk, which situates a little person called "the interpreter" in one side of the brain. This homunculus, ignorant of the input to the other hemisphere, is forced to deal with only limited information, but it can hardly be said to deny or dismiss the activity of the disconnected hemisphere. Ignorance is not disavowal, but it is disavowal and not ignorance that is the essence of the vertical split. Once again there seems to be no way to superimpose the split self of our divided patient onto the anatomical disconnection of Gazzaniga's neurologically impaired one. In this, there is a similarity to the problem of the barrier of repression discussed with reference to Socrates and Freud: the mind that is disconnected owing to a vertical split cannot plead ignorance, but the brain seems quite justified in doing so.

While one could focus upon discourse as a way to cross the barrier between conscious and unconscious content, or could take the silence of the neurons as sufficient reason to dismiss a continuing search for a way to close the gap between neurology and psychology, neither of these options seems to help with the vertical split. Our respectable patient both knows and can speak about his unhappy duality, and might even have different PET scans while living in one or the other persona. But perhaps one aspect of Gazzaniga's research is relevant to our inquiry, one that he describes as "an intriguing idea." He asked his patients how they felt about the right hemisphere making them do things beyond their control. They usually managed to incorporate it into some story like the one noted above. However, the same question put to our vertically split patients evokes a range of dislike and disowning, with only a very rare account or tale intended to justify or explain its occurrence. If we focus our attention in this area, one that reflects a disavowal of reality, we usually can highlight a striking feature of our patients that is far different from those of Gazzaniga's. In its simplest form, our patients do not *understand* their parallel other, while they surely are *not* ignorant of it. They can rarely empathize with the split-off part, and they prefer its obliteration rather than its acceptance. Certainly, at times, each sector may feel that way about the other. This feature of dislike is an essential one in evaluating treatment and also seems to best explain the presence and persistence of the vertical split. We have moved from language to understanding to self-empathy. While the split-brain patient has no *recognition* of that alien part of himself, the vertically split patient has no *room* for it. He recognizes it but wants no part of it.

Moreover, the split that seems to exist in the mind of those divided in a Jekyll and Hyde pattern is misnamed. When one studies such a patient one usually finds not a whole person that has been rent in two, but the presence of a divided set that has never been made whole. The problem is one of integration, and so is the solution. One does not so much heal a split, a figure of speech suggesting an injury, as much as unify a disparate self: a self in need of self-understanding and/or self-empathy.

DISCUSSION

If what we term gaps, barriers, and splits are matters of mere imagery, there surely can be no harm in their use as long as one recognizes that they have no grounding in reality. If, however, the lure of such metaphoric imagery leads many to pursue a course of study and research that is directed along these conceptual lines, then we may be witness to both a waste of talent and a weakening of our own conceptual framework. I should like to briefly point out some of the inherent dangers that lie behind each of these images, all the while recognizing that these images are useful as well as pictorial devices.

The Gap

If one aims to elicit changes in the brain by a psychotherapeutic approach, one must somehow be able to make a claim about a recognition of a corresponding neurological activity, whose detection is simply beyond any presently known scientific capacity. Even the most courageous effort to link neurobiology with personality (Depue and Collins 1999) is presented primarily as a corollary way of explanation; that is, some neurobiology has a theoretical model that can be compared to other models with no causal connection to be claimed (p. 524). To say that psychotherapeutic efforts do change one's PET scan is no different than saying that learning to play the cello does so as well and, quite obviously, so do pharmacologic agents. Brains of depressed people show different scans before and after treatment but, most cogently, they have different lives as well. However, one must be very cautious in claiming a causal link since, as we have said, these facts should not compete with one another. Nor should we equate causes with correlations. Many depressed patients after treatment also wear brighter clothing but correlations of this kind are not regularly causal.

The Barrier

Psychoanalysis, founded upon a concept of the unconscious, has moved from the analyst as midwife to the analyst as coauthor of a narrative (which may or may not need to have a relation to an individual's real history). The first position minimizes the relationship while the second tends to make it everything. This struggle over the proper placement of the analytic or therapeutic relationship leads to extreme positions. There are those who claim the relationship itself is curative, for example, "the patient internalized the relationship with the therapist and thereby was improved." Others explain reactions of the analyst as due to projective identification from the patient and thereby try to reclaim the hallowed neutrality of the analyst. In each of these the unconscious is lost. To base everything upon the relationship moves psychoanalysis to an aspect of social interaction and so ultimately to a diminution of the concept of transference, even to the point of recasting it in a new lexicon (Stolorow and Atwood 1992). To persistently remove the analyst from the dialectic makes for an isolation of certain events as enactments (Chused 1991), as if there could possibly be times in a treatment when the unconscious could operate or express itself without the other. We do best to remember Freud's admonition that begins, "Another person must be brought in."

The Split

Just as Mr. Hyde was heartily disliked by Dr. Jekyll, so it is with most therapists who join with their patients in condemning their misdeeds. When this occurs it regularly leads to a further isolation of the parallel self, which may disappear from the conversation and/or be suppressed through the efforts of both patient and analyst. However, if one takes the stand that there really is "a stranger beside me," then it may be possible to see that neither the embracing nor the dismissal of the other is the answer. Rather, the vertically split patient needs, over time, to integrate that other set of ambitions, goals, and values into a new and unified self. The difference may be subtle, but it becomes striking in those analysts and therapists who are unable to see their own complicity in either encouraging or disliking the wayward other. Seeing a patient's split as real may inhibit one in noting one's own collusion in its persistence, since such a perception tends to consider the parallel self as alien and as something that is not a part of us. For the most part, one fails to help a vertically split patient until and unless one has already allowed that stranger into one's own house. The split is best seen as a failure to integrate rather than an activity of separateness.

CONCLUSION

In the 1920s, when Heisenberg once defended his interpretation of quantum mechanics to Einstein by pointing out that he was simply using Einstein's own method as it had been practiced in the Special Theory, Einstein replied: "Yes, that may be true, but it is nonsense all the same" (Munz 1985, p. 4). We would presume that Einstein knew just how far his theory could take him and just when it became of no further use. What one author claims this remark to mean was that Einstein did not believe in what he was practicing even while practicing it. More to the point is that such uses of models and theories can be as inhibiting as they are helpful.

Neurobiology is an essential field, and its findings can enrich the study of psychology and depth psychology. It is not a replacement, nor could or should the one be reduced to the other. The inaccessibility of the unconscious is a fundamental feature of psychoanalysis. It is neither a place nor a structure, and treating it as such robs *it* of its essence and *us* of its value. Relationships are mere social phenomena without it, while psychoanalysis is itself handicapped by mystifying it to a level of magical exchanges (Bion 1990). The splits in our patients, like the splits in ourselves, enable borders and boundaries to be built and maintained. The true connection for psychoanalysis is neither to close the gap, nor breach the barrier, nor heal the split; it is rather to be open to the world. And so we move now to understanding and how we go about that.

PART TWO

From Understanding
to Enactment
to Interpretation

3

Psychoanalysis as an Understanding Psychology

INTRODUCTION

For those of us who were trained in psychoanalysis during the heyday of Heinz Hartmann, his book of *Essays on Ego Psychology* (1953) had a status and stature that ranked just beneath that of the *Standard Edition*. One of the essays in that book least-read (by myself and my colleagues) was a reprint of Hartmann's early article (1927), "Understanding and Explanation," a paper that seemed to many of us dated and irrelevant because of its critical attack on Dilthey and Jaspers, both of whom were hardly mentioned at all in our curriculum. Yet, if one rereads that essay today, it seems very current as well as very controversial.

Although one may argue whether Hartmann can be said to ever write in a clear and readable manner, this particular essay of his is deceptively complex, and I am not sure if I can easily capture and summarize its content. The main theme seems to be an argument against the restricting of psychoanalysis to understanding per se, something

Hartmann claims is fraught with error and uncertainty. Rather he insists that the theoretical framework of psychoanalysis, one that encompasses the causal issues involving instinctual drives, must be considered and included in order to make for a comprehensive explanation of psychoanalysis. He says that, for psychoanalysis, the experience of the patient (be it of states or processes) is the starting point of scientific work and not, as it is for what is called an understanding psychology, the goal. And he goes on to state that "understanding encounters its limits in two facts of psychic life: in the unconscious life of the mind, and in those processes which are grouped together in the category of 'somatic intrusion'" (p. 389). In this very distinct division of the two problems of an understanding psychology, I think Hartmann foresaw some of the problems of today's psychoanalysis, problems that reflect a bifurcation of our field into a more or less focused concentration on personal conscious experience, or toward a newly reactivated love affair with the soma in the form of brain studies. To be sure, Hartmann's lament concerns the limitations of understanding, while I think today's misfortune is due to the misunderstanding of just what understanding is.

JUST WHAT IS UNDERSTANDING?

Most analysts, along with almost everyone else, claim to know just what understanding is, along with claiming to have a fairly good idea of when they have it and when they don't. Hartmann prefers to say that we understand "meanings," but essentially he wishes to claim that understanding is regularly restricted to descriptions of overt phenomena as opposed to its being an explanation of what must go on beyond description. His critique of phenomenology, or conscious description, leads him directly to a sharp criticism of empathy with all of its baggage of unreliability and impossibility of validation. Today, however, understanding in psychoanalysis is regularly equated by some with the achievement of an empathic connection, an activity by means of which we are thought to be able to capture the experience of another person. And today's sustained empathy has become, for some, the hallmark of proper psychoanalytic technique. The ways of achieving and maintaining such an empathic bond between one person and another have occupied much of recent psychoanalytic and psychotherapeutic training and literature, and the study of the development of empathy and its therapeutic effect has become the centerpiece of much recent analytic work.

Although some philosophers claim that the very phenomenon of understanding is basic to all of humanity as a foundational principle of existence (Heidegger 1946), there has been a good deal of work especially in the cognitive arena to better pinpoint how and when children learn to ascribe motives and meanings to themselves and to others (Rychlak 1997). I think it is important to keep in mind that the attainment of empathy and/or understanding as a psychological capacity is something distinct from how and when that capacity is employed. If, for instance, we understand how a Coke machine works we can claim such cognitive know-how for ourselves. We can even describe the development of that capacity. If we, likewise, understand why a person is sad and tearful we may be equally correct in our empathic comprehension. How we achieved such knowledge depends on both our ability and our correct gathering of the data. It is here, of course, that Hartmann had cause for concern, since he felt that the cognitive wherewithal of such mechanisms as Coke machines could be verified and validated, while that of empathy could not possibly be left to stand on its own. And it is here that psychoanalysts have begun to diverge in their views as to just what could serve as an adequate defense for the successful deployment of empathy. The question then is not so much how we attain the capacity to understand—either machines or men and women—but how we can know when and if we have got it right, and indeed if it is either possible or necessary to worry about that issue at all. More severe critics say it is a colossal affront to human dignity to insist upon an understanding that may be no more than an agreement not to disagree. If it is no more than that, the reputation of empathy is sullied.

Among the many misunderstandings of empathy is that of contrasting it to observation (Meissner 2000). We are always employing a mix of data from both observation and empathy in order to ascertain the psychological state of the other person—as, for example, if we purchase a soft drink from a person who is angry, if we teach a class with a sleepy student in it, or if we give directions to someone who seems unable to comprehend our language. Indeed, all of our human interactions are underscored by empathic data-gathering or observation of a specific sort. In this restricted sense, psychoanalysis is no different from all forms of human communication. Some people are better at reading people than others, and it is simply not true that empathy is inherently unreliable, while only direct observation is trustworthy. It is, however, true that empathy is often a more complex matter than the reading of numbers from a chart or computer screen.

Empathy is misunderstood by others (Grossman 1966) who equate its special role in psychoanalysis with the ordinary employment of empathy. Two factors serve to differentiate the role of empathy in psychoanalysis. The first differentiating point is integral to the foundational tenets of analytic theory, which direct us to notice certain things overlooked or dismissed by nonanalysts. That direction is then coupled with the special sort of interpretations made by analysts, those comments that expose certain phenomena and that are informed by psychoanalytic concepts. The second and more crucial point is that psychoanalysts employ *sustained empathy*, which not only provides different forms of data but also allows for the continual feedback process that is so essential for the realization of the hermeneutic circle.

MISUNDERSTANDING

Putting aside the routine cognitive failures in communication, most psychoanalysts attribute the misunderstandings of a patient as due to transferences that, when interpreted, lead to a better understanding. So too do patients tend to evoke or perhaps induce the misunderstandings of childhood in their analysts, and these occasions become opportunities for further interpretive work as each participant may recognize a joined episode of confusion. In a sense, misunderstanding is inevitable but also essential.

Psychoanalysts regularly attribute a patient's failure to understand as evidence of resistance, and rarely consider that the failure may be a product of a mistake of their own. Also, transferences often tend to make patients more compliant, and it is a common enough occurrence to hear or read of a case that you feel has been thoroughly misunderstood or mishandled from beginning to end, but neverthtless is presented as a success. This brings up another very significant problem that occurs when patients believe that they are understood and/or are in turn understanding their analysts, thanks to some sort of matched fictional scenario. Here psychoanalysis stands full square with those forms of belief system that must depend only on internal coherence and pragmatic features of effectiveness. We simply cannot escape the fact that mutual misunderstanding is not equivalent to clinical failure, anymore than mutual understanding must necessarily lead to success. For the most part we do equate the latter with progress; however, we would do best not to neglect the value of misunderstanding. The decision as to whether we have properly understood ultimately rests on the way we comprehend what we have understood. It is here that we must combine understanding with explanation in order to construct a floor for veridical belief.

EXPLANATION

The complex issue of just what constitutes analytic explanation has certainly haunted psychoanalysis ever since philosophers started to worry about it. Heinz Hartmann was himself a champion of causal explanation, while others have insisted that psychoanalysis is indifferent to the meaning–cause issue (Gardner 1999, p. 496). However, the temptation to look for causes for psychological phenomena, and to go beyond mere description and phenomenology, has never left analysis. Nowhere is this more prevalent and seductive than in the search for what lies *behind* the experience. Such an approach is nicely illustrated by the recent appeal to "procedural memory," which is said to be outside of the realm of conscious or even unconscious experience. Joseph and Anne-Marie Sandler (1998) claim to explain the status of internal objects by a to-and-fro interaction between the experiential and the nonexperiential realms, with the latter being the business of procedural memory (p. 131). This certainly serves as an explanation of some aspect of experience, just as we might well explain procedural memory itself as caused by particular sorts of neurochemical and/or electrical activity. The larger question to be confronted is whether we indeed should explain or even try to explain experience or understanding or empathy by moving to what has been called another universe of discourse, when, for example, "what lies behind," as noted in the previous chapter, is a different area of interest using a different vocabulary.

Is psychoanalytic understanding capable of being explained within psychoanalysis or do we necessarily need to change the subject? Or to put it differently, do we really gain in our understanding of internal objects by situating them in the category of procedural memory? The antidote to the solution offered by the Sandlers and other more radical embracers of nonanalytic territory has been offered to us by hermeneutics.

HERMENEUTICS

Just as phenomenology refers to the manifestations of what presents itself to experience, hermeneutics refers to the interpretive method and stresses the plurality of interpretations associated with the reading of human experience (Changeux and Ricouer 2000, p. 5). It is important to recognize that one cannot oppose hermeneutics and the scientific method as so many naively do (Gedo 1997). Rather, all of our observations are interpreted (Okrent 1988). Therefore, the distinction to be made lies between the interpretation of human experience, and interpretation that is either nonhuman or that falls outside of the experiential or of consciousness, as in the Sandlers' procedural memory. If I may return to Hartmann (1927), it is at this point that he makes it clear that unconscious connections as well as unconscious influences are not experienced and therefore cannot be sympathetically grasped and thus understood by another. (As an aside, the word *Nacherleben* is used by Hartmann to describe the reproducing of someone else's experience as one's own. We could substitute the word empathy as well, since the translation makes them interchangeable.) In relegating the unconscious to the nonexperiential, Hartmann also considers the unconscious as belonging more to the physiological sphere rather than to the mind (p. 390), and so he never really succeeds in separating these two possibilities, although he hopes one day for a link between the two. It seems that Hartmann differs from the Sandlers, who claim that the unconscious is able to be experienced while the nonexperienced or neuropsychological remains truly unknowable (Sandler and Sandler 1998, p. 71).

I think we can now easily see more of the bifurcation that confronts psychoanalysis today. On one side one can go down the road of conscious experience or empathy with a relative neglect of the unconscious (whatever that means). On the other, one can pursue the explanation of mental phenomena in terms of their derivation from one or another nonmental, neurophysiological source or sources. The first is perhaps caricatured a bit in those studies that confine themselves to "the relationship," while the second is openly championed in the hybrid field of neuropsychoanalysis. I believe that they both miss the point of what psychoanalytic understanding is all about. They especially seem to slip away from the arena of understanding that, for psychoanalysis, demands both understanding another as well as the other feeling understood, not to mention considering the critical role played by misunderstanding. The task that Hartmann took on is one that remains with us today, and that is the need to better circumscribe the field of psychoanalysis.

THE DOUBLE HERMENEUTIC

When our faithful Coke machine fails to deliver a product, we interpret this failure either as a mistake of ours in putting in the right coins, or as due to an absence of available soda cans, or possibly another sort of error. The machine is mute and fairly stable. When we listen to a patient we interpret the productions of the patient all the while, in parallel, realizing that the patient is also interpreting us. The latter activity is often, but not always, called transference. We recognize that interpretation goes both ways and that each way may be distorted to some degree. The fact that our patient has a past and language of his own separates him from objects like machines or even brains that can be studied and interpreted in a more or less fixed manner. In contrast, analytic dialogue qualifies as a double hermeneutic, that is, it is bidirectional (Giddens 1976). The back-and-forth between analyst and patient is a circle as each strives to interpret and understand the other. Each participant carries with him a history, a set of beliefs, and a theory to help in understanding the other. This, however, need not be seen as an egalitarian effort, since we assume the theoretical equipment of the analyst is both different and technically superior to that of the patient. Here is where we can incorporate the notion of the unconscious, in that it is a part of the theory the analyst uses to interpret the mind of the patient. The psychoanalyst presumes the existence of the unconscious and proceeds to find what he is looking for. The patient presumes the existence of a transference figure and proceeds to search for it in a manner that resembles what the analyst is doing, but with one exception. The inevitable misunderstandings that emerge are clarified and removed by the interpretations of the analyst. He or she is expert. Indeed, an idealized vision of a psychoanalysis would see all misunderstandings as resulting from patient transferences, which then become dissolved by the interpretations of the analyst. The sequence of understanding → misunderstanding → interpretation → understanding defines and delineates the place or form of psychoanalysis as an understanding psychology. Now to its contents.

CLINICAL CONSIDERATIONS

One lasting memory of mine is of hearing from my analyst, teacher, and supervisor, Therese Benedek, that crying is most often an expression of anger. It is something that I have learned over and over as absolutely true and yet something that I regularly forget. When Hartmann cautions us not to take a patient's presentation at face value, recognizing that certain personality characteristics hide impulses of a quite different sort, he is essentially urging us to be skeptics. Yet my need to see the crying patient as angry is not a product of skepticism as much as it is an effort, over time, of empathic understanding. One moves through layers or levels of such connection with a patient, and yet this is never to be thought of as equivalent to sensitivity or sympathy, or even of a joining of minds. Here is one example:

A middle-aged man comes to treatment after having been arrested for illegal involvement in certain pornographic activity on the Internet. He is a respected businessman, married, and the father of two children. He readily qualifies as a pillar of the community inasmuch as he is active in his church, is a devoted volunteer at several charitable institutions, and has a wide circle of friends who see him as virtuous and responsible. In his initial diagnostic evaluation, he is tearful and remorseful and seemingly unable to account for his misbehavior, which has extended over several years, up to the time that he was trapped in a specific police effort directed at such offenses. I had no doubt that his remorse and guilt were genuine, and he might well have been offered some antidepressant medication by a general psychiatrist had he been seen by one.

Initially one can sketch three areas of concern in terms of being empathic with this patient. The first was his overt remorse and depression over his arrest, the second was what *I* assumed might lie behind his tearfulness, and the third was a puzzle over just what his pornographic pursuits were all about. As to the first, we recognize that the cause of his depression was his arrest. However, in the interest of multiple determinacy one should include the shame of his exposure, the emotional and financial repercussions on his family, and an involved legal process and preoccupation with a possible incarceration. Our literature is filled with case reports of therapists and analysts being sensitive to patients' sadness and crying, up to and including a parallel tearfulness of the analyst (Ogden 1997). That this may sometimes be therapeutic is without question, but particular phenomena of this kind should not be equated with the practice of a depth psychology. Only a sustained empathic approach allows entry into a psychoanalytic explanation of the patient's tearfulness, and that is only accomplished by way of interpretation.

The second task in achieving empathy with this patient was to get in touch with the meaning of his preoccupation with Internet pornography. As those of you who have some experience in the analytic treatment of offenders will know, whether these patients are involved with minor sexual perversions to more serious misbehaviors involving the law, it is often a struggle to properly position oneself in terms of the transgression. For a while, neither of us understood his pornographic preoccupation, which he treated as a foreign part of himself. This material was disavowed rather than repressed, and our mutual approach to it was one of puzzlement. The particular manner in which such split-off material is dealt with is described elsewhere, but the essence of the interpretive work has to do with a transformation of unbearable affective states into more tolerable ones (Goldberg 1999). One striking feature of such experiences is the very specific ability of a therapist to understand and/or be empathic with one form of misbehavior while remaining rather opaque to another. With this particular patient, I found it less difficult to struggle with the moral implications of his behavior than with my own obstacle in comprehending what positive meaning the behavior had for him. Though this may be a more glaring or blatant example of empathic failure, it seems fair to say that something like this happens at some time in every treatment or analysis.

Getting behind my patient's sadness and, at long last, empathizing with his pornographic preoccupations allowed us to reach an even deeper and more profound depression in his psychological makeup. This process, familiar to all analysts, is only achieved by the ongoing interpretive activity by which my understanding of, say, his need to get on the Internet for relief from his dysphoria, is in tandem with his feeling understood, and thus allowing more of his repressed and disavowed mental contents to be revealed and integrated. It is *not* the case that I make an observation from a point outside of the circle of interpretive activity, nor is it sufficient to say that my relationship with him is, in itself, the essence of a cure. More to the point, my own theoretical preconceptions allowed me to uncover the rage that I could, in a word, discover in my patient. I realize that some feel that the very notion of our knowing beforehand what to look for is anathema. I think it is appropriate to once again quote Freud (1909) who said:

> In a psychoanalysis the physician always gives his patient . . . the conscious anticipatory ideas by the help of which he is put in a position to recognize and to group the unconscious material. For there are some patients who need more of such assistance and some who need less, but there are none who get through without some of it. . . . Another person must be brought in, and in so far as that other person can be of assistance the neurosis will be curable. [p. 204]

That is a very succinct summary of the hermeneutic circle in which one person has the foreconception to find what he or she then discovers (Heidegger 1946). And in this process, since this is a double hermeneutic, it is my own recognition of what to find in myself that allows this discovery to be made.

The rage in my patient was understood and explained by me, once again, according to my theoretical predilections. Beyond this point, it is very difficult to claim a validity for one's theory that goes farther than the status of just this mutual understanding. This remains the bedrock of our psychoanalytic science, and efforts to reach beyond it are problematic.

One striking example of this problem of misunderstanding our analytic database is illustrated in an article used to demonstrate how Otto Isakower's description of the analytic instrument can serve as a useful evocative image of the connection between the analyst and the patient. Morton Reiser (1999) uses this model of interaction to demonstrate his explanation of some clinical material. He proposes to explain his interaction with his patient with a description of the information gathered and reassembled in the amygdala and hippocampus, which information is activated when a shared potential evokes similar complexes in both participants. The gap between what really goes on between Reiser and his patient and the neurophysiologic explanation is both enormous and telling. The first—its enormity—is because that sort of neurologic explanation also serves to explain why the two—analyst and patient—smile at one another, smell the same flowers, and bid farewell. It is so true of all human interactions that it becomes an empty exercise. It covers everything. The second—its failing—is because showing how he connects with his patient has no need of a psychoanalytic theory to explain this particular shared meaning. To do so would suggest there was a failure of nerve, as if analytic theory were a sham explanation waiting for the truth. To limit psychoanalysis to some sort of sympathetic resonance and/or to place it in an anatomical area of the brain once again derails us from the goal of a scientific understanding of understanding.

The first empathic union that I experienced with my forlorn patient is a common phenomenon to be explained in many psychologies and may be handled in psychoanalysis with such theoretical tools as projective identification, or trial identification, or a merger state. This resonating state lasts for a variable period of time with many patients, but it was relatively brief with this particular man because of my initial failure to understand his pornographic Internet activity. Without going into details, this was a peculiar perverse preoccupation that few people might readily comprehend. What I want to point to, rather, is the way we as analysts ordinarily explain failures at empathy. Of course, we may claim defense and resistance as obstacles to understanding, but the achievement of a workable union with a patient demands multiple efforts at a match that is always only partially successful. With full credit to my hippocampus and amygdala, I was able at long last to get in touch with what this pornography meant to this man.

Once again, the empathic union that initially connected the two of us was subsequently breached by my own pursuit of what lay behind this particular perversion. My patient experienced my personal restlessness with his state of sadness as a "misunderstanding." This word covers both a failure to initially connect as well as a break in a connection. If we remain at the level of his tearful state, he feels supported and understood and, over time, he becomes less depressed and even less guilty. But misunderstanding is needed to drive the engine of analysis. This, of course, is played out over time in his own very personal misunderstandings of me as a promising parental figure who fails and disappoints. And then one finds the rage that lies behind the disappointment.

With the ultimately more available affective experience that I was looking for, the double hermeneutic is at its apogee. This too may be explained with a variety of theoretical devices and vocabularies, ranging from the wish to destroy the object to narcissistic rage at traumatic de-idealization, and so on. Though these are certainly not interchangeable explanations, they make up the area of our depth psychology in which we live. We would do well to stay inside of it. This sequence of understanding, misunderstanding, and interpretation followed by a new understanding defines the field with no need to reach for a more scientific credibility.

THE UNCONSCIOUS

The other road that Hartmann felt was a threat to psychoanalysis was that of phenomenology, or conscious description. There can be little doubt that there are different ways of interpreting a shared conscious experience, but this should not be equated or confused with the interpreting of that experience with the unconscious in mind. Theories such as intersubjectivity, and interpersonal and/or relational analysis, treat the matter of the unconscious differently. Indeed they seem not to know what to do with it because of its implication of unequal authority, with the analyst as the one who knows. The intersubjective approach moves the area of inquiry to the field between the analyst and patient and claims that each co-constructs that shared field. It is assumed that each participant has his or her unconscious (no matter now the change in definition) as part of this field. The interpersonalist seems less able to pinpoint the presence or absence of the unconscious (Mitchell 1988). The late Stephen Mitchell, who was one of the most articulate spokespersons of the relational perspective, says, "To understand unconscious processes in one's own mind or that of another is to use language in a fashion that actually discovers and creates new experience" (p. 219). And, "The understanding that emerges within the analyst's mind about the patient is embedded in the fluid, interpenetrating mix of their encounter" (p. 219). Here, the unconscious loses its status as a critical aspect of psychoanalysis, since the creation of "new experience" is vulnerable to the same sort of fallacy of generalization as is the assignment of explanation to the hippocampus.

In the efforts these and similar schools make to avoid privileging the analyst's authority and with it his recognition of the unconscious, or the analyst's better hold on reality and with it his recognition of distortion, there is a corresponding push to a more egalitarian view of the shared field or the co-constructed understanding. The problems that result from this aim for equality are twofold. The first has to do with the analyst having to decide when and if this co-constructed or intersubjective field is good or bad. Mitchell (1988) says that he wants his patient to feel safe and/or exhilarated (p. 227). Intersubjectivists also want their patients to be liberated from invariant organizing principles (Stolorow and Atwood 1992). It seems both unrecognized and yet unavoidable that the analyst does decide, and that what constitutes pathology and health are viewed from the eyes of the analyst. Statements such as "psychoanalysis is not a search for the hidden truth about the patient's life, but the emergence, through curiosity and the acceptance of uncertainty, of constructs that may never have been thought before" (Stern 1997, p. 7) are as applicable to an activity like painting or any creative act as to treatment. One cannot escape granting a privilege for the analyst by designating just what he knows that the patient does not. For psychoanalysis, this is the awareness of the unconscious, no matter how the technique may differ among schools.

The second problem has to do with the problem of time. In ordinary relationships, in the here and now, most misunderstandings derive from a lack of knowledge or a lack of clarity. We clear up misunderstanding by better managing the exchange of information. In psychoanalysis, we consider misunderstandings as intrusions from the past, where the past is considered as sequestered in the unconscious. These intrusions take the form of transferences from persons or functions from the past and so this exchange of information must be seen as being conducted along an axis of time. The ongoing hermeneutic circle develops interpretations through and with the foreknowledge of the analyst that he or she is misinterpreted as a figure from the past. Otherwise, the analytic process is indeed a series of "fluid encounters." These may well be ameliorative, but they cannot be a proper area of understanding.

The rage in my patient appeared when he saw me as a replica of the mother who had failed to respond to his childhood feeling of exuberance and specialness. Of course his anger may have emerged in other forms of treatment, although he claimed that he had never before remembered such powerful and hateful passion. And of course his anger could have been explained in a variety of different ways using different words. But essentially I was convinced that his misunderstanding of me as the mother enabled me to understand him and, perhaps more importantly, for him to feel understood.

DISCUSSION

Depth psychology, much like other areas of psychology, has often been thought of as a holding station or place-holder, to be employed only until enough was learned about brain activity to either eliminate the field or else to relegate it to the denigrated category of folk psychology. Ultimately it was to be eliminated or reduced to neurology. Therefore, any effort to see psychoanalysis as a scientific study of understanding seemed from the start to be an oxymoron. Either we could follow one group who explained what was to be known about the amygdala and hippocampus and procedural memory, or we could join up with those who insisted that "the analytic process is profoundly personal and there are many authentic modes of analytic participation" (Mitchell 1988, p. 145). Of course both are right, but in their own way are irrelevant, too. Multiple authenticity does not preclude a coherent theory, and brain physiology need not, indeed should not, compete with psychological explanations. Rather we must recognize that the mind will never be reduced to neurophysiology, and that it can never be understood in depth through conversation, unless we want it to evaporate into a linguistic cloud.

To say that "psychoanalysis works by modifying procedures *rather than* creating new ideas" (Fonagy 2000, p. 923) is to offer a fine example of what I call moving away from the mind to the brain. But the brain does not think, and to say that procedural memory explains ideation is exercising what Ricoeur calls "semantic amalgamations" (Changeux and Ricoeur 2000, p. 14). If I were to add that the activity involved in psychoanalysis involves "highly localized stimulation which elicits the sprouting of felopodia or thread-like protrusions which later convert to dendritic spines which require the presence of NMPA receptors" (Quartz and Synowski 2000, p. 785), I would quickly be laughed out of the club. But that is a very accurate present-day explanation that nicely illustrates semantic dualism. The issue is surely not the correctness of an explanation, which is not presently in dispute. Rather it is the relevance of such explanations for analysts, meaning that it is a question of whether or not they belong in the language of psychoanalysis.

The championing of experience in a developmental or growth-promoting role in treatment lies at the other end of the spectrum from neurophysiology, but seems equally alienated from what is usually thought of as interpretive activity. All interpretation, even apart from the goal of insight, leads to seeing things differently if not necessarily correctly. Since interpretation can be said to include any sort of response to a message or a perception, we readily recognize that psychoanalytic interpretation is of a quite distinct kind, focused in both its causal aim and its interest in unconscious activity. Of course, much that goes on in psychoanalysis is not transference, but it may also be said that much of what goes on in analysis is not psychoanalysis. To make a claim that the experience in the relationship has, in itself, ameliorative or curative powers lifts us away from understanding to areas of intervention such as reparenting, companionship, corrective emotional experiences, and so on. None of this is to be condemned, but it may be seen as falling outside of a science of understanding. Indeed, there is a paucity of explanatory weight in most relational technique, aside from the rather controversial issues surrounding attachment theory. Even there, the explanations offered are in the direction of clarifying developmental achievement, although no clear reason is given why this may not be accomplished better in psychoanalysis, or how it is brought about at all. Again, this is not meant to diminish the efficacy of relational technique so much as to question its place in the science of psychoanalysis.

SUMMARY AND CONCLUSIONS

To say that Hartmann was wrong, and to say that psychoanalysis is indeed an understanding psychology with no need to move either into neurophysiology or social psychology, is essentially to draw a line around the field and to claim that its explanations stand or fall on the basis of coherence and usefulness. It is not to say that any of the explanatory theory that falls outside of this circle is false, nor is it to say that it is valueless. Rather it is to reclaim the proper province of psychoanalysis. Such a reclamation directs our attention to what analysts do. We work within the circle of understanding, and we have a specialized technique to aid our understanding of patients who in turn are led to feel understood.

To describe this specialized technique, I offer the sequence of understanding, misunderstanding, interpretation, and further understanding, formed against the background of transference and countertransference. Although there are and will continue to be controversies with regard to the circle of understanding as to its accomplishment and validation, movement outside this specialized technique is to be avoided. I suggest that the avoidance is necessary rather than optional, because otherwise the siren song of neurophysiology makes us feel that the truth lies elsewhere, while the lure of concentrating on the relationship as such asks us to believe that there is no truth.

4

Understanding Others

Watching the lady in the supermarket lift up a plastic container filled with orange jelly candies, slip one into her mouth, one into the hands of her little boy, and one directly into the open mouth of her friend made me feel that I wanted to do much the same, while at the same time I was registering my outrage at the openness of her offense. I tried to catch her eye to evoke a feeling, at a minimum, of mild embarrassment so that she would know that her thievery was not a private matter. She, however, continued down the aisles, and I stood there with a peculiar combination of my feelings: wanting to do wrong along with feeling proud about not succumbing to the wish. Indeed these two feelings seemed to run along in tandem, with the former held in check by my insisting that I knew how she must have felt, while the latter proclaimed that I certainly was not she. I had no doubt that I understood her and her feeling of entitlement. I just wanted her to feel bad.

To know what it is to be a thief may come easily to many of us. I, for one, remember stealing trinkets from our local five-and-dime store when I was a boy, and I am quite sure that I felt not a moment's guilt until my parents caught me stealing some coins from them. Once apprehended, I never stole again, although the temptation to take a newspaper from an open stand without payment was certainly with me, proven by the fact that I always wanted someone to see me leaving the required amount in full view. So for me, getting away with it or not appeared to be one of the necessary components to this complex psychological state of doing wrong. Somewhere, I, for one, seemed to require some recognition of the fact that I was doing the right thing. Someone had to know it, and that someone was not always me.

In any assessment of wrong, sinfulness, and evil, the list of what qualifies as a misdeed is not easily drawn up. The theft of a piece of candy is certainly of a different order than (say) the abuse of an animal, and that in turn is strikingly different from the torture of another human being. The distance or diffuseness of the injured party may allow some behavior to be rationalized away with the claim that "no one is being hurt," as in the theft of that piece of candy, or the close cousin of that defense, which takes the form of "it can't amount to much." Carrying around the standards of society in our psyches provides us with a convenient map for the negotiation of moral behavior. Indeed it seems that such a map is constructed on the basis of the prohibitions of some of our own desires, those that we know about, either from experience or from imagination. Temptation or desire is the source of the code of propriety according to some, but not to others. Aristotle felt that our ethics were a part of our "practical wisdom" or, in modern parlance, the built-in programs of our mind that let us find our way in the world. Our ordinary upbringing brings the demands of ethics into view (McDowell 1994, p. 83). And so one would suppose that faulty or neglectful or deviant upbringing would not do the requisite job of creating a properly moral individual. The line of development that draws the moral map travels from someone telling you and showing you what is right or wrong, to your knowing it yourself, to your feeling good about doing right. The problem occurs when the line deviates to that of your feeling good about doing what is wrong and proceeds back to not even knowing what qualifies as wrong. Is it possible not to know good from evil?

In truth the question of what needs to happen for one person to understand how another one could enjoy doing what he knows to be wrong is rather easily answered if the person who is offended can be removed from the equation. The supermarket, for example, is so anonymous that one can readily dismiss the question of harm from consideration. Indeed this may be the most crucial issue in an explanation of how and why people seem able to do things that seem horrible or unspeakable. The act divides both into what is done and to whom it is done; stealing candy from a baby turns a simple theft into a more serious offense because of the nature of the victim. The marriage of act and victim gives a special meaning to wrongdoing. Here we encounter a fundamental fact about wrongdoing: it connects one person, the perpetrator, to the another, the victim.

UNDERSTANDING ANOTHER PERSON

What does it mean to say that we understand another person? For a start, we regularly employ what is called a normative procedure (Haugland 1998), or an anticipation of what most people do in that set of circumstances. Psychoanalysis adds to this normative procedure by including a host of additional information derived from knowledge of the unconscious. Thus if we see that another person laughs instead of cries or cries instead of becoming angry we are better able to understand what a nonanalyst would possibly misunderstand or might consider to be a sign of craziness or "something wrong." The irrational becomes rational in light of the unconscious.

The psychoanalyst's failure to understand derives from a failure to develop a procedure that enables her to "see" what makes sense, and/or—from a conviction similar to that of the nonanalyst—to declare "this makes no sense and so something is wrong." Understanding another person is launched from a set of standards of operation that allows us to be that other person for a moment of comprehension. However, we all find we have a line of demarcation that ultimately trips us up as we venture too far afield from our own base of normative procedures. Psychoanalysis allows one to go a bit further as, indeed, does all learning about others. However, we regularly meet people who seem to elude our understanding, with whom we are unable to connect.

Case Example: Alan

Alan was a middle-aged man whose life, by virtue of his lifelong pedophilia, seemed to be an outstanding illustration of one response to the questions that come up when purposeful harm to others occurs. Alan maintained his active pedophilia along with a long-standing incestuous relationship with his daughter from age 4 onward. He had already spent some time in prison when I first met him, and he was able to be quite open about his past life. Although he readily and eagerly admitted the error of his ways along with a resolve to never repeat the behavior, he unfortunately could not succeed in convincing anyone else, or at least anyone who mattered, to believe him. It was not so much that the people involved—the judge, the lawyers, and myself—were so hardened and cynical that we were not able to be moved. It was more a case of Alan himself being quite unable to comprehend the impact of what he had done. When he was more comfortable in his talks with me, he admitted that he felt that he had done no harm to anyone and asked me in all sincerity why the judge was so upset about this lack of remorse. Alan puzzled over this and tried mightily either to be remorseful or, at a minimum, to at least show some semblance of remorse. Alan was not a good actor. It seemed apparent that for Alan to show a genuine regret, he would have to know how those little girls felt, and this was clearly not something that he could do. That he said that he did no harm to them was, amazingly, not only a defense of his behavior but an honest opinion of his as well. Alan would be the first to admit that he, for one, did not understand others or, at least, some others.

Alan is representative of a group of perpetrators of misdeeds who are said to be lacking in empathy for others. Some of these individuals may be seen to have a circumscribed capacity to feel for others (perhaps a few friends or family members), while others appear to be strikingly unable to take that step of trial identification, of putting oneself in the other's place. It is not the case that these individuals are incapable of ascertaining the motives and thoughts of others, since they are often anything but innocent. In fact, being able to know about someone else without necessarily feeling for or with that person can be advantageous in certain situations. Alan, for instance, was a good businessman and had a number of friends. But he walked through life without the burden of caring very much about others. For the most part his life seemed not too hampered by what may well seem a horrible deficiency to others, but in the particular arena that led Alan into legal and ethical problems, it was a monumental burden. The crucial question of why he did one particular act of awfulness rather than another cannot be answered here, except to mention the possibility that his deficient empathy was not operant in all areas, and the probability that his moral code was also not imbued with the feelings that readily go hand in hand with certain kinds of behavior. Though the judge and almost everyone else wanted Alan to feel bad, he simply did not. And was he to blame for that? Alan could not understand.

Case Example: Bernard

Bernard had no trouble at all in knowing just how he wanted his adversaries to feel. He was a cruel and abusive man who was quick to scream and yell and debase anyone who might offend him, and so he knew exactly how he wanted his opponent or victim to feel. That feeling of displeasure that Bernard had for others, be it of guilt or blame, was to be situated in the mind of whoever had offended Bernard, and having this impact on others was a source of pleasure for him. It certainly was not true that Bernard was lacking in knowledge of how his abuse was experienced, but it was just as equally true that he himself had no willingness to share in that experience. Bernard's misdeeds were justified or rationalized in myriad of ways having to do with people getting their just desserts, but he never took the added step of recognizing how it felt to endure the blame that he insisted was their due. We may be able to say that Bernard had just enough empathy to recognize the effect of his assault, but it was so short-lived that it gave him no real discomfort. In fact, it seemed to have the rather peculiar quality of giving him comfort because, along with the pleasure in venting his spleen, Bernard seemed relieved of whatever blame or dysphoria he may himself have been feeling. Thus his abuse was cathartic and was hardly something that he wished to examine, much less to the point of losing it and its effectiveness. When he became more comfortable in talking to me, Bernard could imagine how his adversaries experienced his wrath, but in doing so, and in understanding, he felt robbed of what he seemed to require from these encounters: something that made him feel good while his victim felt bad. This feeling good that Bernard achieved was not yet a pleasure in hurting someone else. It was a feeling that seemed to reside almost totally within Bernard and was best described as energizing. He felt alive, triumphant, righteous, and strong. Where there once was an aggrieved, passive, and vulnerable person there now stood a man of stature and conviction. It took no special insight to sense the fearfulness with which Bernard regularly lived and that he resolutely kept hidden. It did, however, demand an extended effort of personal empathy to look beyond his nasty demeanor and to approach the anxiety that he himself could not recognize or talk about.

DISCUSSION

The interplay of my understanding with these people, who were a mixture of the familiar and the foreign, was composed of a trial identification as well as some sense of disdain—that is, I felt myself both to be them and not to be them. If I were to ask each of them if and how they understood themselves—something I succeeded in asking Alan and Bernard—they would fall far short of my own assessment, and so I was convinced that I knew more about them than they themselves knew, at least in the sense of this moral dimension. The moral map of Aristotle and/or the superego-ideal of Freud could be known to me no matter if I saw these others through their development or through some innate program of morality. What they themselves were was either not known to them or was unavailable to them, but, nevertheless, in each case, someone else was needed to make it known. Alan could not make much of that someone else, and while it may be an oversimplification, we ended up wondering if his impairment was indeed best seen as neurological. Bernard, on the other hand, seemed to know that other part of himself while hoping never to have much to do with it. His was a parallel and vertically split personality. My unknown lady in the supermarket had no idea why she committed her minor theft but never seemed to quite shake that guilty feeling for doing so. Yet I did have some sort of connection with them all, each beginning with misunderstanding and ending with less of it.

I had an imaginary conversation with the angry judge in Alan's case, as I carefully explained to her that my patient and the judge's guilty offender could be neither a real and complete patient nor a person feeling guilt. The regret that Alan felt was a long distance from the re-morse that the judge demanded. The judge scoffed and insisted that this failure of remorse was more like a childish indulgence that must be re-linquished. A colleague of mine entered into the imaginary discussion and explained to both the judge and to me that Alan's guilt was indeed there, but it was unconscious. It would require therapy to unlock it from its hiding place and so permit Alan to share that human quality or moral map that would allow him to be one of us. One can see that I felt Alan's problem was more like color-blindness, or a neurological limitation; my colleague's opinion was that it was more akin to hysteria, or a psychic conflict, while what the judge felt was psychological was a simple case of conscious self-centeredness. The judge saw no place for psychoanaly-sis and the unconscious while my colleague, I felt, misunderstood what psychoanalysis and the unconscious were meant to explain. My own position was that of someone regularly expecting to see the supposed effects of the unconscious by way of the transference. Alas, there was nothing there; and thus followed my conclusion of a simple lack or deficit. Perhaps one day neuroscience can pinpoint the exact problem in Alan's brain, but, for now, it merely demonstrates the limits of our psychological efforts along with the limits of seeking answers in brain structure or chemistry.

One should mention, however, that the beginnings of a connec-tion of sorts between neurology and psychiatry is developing for cases similar to that of Alan. The basis of this linkage is a correlation between what we sense as a defect in Alan and some evidence of reduced pre-frontal gray matter and reduced autonomic activity in persons diagnosed as having antisocial personality disorder (Raine et al. 2000). It is im-portant to recognize that even the presence of such a structural brain deficit would not in itself reveal a corresponding disorder; rather, a whole series of intermediate psychological steps must be posited. Hy-pothetical considerations are given to ideas such as that of a low level of autonomic arousal making for a certain blunting of emotional reac-tion to scenes of violence that might upset an ordinary person. Also, the prefrontal cortex modulates emotions and attention, and damage here could conceivably allow for more aggressive or violent behavior. In a parallel manner, we may be hard-pressed to empathize with per-sons who do not correspond to our own affective states. This is a good example of how neuroscience enables us to see the limits of psychology as well as the correlations. It is equally important to recognize that the presence of these or similar neurologic defects is no sure indicator of any form of pathological behavior. Once again one must be cautious in aiming for a linear connection between the brain and the mind. But Alan surely represented a line that I could not cross.

It was different with Bernard; he managed to have scores of people who were quite able to evaluate and explain his obnoxious behavior. While Alan was quite incapable of reading others, especially those whom he mistreated, Bernard had an exquisite awareness of the impact of his actions. He aimed to hurt but not for pleasure. It took awhile for me to understand Bernard, to be able to connect to his desire to make others feel bad in a spirited act of justification. The temptation to bring him together with Alan as a subspecies was a strong one, but I could not dismiss another part of Bernard's impact upon me: one of sadness and emptiness.

My function as an instrument of evaluation and thus of understanding with both of these men becomes the psychological correlate of PET scans and EEGs. With effort, one could recognize Bernard's divided aspects, which could easily be seen to alternate between bombast and vulnerability, between warmth and dismissal and so forth, as related to a division between guilt and blame. Once I was able to find a matching and contradictory split in myself, I was equipped to join in a recognition of him in a totally different manner than was possible with Alan. Alan's inability to read others, or to recognize any part of himself in others, was in sharp contrast to Bernard's; Bernard literally had to see something in others. Thus I was a natural illustration of the capacity of these men to connect, one with pain and unhappiness and one not at all.

And what of my lady in the supermarket? She and I instantly yet mutely knew one another. If I had caught her eye, I have no doubt that a perfectly predictable conversation would have taken place with no need for words or further gestures. The minor difference between us—that she committed the theft while I did not—hardly qualified as one that made a difference in understanding; only in action were we that separate from one another. I take this interchange as an example, albeit a somewhat unusual one, of the phenomenon of basic understanding that subsumes most human contact and connection. It might be pertinent at this point to again refer to Hans-Georg Gadamer (1989), who developed Martin Heidegger's thesis that understanding is the mode of our being and so embraces the whole of our experience in the world. One's ability to live in the world and cope skillfully with it is what is meant by understanding. This primary understanding runs through all of our life, and interpretation occurs at points where we do not understand. Thus interpretation may be seen positively as a capacity to move from a state of misunderstanding to one of understanding. If I were to be puzzled by my friendly supermarket thief then I would be moved to find some interpretation to explain her action to myself. But I had no such bewilderment because I immediately caught on, even though I may have been unhappy with what I quickly knew.

PRIMARY UNDERSTANDING

To establish the status of a philosophical position that speaks to the existence of a basic or "primary" understanding calls for some psychological underpinning. Is this form of understanding an innate property of the mind or is it a developmental phenomenon that has a timeline and various stages? Michael Basch (1973), following Kohut, felt that it was a first stage in selfobject development called kinship, a stage in which one feels oneself to be a human being among humans. Yet this kinship stage requires some cognitive recognition of the sameness or similarity of one's fellow humans and so could be said to take place further along in development than earlier stages involving experiences of safeness and security, which themselves might well predate the cognitive capacity to compare and contrast oneself with others. Nevertheless it seems safe to say that there does seem to be a fundamental grounding of our existence in the experience of being able to feel connected with one another and so to feel understood and to be able to understand others. In that sense, Alan was a fairly isolated individual who both puzzled over and groped for connection. As an aside, he loved to be alone in his basement with his ham radio that allowed him to speak, and to connect with anonymous voices all over the world. Bernard surrounded himself with lackeys and subordinates who jumped at his orders, yet who were amazingly loyal to him, as he was to them. Each of us seems to manage a certain circle of safe connections, and in this sense connection is more than a relationship: it is a unity, a being as one.

When we step outside of the circle of understanding and/or we enter the arena of misunderstanding, or experience the break in connection, the preferred or perhaps the sole treatment for this state is interpretation. Yet because interpretation itself may be seen as endless as well as subjective, it must come to an end when a particular shared meaning is captured, or simply when understanding is regained, as when connection is established. Inasmuch as the task of interpreting the unconscious may be limitless as well as individually controlled, interpretation too must be seen as directed toward a resting place. Therefore interpretations of whatever sort that merely make a claim about one or another contents of "the unconscious" without the achievement of furthering understanding fall outside of the arena of activity that psychoanalysis attends to since they are distinct from true understanding. As David Hoy (1993) says:

> Understanding should not itself be taken as a mental operation that is distinct from interpretation. Understanding is itself realized in interpretation and is not a secondary operation of interpretation. . . . Interpretation is the concrete working through of the possibilities projected by the understanding. That is, the context of intelligibility that is tacitly understood provides the background against which specific interpretive actions make sense. This tacit background and the explicit interpretive action are integral functions of any instance of interpretive understanding. [p. 187]

The sequence of moving from one interpretation to another is a sign that we do indeed understand, since the world is never static and demands constant interpretive activity.

My imaginary conversation with the judge in Alan's case was to no avail, because she had failed to understand. This nicely frames the difference between explanation and understanding, since all explanations that do not follow from understanding, while they may seem to work quite effectively in some areas outside of human relations, are felt as free-floating and groundless when we discuss our dealings with one another. Indeed the judge may have said that she agreed with me—but there are no real agreements without understanding, and good explanations are much like good interpretations, in that they make for understanding.

If I were to have another imaginary conversation, this time with my supermarket thief, the most likely initial result would be that of a break in understanding. No matter how much I may have resonated with her in her act of larceny, I would move to an alien position if I were to confront and accuse her. Now one can certainly imagine and construct all sorts of scenarios in which a criminal begs for confrontation, but they usually require either a Hollywood scene of blinding insight or a more plausible script involving a gradual recognition of a wish for apprehension. Neither was the case with my larcenous lady, who could only deny any wrongdoing, dismiss me as a meddler, and complain all the way home to her friend and child that people ought to tend to their own lives, and that she could not understand what business this was of mine. At that moment, I grew apart from her.

From the basic primary understanding or kinship that serves to connect us to one another, we grow to have a medley of differences that distinguish us from each other. Even the effort to squash these differences, whether through claims that we are all fundamentally alike, or by posing the essentials of "human nature" as a whole, may be seen as directed toward maintaining these linkages between people. So, too, is the effort to champion empathy as the pathway to understanding. It becomes proof of our sameness. But caution is required here since the word "empathy" may be overused and so obliterate a host of distinctions. One potential source of confusion can be seen with the aforementioned work of Flanagan (2000) and Gazzaniga (1998), both of whom explain brain activity through the employment of homunculi or, perhaps more accurately stated, through an anthropomorphization of entities that they claim to understand. It is not at all uncommon to slip into such "human talk" when one wishes to consider issues such as motivation or desire, yet one wonders whether empathy is operating here. It is certainly possible to say that I understand Alan with his inherent limitations, Bernard with his vertical split, and my supermarket lady as well. Yet I really could not be empathic with the first, nor able to sustain my empathy with the second. The practice of assigning aims and goals or attributing intentionality (Dennett 1987) is a common one that we use in situations that range from explaining why the soft drink machine failed to deliver a container all the way to interpreting how a neurotransmitter adapts itself to a changed serotonin environment.

Third-person, objective, impersonal data is not empathy. Analogous or similar models of operation cannot be assumed to be derived from empathy. Empathy is a complex activity confined to humans who are able to see themselves as other humans in a similar setting. It is a trial identification rather than a scrutiny from outside.

Nor is empathy agreement. When we see eye-to-eye with a person, we need to distinguish our understanding from our agreement. The former is an emotional attunement while the latter is an intellectual meeting of the minds. The two may indeed co-occur, but often they do not. This is especially true in cases of divided selves such as Bernard, who managed to make me feel that as much as I understood him, I could not always agree with him; not surprisingly, he felt the same way about himself. Thus, one possible problem with empathy and agreement is that both can reside in a single person as well as in two individuals, but one does not require the other.

Freud is often said not to have understood Dora, and so his explanations missed the mark. His supposed understanding came from a set of convictions he held about women and the unconscious, and so he fell short of a real connection to her. The two people were too different. Yet if they had been too much alike, he may have been equally unable to understand Dora, since we must assume that some semblance of difference is essential for an interpretation to be fashioned. If understanding is to be realized by way of interpretation, one must somehow start from an inability to understand: a misunderstanding.

Just as my understanding of my supermarket companion was conducted in silence, so too does much understanding take place outside of conversation. The talking cure involves more than mere talking inasmuch as so much is left unsaid. We turn next to that remainder of action that is outside of language as revealing another example of a dualism that restricts psychoanalytic theory.

5

Enactment as Understanding and as Misunderstanding

Most of us, most of the time, aim to understand others, and we acknowledge our understanding by some form of affirming communication, verbal or otherwise. Normal conversation proceeds by a series of exchanges that try to clarify any misunderstanding and to change it into an agreed-upon understanding. The gestures and words that compose our everyday discourse are, however, necessarily decreased and minimized by the structured form of psychoanalysis, which is regularly conducted without face-to-face contact and in an atmosphere of much-reduced verbal exchange. Over the years, our attention as analysts has been increasingly drawn to an investigation of the inevitable impact of the out-of-sight and often mute analyst upon the analytic process, and we have profited from this. We also owe a considerable debt to those who have tried to isolate and demarcate the so-called enactments of analysis as these situations serve to illustrate special times of inter-action (Chused 1991, McLaughlin 1991).

Enactments, characterized as somewhat circumscribed moments of behavior, are defined either as "symbolic interactions between patient and analyst which have unconscious meaning to both" (Chused 1991, p. 615) or as "regressive interactions experienced by either as a consequence of the behavior of the other" (McLaughlin 1991, p. 595); or are further circumscribed as "enact[ing] rather than maintaining the separate thinking and inquiry necessary to the analytic stance" (Anderson 1999, p. 504).

If we turn a bright light on these definitions we see that only the terms "regressive," "unconscious," and "symbolic" serve to differentiate that particular type of behavior from what would otherwise be an ordinary run-of-the-mill action. And if one turns an even brighter light on those particular words, it is difficult to claim that any single bit of action could be free from the qualities ascribed to enactment. Indeed action or behavior itself seems to be by definition disqualified here, inasmuch as silent inactivity can readily be seen as regressive, symbolic, and laden with unconscious intent. The claim that psychoanalysis can theoretically be divided into a time of thoughtful inquiry and a time of regressive, defensive action may well be more of a hope than a reality. Here, another dualism has taken hold of our field: acting vs. thinking.

The ordinary activities of arranging schedules, setting fees, and managing the day-to-day conduct of a practice, coupled with such extraordinary actions as extra appointments, phone conversations, disclosure of personal information, and so on, are never easily compartmentalized into what is or what is not an enactment or an interaction. If a patient offers a hand to shake, our response is surely an enactment, and it has, just as surely, an unconscious reverberation. If we agree to modify a schedule or reduce a fee, we are behaving as a consequence of a request and so can hardly claim that our responses are not regularly a mixture of regressive as well as thoughtful behavior.

Indeed the entire conduct of an analysis seems only to allow one person—the privileged analyst—to highlight some forms of behavior as enactments, while simultaneously dismissing or disregarding others. The crucial issue seems to be more one of determining why we choose to select certain forms of behavior as enactments, and understanding what *this* choice and *this* behavior may mean. It would seem folly to consider all enactments as bad or infantile or defensive, since they may be initiated by either party (Jacob 1986), and in fact they might more properly be seen as efforts at understanding—from the one to the other, and in both directions. For a start, we must agree upon just what constitutes the understanding that was outlined in the previous chapter.

UNDERSTANDING

Psychoanalysis regularly makes a place for understanding in the realm of cognition; that is, one knows something that was heretofore hidden or repressed, as illustrated in our making the ego aware of the contents of the id. Yet we also know that understanding, or *Verstehen*, is at least one half of the understanding-explaining complex and, for some patients, is said to be the most crucial part of treatment. Much effort has been directed toward a better positioning of understanding, especially in psychoanalysis, and particularly as it relates to interpretation (Hartmann 1950). One perspective maintains that interpretation is the link between understanding and explaining, so that one interprets something, say a transference resistance, that allows understanding to emerge, and this in turn is explained, say, by a genetic reconstruction. Another perspective says that we understand one another by way of empathy and that this connects us to one another. The connection that results is then the area of explanation, both in its origins and its vicissitudes. Both these perspectives allow for understanding to be seen as moving us from one place to another, not so much or only in the form of increased knowledge, but more in terms of opening us up to more possibilities, or perhaps better said, freeing us to be and do more. It may not be too far afield to say that understanding makes one a different person. No matter how one chooses to conceptualize the status of understanding, it clearly serves a central role in analytic therapy.

In most analyses, the achievement of understanding is a product of verbal discourse, and the failure of this achievement is sometimes attributed to action, or behavior that is not, for whatever reason, reformulated in discourse. Indeed, it is often the case that mere action, when it occurs in place of words, is felt to be inconsequential, or even deleterious, either because the activity as such does not contribute to understanding, or else because it is misunderstood. It may also be true that certain actions or behaviors are themselves efforts at understanding, and these bits of behavior may be successful even if they are not made a part of the talking cure. If all enactments are seen as efforts at

understanding, then some are successful, albeit of little or no consequence; others are successful and remain quite outside the analytic
discourse, while some few are unsuccessful and become the locus of misunderstanding. These last instances are the usual places of concern for
many analysts. It seems that enactments are more likely to be defined
(although perhaps erroneously) as behavior that is misunderstood rather
than behavior that is understood. Much behavior falls inside this particular definition, such as acts of misunderstanding that are open to
understanding, and that may either be of no import or become objects
of investigation that are resolved, or understood. Some acts, however,
remain misunderstood and unresolved. Action that lies outside this
circle of concern may or may not be attended to, but rarely does it join
in the discourse of the treatment. Misunderstanding therefore is characterized as something that stands out or calls for recognition, and is
sometimes properly reckoned with. Understanding is regularly left
as-is—that is, left unexamined and taken as a matter of course.

MISUNDERSTANDING

Hans-Georg Gadamer (1962) discusses misunderstanding as a state
that must itself somehow depend upon understanding, since we are only
able to claim that we misunderstand or are misunderstood if we have
some baseline of reference. Most psychoanalysts and psychotherapists
can differentiate cases that they would describe as not at all understood
from those that are misunderstood. With one patient we may claim that
we simply do not "get it," while we may be just as likely to insist that
we misunderstood another. And clearly these casual descriptions do aim
to differentiate two quite separate sets of conditions. The first is not so
much based upon error as it refers to a lack or absence of a connection.
The second lies more in the direction of a faulty connection. To be sure,
there can be no black-and-white distinction between "not getting it"
and "getting it wrong," but the latter has more to do with the area of
interpretive work, while the former points to a complete empathic failure. When we are out of touch or completely lost, we try to make a
connection. When we are a bit off, we try to clarify. Without in any
way dismissing or not recognizing the many shades of gray that exist
in this area, it may be possible to better understand why some enact-

ments stand out as significant and worthy of examination, while others are readily classified as trivial and of no import.

To be sure, one analyst may more readily struggle to comprehend a patient than another analyst might with the same patient. We all differ a great deal in our "getting it." Something similar may occur when one analyst deals with a number of patients, some of whom are a challenge to comprehend while others are more easily grasped. The psychology of the analyst varies in terms of both her wish to understand and her propensity to ignore what is not understood. The same is true of a patient who feels understood and who, in turn, understands the analyst. Seeing the analyst–patient dyad as an effort to enhance mutual understanding and to diminish misunderstanding may allow for a changed perspective on the problem of enactments. And in analysis, such actions may then be recast into moments of misunderstanding that break the connection between analyst and patient, *or* bring about efforts to reconnect without the use of interpretation. That is, they are acts centered upon the mutuality of understanding.

One way to maintain a connection that is in danger of being broken, or to reestablish one that has been lost, is to disregard whatever occurs that threatens it. This disregard can be classified along a continuum as anything from a minor issue to which we turn a blind eye, to something on the level of a disavowal that may qualify as pathological. Thus two persons who seem to understand one another may approach an area of potential disagreement, one that is temporarily not amenable to negotiation or resolution by interpretation, and reckon with it by implicitly agreeing to exclude it from being noticed. The result is that a silent conspiracy or collusion develops in which each participant is drawn into splitting off or disowning the troublesome area. It is achieved by an act of disavowal. We shall call this pseudo-understanding. It seems necessary to invoke this experience of a silent (that is, unspoken) agreement if we are to comprehend the broad range of definitions and recommendations about enactments.

CLINICAL EXAMPLES OF MISUNDERSTANDING

In an extensive review of the many contributions to the problem, Frank (1999) notes that because all patient–therapist interactions can be seen as enactments, one runs the danger of a too-broad or a too-limited conceptualization of them (pp. 45–65). Over and over, the decision as to what counts as an enactment seems to be either arbitrary or somehow involved with self-deception. Setting a schedule is a good example of enacting that can be dismissed as trivial or else can become the site of a significant unconscious conflict. Here is an example taken from the psychoanalytic literature.

Case I

This case is taken from an article describing enactment from a Kleinian point of view (Anderson 1999). The author reviews much of the relevant literature on enactment and proposes the idea that enactment derives from a pressure upon the analyst to avoid sensory bombardment issuing from the patient. Without pursuing the theoretical issues discussed in the paper, one can focus upon the clinical material, which involves an initial compliance by the analyst to the patient's requests for what are called "minor deviations from the analytic frame." These are usually changes made in regard to schedule alterations. The dreams that follow these "enactments" are of a debilitated analyst, and they led the analyst to decide to refrain from further complying with the patient's requests. The analyst's refusal of the patient's next request led to new material from the patient about the analyst's "cruelty" and other important "hidden elements." Thus the analyst's changed position, characterized as a move from enactment to neutrality, was said to have solved the mistaken initial compliance or neutralized the disequilibrium set in motion by the agreement.

One need not subscribe to (or dismiss) the Kleinian considerations in order to briefly pursue some critical points. To begin with, the author seems not to make much of the fact that her later refusal to comply is just as much of an enactment as was her previous agreement. That evidence of supposed primitive hate, with attributions of cruelty to the analyst, might ensue from a refusal would seem to be fairly expectable. But would an enactment of generosity or indulgence on the analyst's part have evoked material that would also support the same theory? Enactments that occur between patient and analyst that are said to no longer avoid "painful reality" seem peculiarly to center on the analyst as the one who does less or gives less. Need this always be the case? Is all compliance an avoidance of reality? The enactment is not only the refusal of the request but is also the very act of the analyst in either accepting or refusing, that is, it is the delineation of a frame and the change in the frame. This delineation and subsequent change must take precedence in becoming the focus in the analysis, since the analyst says that "her best analytic judgment" caused her to change her mind, and the patient agreed with this judgment. Although one need not take issue with this judgment, it would seem obvious that such an agreement between analyst and analysand is the stuff of transference that could well be the central point of the enactment, that is, unless it is disavowed. Yet this clinical vignette is offered as if this central point of agreement were but a preamble to the real one, which would mean the cessation of complying with requests and the resultant rage. In truth, one is no more real than the other. To insist that the analyst enacts as a defense against the patient's terrorizing threat may open the door to questioning whether both the analyst's refusal *and* her earlier compliances also allow for another defense, that of disavowal; and whether disavowal may be the more significant arena of inquiry. Thus a seemingly minor act of schedule arrangement illustrates a sequence of supposed understanding or agreement followed by misunderstanding with a solution of compliance. This compliance may then be a sign of objectionable material that is split off and disavowed.

The analyst and patient begin the treatment with a set of understandings about the frame of analysis, although surely much of this remains in the background. The analyst may feel a struggle within herself over some of the niceties of the arrangements, but nothing need be an issue until the emergence of a moment of misunderstanding. In the above case, it took the form of a set of dreams, and in addition there were said to be further requests from the patient. One might say here that these changes and/or requests had unconscious meaning to both patient and analyst (Chused 1996), and that in one sense they each misunderstood the other at this juncture. This mutual misunderstanding is the ideal occasion for an interpretation that can lead to or restore understanding. Too often, of course, such misunderstandings are not seen as mutual, and so they become arenas for what may be misguided analytic work aimed at a compliance, which then masquerades as understanding. In this case, this misunderstanding took the form of the analyst introducing a new rule, one of refusing requests.

Enactment can be said to move from a mutual understanding to a misunderstanding on to further enactment without mutual understanding—although the analyst would claim that she well understands her patient. I suspect that assertion would only be valid if such understanding could be confirmed by the patient and had been achieved by interpretative work.

Here is another example that includes how understanding can result from interpretation.

Case II

This young professional man came to see me upon referral from an analyst whom he had been seeing in another city. My prospective patient had had to move because his wife had been offered an important and promising position in this new location, and he felt that up to now she had sacrificed her career for him. Their finances had not improved at all with this move, and finances became of immediate concern in my taking on and treating my potential new patient. He told me that his previous analyst had begun seeing him on a one-time-per-week basis at a somewhat reduced fee and had proceeded to further reduce the fee as the frequency of hours increased to four times weekly. He said that this was a common practice in the community from which he had come, and he wondered if the same were true here, and if I could accommodate him in an equally negotiable manner.

Reducing a fee for a patient was not a new experience for me, and the financial issue itself could not be considered significant. Therefore, it seemed reasonable to put aside any question of this action having much of an impact on me. The patient seemed interesting, my self-esteem was enhanced by the referral, and so I agreed to start at a lower fee and then possibly to increase the frequency of sessions and so, too, agreed to the decrease in fee, just as the other analyst had done. In retrospect, I felt uncomfortable from the very start at having to make accommodations that matched those of the other analyst rather than offer a setup fashioned by myself. I tried to put this nagging discomfort to the side and attributed it to my competitive feelings toward the other analyst. I therefore tried to convince myself that no matter who made the decision, it was all for the patient's good.

I was wrong. As the once-per-week meetings began, the patient spoke more and more of the burdens that he had assumed with this move, which was made primarily in his wife's interest. As his anger toward his wife became more open and focused, I found that my initial mild discomfort with the financial setup seemed now to make me feel even more uncomfortable. At what seemed an appropriate moment in the treatment we began to discuss money—first in a general way, then more specifically in the here-and-now with his wife and family, and then even more specifically in his lifelong relationships with his father and mother. It was interesting and revealing to learn that his parents gave him and his wife a yearly gift, allowed as a tax deduction by the IRS, but with the stipulation that it was really a loan that would have to one day be repaid. These parents were well-off financially but seemed unable to give any gifts without the attached strings. When this was brought into the arena of treatment we were able to discuss the patient's feelings of guilt at receiving along with his rage at "not getting." We could next see how I was feeling a similar set of feelings at being placed in a position akin to my patient, and we saw how others were likewise putting my patient in a situation much like that he had experienced his entire life, that is, making a sacrifice, feeling angry at having to do it, feeling guilty that he was angry, and feeling ungrateful as well. However, the more basic component, and one essentially absent from all of the interactions in his family, with his wife, with his first analyst, and initially with me, was that much if not all of this remained unspoken. For awhile it was segregated in our work, but finally it took its place in the conversation. It should be mentioned here that this discussion did not entail changing the agreed-upon fee in any way.

This single event (of lifting behavior into the therapeutic dialogue), which is sometimes routine but is often a source of surprisingly great discomfort, can become a crucial turning point. The particular enactment described here was thus different from other enactments, in that it was not allowed to rest among the "usual and ordinary" behavior of the analyst. We see how the material moves from the status of the disavowed to a place of importance and recognition. The crucial element of the analyst's reluctance to bring the material into the discussion is one that is basic to the problem of enactments.

This next case is of an enacting that is never addressed either by action or interpretation.

Case III

This case is an example of a mutual enactment, and what initiated it was unclear although it probably belonged to the therapist. It is an example that would appear to present no particular moral issues and so could readily be classified as innocent on that basis. It does, however, qualify as an enactment that passed as unnoticed and that remained so.

This case of a middle-aged and well-known female theatrical celebrity was presented for consultation because the therapist felt the treatment was at a stalemate. The hours with the patient were said to drag on and on, with the mere reporting of events and with little time for any sort of intervention, along with no tolerance whatsoever by the patient for transference interpretations. In the recounting of one hour, the therapist began by focusing on his patient's infidelity to her husband, primarily with a much younger man whom she would meet in out-of-the-way and/or secluded hotels in order to avoid discovery. These secret liaisons were of vital importance to the patient, and her therapist often attempted to contrast their significance with his own insignificance, which the patient had often asserted. This woman felt it to be vitally important that she not be seen with her young lover, since not only her marriage but also her public persona would suffer.

In a more detailed examination of a representative hour, the therapist began with a description of his letting his patient in by a private door so that she would spend no time in the waiting room and so that her entrances and exits could not be observed by other patients. The therapist recounted this in a matter-of-fact manner and could not recall if the routine had begun with the patient's request for secrecy or the therapist's offering it for the same reason. When the supervisor called attention to the fact that this bit of behavior seemed to exactly parallel some of the activity associated with the patient's secret rendezvous, the therapist seemed quite literally stunned. He had never noticed, and he certainly would have never chosen to discuss this with his patient. Yet he had no difficulty in seeing that this bit of behavior that was going on in a regular fashion between his patient and himself might well be connected to his own feeling of frustration over the lack of meaningful discussion of important issues with the same patient.

Without now going into the case discussion in any greater detail, one can pursue a more careful inquiry into the therapist's conduct. He could readily see that he had engaged in an action that he then proceeded to deny or disavow. Indeed he openly said that he felt somewhat alien to that action and decision of his, almost as if it had been made by someone other than himself. He felt embarrassed at this disclosure but, perhaps peculiarly, did not at that moment feel able to confront his patient with his new observation. He could consider the entrances and exits of his patient to be behavior that might conceal a host of other complex meanings, in that (1) it was symbolic and carried unconscious content; (2) he was convinced of the need for this enactment to be discussed; and (3) he knew it should be brought into the therapeutic discourse. But nevertheless he felt a clear resistance to contemplating the symbolism and a reluctance to pursue it in the therapy. Essentially this enactment would seem to qualify as significant nonverbal behavior that remained outside the arena of interpretive activity, as it was disavowed and kept hidden away.

It is important to recognize and underscore that this particular enactment might mean little or nothing for one patient and might well be discussed with another patient. There is nothing inherently deleterious about the behavior save as it exists within the context of the treatment.

EXPLAINING ENACTMENTS

It would be foolhardy to attempt to offer a single explanation for all enactments, especially if one appreciates their ubiquity. However, it may be possible to focus upon those that occur in a specific analyst and are experienced as unusual by that particular analyst. Such personal experiences may involve external scrutiny, as happens in supervision, or may be recognized as an individual sense of uneasiness or guilt or embarrassment. For each person there is thus a sense of disruption as one moves from personal comfort to unrest, from innocence to blame, and from understanding to misunderstanding. From the outside, the corresponding view may of course be one of a more or less moral or ethical evaluation. Within this area of judgment are the rules and regulations of whatever system of psychoanalysis or psychotherapy the analyst embraces. Therefore, if one assumes that anything from a handshake to a hug belongs to the ordinary routine of practice, then this imaginary line of meaningful enactment has not been crossed. Although one person's enactment may be another's routine behavior, short of clearcut ethical misbehavior the proper explanation can only belong to that one person. Thus this particular approach to understanding concentrates on the psychology of the analyst and to the way he somehow steps outside of his "ordinary and usual" behavior. Each of these cases allows for different responses, responses that enable us to categorize types of enactments, such as those that can be ignored, handled by counteractions, or resolved by interpretation.

DISCUSSION

Enactments may be placed within the larger category of interactions between analyst and patient, but are distinguished only in terms of their having a special psychological significance; however, this aspect of significance is one that is assigned by the analyst. If both enactments and interactions are ubiquitous, then we must separate out special types of interactions that are therapeutically meaningful. The arbitrary nature of such a decision has led to a plethora of literature that struggles either to make of enactments something unusual or to see them as having some special status. The problem here is that while some enactments certainly do escape the notice of analysts or are disavowed, either owing to the theoretical stance of the analyst and/or to his personal psychology, others seem to defy being ignored. Thus, rather than remaining at one or other of these poles of recognition or nonrecognition, we need to carve out a better way to conceptualize enactments. When Chused (1991) says, "To want anything from patients . . . even to be understood accurately, is to be vulnerable to the experience of one's own transference and thus be susceptible to an enactment" (pp. 616–618), she suggests that "not wanting" can be a pure, albeit unattainable, state of neutrality rather than a very powerful form of interaction of its own. Alas, not wanting is no protection from enacting.

In my effort to reformulate the concept of enactment in terms of understanding and misunderstanding, I have placed interpretation at the center of the solution to the conundrum. Thus the core concern of the analyst need not be directed toward restraining action or "not wanting," but rather toward the more liberal action of understanding what he or she did or did not do.

ENACTMENT AS PSEUDOUNDERSTANDING FOLLOWED BY MISUNDERSTANDING

Much of the interaction in psychoanalysis may be felt to be trivial and thus may not be considered to be a part of the analytic discourse. When patient and analyst are "in sync," they usually are involved in periods of information gathering or in the consolidation of new information. They feel connected and, ideally, understanding goes or should go both ways. In these states, we are loathe to speak of enactments as such. Yet one problem that may occur during these periods is that of disavowal, which occurs when disturbing material that has the capacity to disrupt the connection is allowed to remain outside the treatment. The case of the celebrity let in by a side door illustrates this form of disavowal. The case involving reduced fees illustrates an apparent understanding—a pseudounderstanding—that clearly negatively affected one participant; however, it was never allowed to be completely split off from the analysis. In each of these cases an effort was made to maintain a comfortable connection with the patient and so not to rock the boat. The analyst's reaction was aimed at better understanding the patient, but this necessitated having to split off disruptive material from discussion. If and when such material is brought into the discourse, it leads to misunderstanding.

This misunderstanding derives from or follows understanding and is often the occasion for enactment, as the word is commonly used. *Something happens.* These occasions of disruption may or may not be behavioral, but something called "enactment" is often noted at these times, especially if the misunderstanding is seen as somehow lying outside the ordinary conduct of analysis. This is best illustrated in the case involving the changes in schedule, where the analyst acceded to other requests of the patient, became troubled, and herself moved to action, although one problem in such instances occurs when action is met with reaction, which then leads to resolution by compliance rather than to a return to mutual understanding. Analysis must necessarily move away from understanding to misunderstanding if change is to be accomplished. The inevitable misunderstanding that follows understanding is the engine that moves the treatment.

INTERPRETATION AS RESOLVING MISUNDERSTANDING

There is no doubt that the usual concept of interpretation is broad in its scope. It can be either behavioral or verbal, and what constitutes an interpretation per se may run the gamut from a casual nod of agreement to a meaningful recognition of an unconscious configuration. Psychoanalytic interpretation, however, is different, and this is seen in its restrictiveness and focus. Moving from a state of misunderstanding to one of understanding in psychoanalysis, as opposed to the process in a host of other forms of resolving differences, demands a concern with transference and countertransference and a recognition of the unconscious derivatives of the misunderstanding. We know that we need not have a dream presented to us to engage us in interpretation, but we are often reluctant to recognize that much of the supposed minutiae of psychoanalysis have equal value in offering access to the unconscious. When something goes wrong in our procedures, we tend to right them in order to attain our usual level of comfort. This pull on us to react should also, of course, be a pull to understand and to interpret. If one moves from allowing schedule changes to no longer allowing them, that is, from one kind of enactment to another, one simply provides an example of handling misunderstanding without psychoanalytic interpretation. The same thing goes for all forms of abstinence and/or gratification that alter or resolve a problem without an increase in mutual understanding. Too often, all that is achieved is comfort for the analyst. Doubtless most analysts do interpret with a personal conviction of understanding their patients, but there exists an added requirement in psychoanalytic discourse, and that is that the patient too must feel understood. Ultimately this understanding is raised to a cognitive level by way of explanation. But that is another story.

INTERPRETATION IN DEPTH AND BREADTH

The usual perspective on psychoanalytic interpretation sees it as one of unearthing something that is hidden by allowing the repressed unconscious to be raised to consciousness. But in addition to this image of movement from the depths to the surface, interpretation can be a gathering of separate or split-off segments into a congruent whole, so it can also offer an image of integration. This latter conceptualization corresponds to what happens when disavowed contents are included in an ongoing scrutiny of attention. Just as we know we need to bring unconscious issues into the ongoing transference relationship and subject them to interpretation, so too must we recognize that disavowed content must join in the conversation. Enactments are regularly left out of the ongoing verbal exchange whether by choice or by virtue of psychological resistance. Our faith in "the talking cure" is rewarded by recognizing that everything counts and so it all deserves a place in the dialogue. Both repression, or horizontal splitting, and disavowal, or vertical splitting, demand integration into a more complete understanding.

SUMMARY

Enactment, like so many overused words in psychoanalysis, has an undeserved popularity. From its original status as an indication of something gone wrong, it has, over time, come to be used to merely describe the normal range of interpersonal occurrences (Frank 1999, p. 55) and sometimes is even encouraged as therapeutic (Bacal 1985). Inasmuch as we may have a legitimate right to say that everything is an interaction (Goldberg 1996), we can perhaps do better to circumscribe enactments as interactions that participate in the analytic dialogue, and that may be conceptualized according to the prevailing analytic theory either as transference and countertransference issues or as what occurs in the pseudounderstanding–misunderstanding sequence. In choosing the latter terms, we may come a bit closer to the mutual experiences of the two participants and therefore be more able to grasp the state of something as amiss.

When something is wrong we can usually agree that one of us—patient or analyst—does not understand that "something" that may have been brought about by an enactment. The ensuing state might be resolved by an interpretation or by yet another enactment. Enactments can thus be positioned as part of the sequence of creating and resolving misunderstandings. The critical point for psychoanalysis is to recognize that interpretive work is called for to resolve whatever is amiss. Thus enactments are never right or wrong or good or bad. They are properly seen as spurs to psychoanalytic understanding, and as such they lose their special status, except as they serve to remind us of what we occasionally forget with respect to our primary effort. Undoubtedly there is nothing new in this way of thinking about enactment. But I offer it in an effort to better understand a word that is often misunderstood. We next turn to a hidden sort of enactment.

6

Form versus Content

INTRODUCTION

One of the great divisions that is helpful in the examination of everything from novels to corporations is that of form versus content. Each of these aspects is said to allow one to gain a different perspective on whatever is being studied, and when taken as separate and distinct views they often enable one to learn more, perhaps by a studied effort to momentarily ignore either the form or the content. An investigation, say, of a corporate structure may reveal problems that have little or nothing to do with the particular qualities of any of the individuals serving it in one or another capacity. A narrative that is less than compelling may well be transformed by moving a character or a scene from one point to another while yet retaining the sense of the story. This duality is no novelty in psychoanalysis, which, perhaps unfortunately, often considers content to be supreme and relegates form to a position associated with more severe pathology. It may, for example, be said that borderline patients have problems in regulation while neurotics have difficulties in oedipal dramas. To be sure, there is a great advantage to be gained in the utilization of such divisions, but there may also be disadvantages in such a divide. Taking a step back from this duality will sometimes yield an understanding that overrides the division and changes the form and content, or the struggle of form versus content, into the sequence of misunderstanding to understanding. The form, as we have seen, is likely to be classified as enactment and so possibly be misunderstood.

GETTING THE STORY

Psychoanalysts and psychotherapists love to hear stories. Some of them are equally enamored of the telling of stories, but the bread and butter of most clinical practices involves listening to a patient's story, helping him fill it in to make it more reasonable or sensible or at least understandable, and, over time, telling it back to the patient in a new and improved version. Indeed, some feel that the retelling of stories is the essence of cure. However, we regularly meet patients who cannot or will not recount a coherent story, and whose conduct before, during, and after a therapeutic hour seems to make storytelling an impossible venture. Indeed, it is not necessarily the case that this particular patient does not need to tell a story or does not have a story to tell. Rather, what seems to transpire is that the proper atmosphere for such storytelling does not exist. Such patients either come late to the hour or come irregularly. They either are in the midst of a crisis or simply are unable to talk at all. They either cannot get started talking or else tarry at the door and continue talking until you have to gently close it in their face. In brief, they seem never to settle down, to come regularly, to arrive and leave on time, to behave like a proper, practical, and yes, peaceful patient. These are clearly patients for whom the content or stories of their lives are less revealing than the patterns or forms of their daily existence. Essentially it is of little moment for such a patient to have something unconscious or unknown interpreted and revealed to them. They are not so much in need of revelation as they are of regulation.

When analysts or therapists encounter one of these patients they may react either by exerting some external control or else by resorting to some theoretical principles that allow them to simply "wait it out." Here is one example.

CLINICAL CASE EXAMPLE I

Dr. J. came for supervision to discuss a new analytic patient, a young man who was scheduled to be seen by her four times a week. This patient, a successful executive who had all sorts of problems with women, entered analysis with an eagerness and willingness that served to delight and charm Dr. J. Alas, her enthusiasm was short-lived, because her patient rather quickly settled into a routine of cancellations and misses, all of which seemed to be quite legitimate as well as carefully and considerately phoned in by this executive's secretary. Initially Dr. J. seemed only a little fazed by these missed sessions inasmuch as her analytic training was a classical one and allowed her to suffer no financial loss from this or any patient's erratic attendance. When the patient did appear, he mainly talked of one or another problem with a girlfriend and, interestingly, most of these problems were centered on the patient's own chronic and repetitive infidelity. However, he loved coming to analytic sessions, felt wonderfully relieved after such cathartic exercises, and had no doubt that his analyst was wise and helpful. As much as she might have enjoyed such admiration, Dr. J. felt that she hardly knew her patient at all and was mainly concerned with whether or not he would show up. Her response, more than anything else, might have had to do with what she had been taught about transference and countertransference. She decided that he just needed time.

Dr. J. did manage to get a history of sorts from her patient and, not surprisingly, it was that of a childhood characterized by multiple developmental irregularities. His father was a brutal and alcoholic man who had spent time in prison and who often behaved outrageously in front of his son. His mother was equally unreliable and also quite unprotective of her son, who was repeatedly verbally and physically abused by the father. The patient recalled an intense and lifelong feeling of his being a physically ugly and repulsive child, and he vowed to himself that he would one day be important and worthy of admiration. He was a brilliant student in school and single-handedly formed a computer company that roared to prominence and financial success. Along

the way, he was able to be charming and winning with clients and cus-
tomers, although he was an abysmal failure with women and intimate
friends. He finally sought treatment upon the insistence of his latest
girlfriend, who had discovered him in an involvement with another
woman and who threatened to leave him unless he changed and mended
his ways. Although the treatment was initiated by this latest fiancée
of his, it was not at all resisted by the patient who himself felt troubled
and in need of help. He was a most cooperative and compliant patient
who had little disagreement about all of the niceties of treatment save
for what seemed to be that single overwhelming problem: he simply—
and often—was just not there.

The failures in attendance did not suddenly appear in this treatment
but were there from the start, and so Dr. J. could hardly feel that she had
unwittingly participated in any sort of intersubjective or co-constructed
phenomenon that was somehow derived from an unconscious communication that was outside of her ken. Rather she felt quite innocent, although impatient. In fact, she had no doubt of her neutrality and as a
matter of fact was a little pleased with how objective she had been.

This reaction of Dr. J.'s, initially merely that of impatience, caused
her to mull over her options. For one, she could readily see that the early
traumata of her patient's childhood might inevitably result in such a
chaotic adulthood, and so felt that what was required according to her
theoretical training was a prolonged "holding environment," somewhat
akin to a corrective emotional experience. She thereby would conduct
herself in a friendly and unemotional manner that would allow her patient over time to feel safe and protected and so to work on his (possible)
traumatic deidealization. This seemed to her to be a reasonable and wel-
come road to travel, but unfortunately it was a plan that she seemed unable to launch, since the patient's absences hardly lent themselves to long
periods of her being "understanding." Her impatience did not seem to be
fertile ground for an exercise of her patience. She was stymied.

Another and alternative solution to her quandary was offered to
Dr. J. at a case conference conducted by a well-known no-nonsense
analyst. He explained "enactment" to Dr. J. He scoffed at the passive
endurance of Dr. J. and instructed her to lay out the rules of analysis,
especially those of attendance required of this or any other analysand.
Dr. J. knew that this sort of aggressive advice worked best for analysts
in those olden times of plentiful patients, but it seemed out of touch

with the current state of analytic practice. Dr. J. admitted to herself that she rather liked this hard-headed approach, but felt it did not suit her personality; she was also reluctant to risk her personal pleasure in having such an agreeable and well-paying patient by antagonizing him.

There seemed to be a very clear and obvious third alternative available to this analyst to get the analysis back on track (although in truth it had never really been on track), and that was to interpret the meaning of this irregularity in the transference. In fact, most of what she gained from her initial supervisory hour was the direction to focus more upon the goings-on between the two of them, and that was what Dr. J. quickly herself attended to, directing the patient to do the same. The particular nature of this special focus had to do with an assortment of interpretations having to do with feelings of disappointment in the analyst and/or anger at the analyst. When these seemed to have little impact beyond the dutiful listening of the patient, alternative sets of interpretations having to do with loving feelings toward the analyst and/or jealous or envious fantasies about the analyst were offered in their stead. The impact of these interpretations on the patient was equally unimpressive and so Dr. J. began to read through the literature to learn more about patients for whom the awareness of unconscious contents was either of little help or was even disabling. Her patient seemed to fit that category, but for the fact that the revealing of unconscious content to him seemed to matter not a whit. And then she noticed something else in this treatment that she had failed to confront.

As a background to this something else, it is important to know that Dr. J. was something of a stickler about paying and getting paid. She told her patients that she preferred to get paid by the tenth of the month, and most of them, including the one being discussed, complied with her request. The only problem was that she soon realized that he never paid the entire amount: it would sometimes be half and sometimes three-fourths, but never all. He would occasionally follow this partial payment with the remainder in the next month, but there was clearly no rhyme or reason to his chosen procedure. When Dr. J. would bring this up he would often miss the next appointment and/or have his secretary call to say that a check was on its way. And it often was. In fact Dr. J. learned that he treated everyone in this idiosyncratic, controlling manner. Dr. J. began to realize that this patient's habits had no particular personal meaning or significance. He treated everyone as he did her. He was "enacting." It was a way of life.

Slowly, Dr. J's impatience changed to irritation, dismay, and ultimately to bewilderment. Let us imagine her visiting London and speaking to a Kleinian supervisor. With a little literary license, this particular Englishwoman would advise Dr. J. that the patient had, by projective identification, taken control of Dr. J.'s mind and had deposited his rage at the mother (and/or the maternal breast) into Dr. J. This seemed to make perfect sense to Dr. J., but she was at a loss as to what to do about that particular state of affairs. She was then advised to return to her patient and tell him exactly what he was doing to her. Although there is no doubt that J. was not quite at ease in the delivery of this sort of interpretation, and that this particular inadequacy may have led to a less-than-committed sense of genuine sincerity in its delivery, the result seemed to be a chastened patient who continued to miss appointments but now with a new-found sense of guilt.

If we put aside for the moment the somewhat magical or mystical components of the process of projective identification, it does make some sense to conceptualize Dr. J.'s state as somehow caused by the patient and indeed as a result of and resulting from the intention of the patient. Somehow the patient had induced or evoked a set of feelings in Dr. J., although this evocation might be no more than a demonstration to Dr. J. of just what this patient's chaotic life is all about. It is vitally important to recognize that such an unconscious or implicit set of messages to a therapist should be read solely as indicative of an illustration or a demonstration of the patient's life. These communications are not to be seen as something that is unwittingly *done* to the therapist. Although this difference may seem to be a subtle one, it has wide implications in terms of any interpretive work that may follow from the recognition and understanding of such messages. The patient does not wish to upset Dr. J. or get her angry any more than he is disappointed in Dr. J. or in love with her. He merely wants her to know what sort of life he lives, and in this very important sense, his irregular behavior really has nothing to do with Dr. J. It is not personal at all. Rather it is his only way to communicate to her the nature of his own psychic organization. It may be said to be personally impersonal.

Interpretations that recognize the essential nature of the patient, or what may be better conceptualized as the patient's psychic organization, are those that deal with form rather than with content. One is here recognizing the behavior of the patient as an indicator of his own sense of internal disorder, and the recognition becomes, in itself, an entry into better regulation. Such understanding on the patient's part of how he makes his way in the world is transformed into a modicum of control. In brief, self-understanding over time equates to self-control by way of self-reflection. Thus the form becomes the content. Action takes on meaning.

Discussion of Example I

The particular way one constructs and delivers an interpretation about form is something that may be familiar to many analysts and therapists but frequently is not conceptualized with equal clarity. One must plan to develop and construct an explanation that is essentially an impersonal one, an explanation that consists of a certain vision of the patient's psychic organization with no intrusion of the therapist's presence. We say things that reflect how it must be for a patient to endure such chronic chaos, while we in no way need include ourselves and what it also does to us. We should aim to steer clear of involving ourselves in the illustration except for our function as a witness to the phenomenon. This is only a step away from the Kleinian supervisor's somewhat accurate but accusatory interpretation, but it allows the patient to, in parallel, take a step back: one that makes for self-reflection. Empathy here involves a simple declaration of what it must be like to live in that patient's shoes.

To be sure, this sort of advice about the interpretation of form rather than content is not applicable to every patient with some kind of disorganized or disordered psyche. The goal must be one that subsumes both form and content. When we investigate several such cases of dysregulation, we soon encounter a variant of the problem. Here is another example.

CLINICAL CASE EXAMPLE II

Dr. K. came for supervision to discuss a patient who was anything but a source of pleasure and enthusiasm. His patient was an attractive and bright woman in the midst of a bitter and messy divorce who had little patience for discussion of anything aside from the nastiness of her soon-to-be ex-husband. Dr. K. had initially scheduled her to be seen twice weekly, but this arrangement never seemed to be easily accomplished, in part because of his own limited flexibility, and over time this woman had become a once-weekly patient. In his heart, Dr. K. was ever on the alert to remind her of her twice-weekly commitment, but he found that opportunities to do so were few and far between and reminding her of it always seemed to carry an accusation of her failing to fulfill an obligation. He kept his discontent to himself. In addition, besides his unhappiness at the frequency of her attendance, Dr. K. was regularly dismayed by the patient's late arrival to her sessions. If one were to characterize Dr. K.'s presentation of this patient to the supervisor, it would be that of a disappointed therapist who felt that his patient did not attach enough importance to him or to the therapy. Much like a discarded lover, Dr. K. felt that he did not seem to count, and he could only conclude that this was a deficiency of his patient in her own inability to really care for others. He decided that hers was a primitive personality with little capacity for intimacy.

Rather than detail this patient's individual history or much of her present troubled life, I wish to concentrate upon a particular issue in the treatment having to do with the missing of appointments. Although it is not uncommon to have patients respond to a therapist's canceling an appointment with reactions that range from a counterreaction of cancellation to a whole variety of parapraxes such as forgetting not to come, it is somewhat less common to have patients react to their own cancellations. When Dr. K. and his supervisor examined the move from twice-weekly to once-weekly sessions, along with other reactions to holidays and vacations, they discovered that any sort of disruption in the schedule was followed by a period of lateness, irregular attendance, and efforts of his patient to change the appointment times. When Dr. K. would suggest to the patient that she might miss seeing him or might have fantasies about what he was doing during the absence, she was less than hospitable to any of these ideas. What did characterize this treatment was a series of somewhat stable hours alternating with periods of erratic ones. The latter were primarily those of lateness, canceling or forgetting, and arriving with nothing to say or too much to comprehend. If Dr. K. looked at these hours primarily in terms of their form, he discerned a pattern that at its simplest seemed to say that any sort of break in continuity or regularity led to an unstable period that required a certain amount of time to settle down. Nothing that he said or did had much of an effect at all.

For this patient, the regularity of the sessions and the presence of the therapist had, in themselves, an ameliorative effect, while any sort of deviation from this somewhat stable state revealed her psyche's underlying vulnerability, after which she needed a period of time for an equilibrium to be restored. Thus Dr. K. was actually quite important to the patient, although more as a bit of psychic structure than as an imago from the past. Interestingly, and not surprisingly, this patient is representative of a group for whom vacations and all sorts of traveling, of coming and going, are inherently disruptive. One such patient characterized her problems as those of entry and re-entry, and she approached any trip fully anticipating being thrown for a loop. These patients are, however, able to regulate themselves with available others who function as structural components or selfobjects. In treatment, the disruptive effect results not only from experiencing the familiar fate of being misunderstood by the therapist, but is also seen as a response to the sheer alteration caused by the organizing effect of the treatment. Although Dr. K.'s patient had a childhood much like that of Dr. J.'s, one is often at a loss when attempting to correlate these fragile psyches with any particular diagnostic category. There is often a temptation to classify such patients as borderline personalities because of the intensity of their affective states and the apparent paucity of close and meaningful relationships. However, it is well to be cautious in any such appraisal, since the fragility of the psyche is not readily connected to any particular psychodynamic formulation, and it is best to understand these elements as part of a total conceptualization of the patient. For one exception to this generalization, here is another clinical incident seen in the same patient.

CLINICAL CASE EXAMPLE III

Dr. K.'s patient also serves nicely to demonstrate an element that is striking in the long-term treatment of problems of dysregulation. Dr. K. had noticed that his patient's recounting of troubles with her husband was easily and obviously seen as often following some provocation of the patient, and this sequence soon seemed to evidence itself in the treatment. The two had been about to talk about a particularly unhappy time in the patient's life, with no anticipated foreseeable breaks or disruptions in the treatment, when the patient inexplicably brought about a schedule struggle. At one level it was readily apparent that the patient was avoiding a re-confrontation with unhappiness, but that explanation seemed a bit too pat and inconclusive. What Dr. K. noticed was that over time, this fight, like any other sort of fight the patient had with her husband, had an enlivening and invigorating effect on her. Her utilization of a struggle was initiated by a barely recognizable descent into depression that could be relieved or even obliterated by an argument or an affect of intense anger or hatred. If Dr. K. were able to approach and investigate the depression of his patient he would be unlikely to see or hear anything reflective of guilt and self-abnegation. Rather he would probably hear of a feeling of emptiness and isolation that was unbearable and intolerable and that needed to be immediately dissipated. Sometimes drugs worked, but for Dr. K.'s patient as well as others, the evocation of a feeling of chaos and disorder could often be counted on to obliterate the underlying depression. Activity was a cure, no matter how it came about. Here one could pinpoint and assign a particular meaning to the form.

Discussion of Example III

There is something of an addictive quality about states of disharmony and even of rage. As much as patients suffering from the latter claim to wish to avoid such mental anguish, they seem to regularly find themselves unable to escape from thoughts of revenge, of memories of mistreatment, and of an endless search for serenity. Treatment of persons captured by chronic rage is best conducted by keeping in mind the aim of reaching the underlying depression. The angry preoccupations of these individuals are essentially a form of self-medication, and are easily conceptualized as such; that is, some biochemical alterations are surely responsible for the cessation and replacement of the much more painful depressive states. It is, however, a gross error to consider pharmacological treatment of any depression that is merely an hypothesis rather than an experience.

A situation that is a step away from purely psychoeconomic issues yet still remains within the concept of form is illustrated by the next case.

CLINICAL CASE EXAMPLE IV

Dr. S. came to supervision in the midst of what can only be called a personal crisis, in that he felt that he had committed a grievous error in his handling of a case, an error that led to his being chastised by a colleague and feeling personally puzzled over how he might otherwise have behaved. It all started with his seeing a couple for marital therapy, or, more accurately, for an evaluation for some form of therapy. After one or possibly two visits, the husband asked to speak to Dr. S. alone, and he thereupon immediately confessed his infidelity. Dr. S. felt torn about being in possession of such information and, not having fore-warned his errant patient about what he might do with this knowledge, decided to do nothing. Subsequent to this meeting Dr. S. suggested that each member of this discordant couple should be in individual treat-ment and chose to himself treat the wife in psychoanalysis and to refer the husband elsewhere. Not surprisingly, the couple's problems got worse, the husband asked for a divorce, and simultaneously confessed his illicit affair to his wife, now the patient of Dr. S. The husband also chose to tell the wife that Dr. S. had been privy to this information, and indeed he had accordingly assumed that Dr. S. would tell the wife. Upon learning of this, the wife became furious at Dr. S., who was then also lectured by a colleague on the proper way to handle these marital communicative misconnections. Dr. S. felt guilty and bewildered and turned to his supervisor for guidance and relief. He felt trapped in a web of intrigue and conspiracy; indeed he felt very much like the unfaith-ful husband who had betrayed his wife, and his new patient accused him of that very misdeed.

When Dr. S.'s supervisor asked if it was really likely that this be-trayed woman was blind to her husband's unfaithfulness, he learned that this husband's particular moment of straying from the marital vows was but one in a string of such occurrences. That made it quite likely that Dr. S.'s patient was herself somehow complicit in her unhappy state—one that involved both knowing along with not-knowing. In fact, Dr. S. was now accused of hiding information from his patient, information that was hardly a secret from anyone. Yet had Dr. S. told the wife what he had learned from the husband, he might have betrayed the confessor. In sum, Dr. S. felt that he had become an actor in a script written by this couple that allowed no freedom for improvisation or correction. Thus, long before Dr. S. could presume to investigate the development of one or another transference configuration, he found that he was a participant. The form dominated the search for content.

In fact, there may be no clear representative person from the past who corresponds to the present status that envelops Dr. S. Rather, the form of the network of relationships, one that involves disavowal and contradiction, may be the more pertinent point to pursue here. Surely there may be a particular set of memories of similar relationships yet there also may not. It could well be that the emergence of the form is crucial, and that this is sufficient for the therapist to reach some understanding.

As Dr. S. mulled over this case, he quickly brought up another one that also involved a couple, one that also made him feel trapped in a script authored by another, and one that also puzzled him—but now with no hint of guilt or shame. This second couple was involved in some periodic couples therapy, but in their case Dr. S. had made it clear that he could keep no confidences when and if he saw a member of the duo alone. Indeed he did so on occasion, and regularly struggled with the fact that the wife, the one who did see him individually, could not commit herself to a frequency that would allow for much depth of understanding. It was not so much that she felt that Dr. S. would reveal her thoughts to the husband but rather that she seemed to recognize that the solidity of the marriage demanded a sort of "this far and no further" stance on her part. Now perhaps all marriages have taught their partners to subscribe to this principle, but in this case Dr. S. felt that the solidity of the marriage had become a particular assignment of his. Once again, Dr. S. felt more like a function than an observer who can exit at will.

THE POSITION OF THE THERAPIST OR ANALYST

Rather than listening to a patient weave a narrative of his life and rather than our co-constructing a new narrative without the original amnesias and distortions, we are sometimes best served by listening to the music instead of the words. The knowledge that we bring to some of our patients is not only that realized by making conscious the contents of the unconscious. The raising of such contents to consciousness seems of peculiarly little help to some patients, and it is best to think of such wasted insight as just the wrong sort of knowledge. In our efforts to understand patients, we usually formulate an imagined scenario of what we might do if we were in their shoes. This temporary trial identification is one that changes from moment to moment until that inevitable moment of misunderstanding, the time of bewilderment and uncertainty that is a necessary part of any psychotherapy or psychoanalysis. What is required of us at these times of being with and then losing the patient is an effort to find the form or the pattern that we are now a part of. More often than not we find ourselves unable to make this effort of abstraction or decentering, and we seem to insist on our being something more meaningful to the patient than a mere node in a network. At this juncture, where our being is assigned a functional role in the psychic structure rather than having the role of a character in a play, we tend to impose our own pattern of existence upon the patient. We regulate from the outside and establish an order of our own, thereby reasserting ourselves in the interaction. Here again, we need to encompass both form and content in our interpretive activity. Action must be understood rather than prohibited.

It is instructive at times to work at differentiating what one means to a patient according to this formula of form versus content. Especially when a separation occurs, it is commonplace to interpret something that qualifies as "missing" or "being missed." Yet we regularly stumble over the inexactness of the term inasmuch as missing a function differs markedly from missing a person. One good example of this difference can be seen, sometimes quite readily, after the dissolution of a marriage from divorce, death, or whatever cause. In most cases we can see two separate forms of mourning: one over the loss of the person, with all of its concomitant grief, and another over the loss of all of the support and meaning of being married. These are separate losses that in some people have quite different valences. They vary from the individual who is so wrapped up in his or her devotion to a single person that another marriage is never considered, to another individual for whom just being married, with all of its privileges and institutional standing, is clearly more important than the particular person involved in the union. So too is the connection to a therapist to be distinguished—as to his or her importance as a transference figure from the past, versus a bit of psychic structure from the present. But beware: neither alternative is healthier or sicker, or desirable or undesirable, they are just different.

We are all familiar with analysts and therapists who have a set of rules of performance and behavior for patients and for whom deviations from these procedures are treated as serious breaches of conduct. On rare occasions these therapists chastise their patients for their misbehavior and so insure their conformity. On less rare occasions these therapists interpret such lack of conformity as resistances due to a variety of negative thoughts and feelings, and some patients join in this characterization of themselves. Sometimes these or other therapists feel it necessary to allow deviations from the rules as a sort of exercise in their being truly empathic with patients. All of these therapeutic exercises, which may range from yelling at patients to mollifying them, are essentially directed at aiding the therapist in regulating herself.

Inasmuch as dysregulation and regulation work in both directions, it is important to realize that our use of patients to organize and regulate ourselves is a much-unrecognized form of countertransference. It remains unrecognized because it is easily rationalized as an important part of the treatment, and it is often institutionalized in the form of one or another theories of conduct. We should be very cautious of therapeutic advice that urges us to allow patients to mistreat us, just as much as we need to be wary of those who would have us mistreat our patients. These are not to be thought of as ethical or moral issues and certainly not as boundary problems that need to be matters of adjudication. They demand an understanding that resides alongside the story that we prefer to listen to: an understanding of pattern and form.

It is often a wrenching experience to realize that there is no proper way to conduct an analysis or psychotherapy, and operating according to the sole requirement of understanding holds everything potentially up to scrutiny. Since there is no possible way we can do the impossible job of such total understanding, we tend to carve out areas of particular interest and disregard others as irrelevant. Some of us get particularly attuned to the so-called enactments of treatment which, of course, are only considered as such by a decision of the therapist. Some of us like to interpret dreams; some look for sadism and hate; some care only for love. However, it seems that all of us want to concentrate on something or other while stilling the interference of the irrelevant. For some patients, however, this irrelevant interference is nevertheless the essence of the treatment, yet it is often not seen as such.

DISCUSSION

One often hears anecdotes about the way patients who have finished an analysis or treatment respond to a question about what they got from their treatment. Usually their answer consists of a particular minor statement or bit of behavior that emanated from the therapist. They remember the time that he kept them five minutes extra or telephoned them in the hospital or asked about the welfare of their parents. These seemingly trivial memories often seem to be the sum and substance of their recollection, and they regularly triumph over stories of oedipal rivalry, aggressive attacks on the maternal breast, and even castration anxiety. Such incidents of selective memory may then be seized upon by those who insist that treatment and cure lie solely in "the relationship," and all that matters are whatever elements compose that nebulous entity. I think that another explanation is possible, one that does include the fact that complex psychodynamic formulations are either forgotten or of no apparent account in the improvement of some of our patients. Those bits of memory they report regularly include the therapist as standing out, either as thoughtful or gracious or generous, and in some way different from the ordinary. One rarely or never hears of a patient attributing his improvement to the fact that the analyst was always on time or gave out bills on the first of the month or any of the routine pieces of the business of therapy. But I would like to make a plea for the ordinary. The supposed extraordinary acts of memory are really the ways of ordinary folks. I think the routines of treatment are much more meaningful to some, if not all, of our patients than we may recognize or choose to believe. It is these routines themselves that crystallize around these memorable moments. I think some of our patients become better organized through the sheer regularity of attendance in a therapy or an analysis, and that this, along with the minutiae of the therapeutic ritual, becomes an essential part of the entire psychic self. Since the mind is not coexistent with the contents of the skull, we can see it more as an activity that extends far beyond the confines of one's skin and includes the presence of the therapist along with the entirety of the process. Even though this is the more fundamental feature of some of our most disorganized patients, it is not ever a feature to be discounted.

SUMMARY

The major types of anxiety that are taught to students of psychoanalysis usually boil down to only two: separation anxiety and castration anxiety. Where once castration anxiety was seen as central to every neurosis, over the years separation anxiety has seemed to dominate and so to steal the show. And as separation began to be more carefully investigated by writers from Margaret Mahler to Heinz Kohut, we saw it as a quite complex set of circumstances that involved much more than the mere fact of one person leaving another. It has to do with one's delineation as an individual, and, in a somewhat contradictory fashion, with one being able to be meaningfully connected to others. As we unpack the various facets of separation we are sometimes able to see it in a purely psychoeconomic perspective, and this is the perspective that best reveals the sustaining role that one person often plays for another. We sometimes literally hold others together and separation causes them to start to fall apart. Perhaps for the majority of patients this psychoeconomic factor can remain in the background and be left unsaid, but for some it is the key to a successful interpretive effort. I think that it is important to include this sort of interpretive work alongside of that which deals with conflict and empathic failure. It probably can even be seen as a variant of the latter, but the risk of separation is so regular a part of the background that it is easily lost and discounted. And, perhaps unfortunately, it may be the reason that some god-awful treatments seem to help patients despite the therapist.

What we learn over time is the simple fact that, out of the multitude of interactions that occur between patient and therapist, certain salient issues do tend to precipitate out. But the features that present themselves for concern and attention need not be the ones that in the end matter the most. Rather, patients often have a capacity to select what has the greatest meaning for them. A therapist who centers his attention on one or another content issue can readily enlist a patient in the pursuit of a topic while being unmindful of the fact that his or her tone of voice or level of enthusiasm is the essential factor that is impacting the patient. In a way, we are most fortunate when it comes to the peculiar manner in which patients are able to profit from a treatment whose design is other than what benefits them the most. Seen in this way, much therapy and analysis resemble the offerings in a cafeteria where we need not finish everything on our tray.

The multiplicity of interactions that occur in every sort of treatment allows us to pick and choose what we wish to make central and critical. The popular option of constructing a narrative often competes with one in which insight is gained from making the unconscious conscious, and lately we have a new contender in the form of the proponents of what is called procedural memory. It may well be true that all of these have a place in helping patients and that the difference lies less in the particular procedure than in the patient. No one has to give up listening to stories or unearthing repressed fantasies or even developing new neuronal pathways. Most likely, the real decision is always one that remains with and is determined by the patient. An interesting by-product of this choice is the fact that therapists often seem to prefer to champion not only what interests them most but also what appears to help them most. I guess I like regularity. But that should not lull me into thinking that it can ever stand alone. Instead I consider it an aid to my understanding. It allows me to champion one sort of interpretation over another, and it is a necessary limit lest I think that I can ever abstain from interpreting, although as we see next that is an impossibility.

PART THREE

From Interpretation to
a Place for the Mind

7

Interpretation Is It: There Is No Beyond

Try to think of it this way: it is all interpretation. There is no before and after, no preparation and follow-up, no cessation and no respite. We are all interpreting animals, and just as some animals are preoccupied with grooming one another, we are forever reading one another. Sometimes we get it right, and quite often we get it wrong, but we never stop trying. When we are not directly interpreting one another in this constant effort at decoding, we direct our attention to the cultural and social artifacts of others. If a man's mind wanders during a conference or a concert, he usually finds himself thinking about interpreting the luncheon menu, the direction to the washroom, or how to work the cellular phone. Sigmund Freud did not so much isolate and insist upon the uniqueness of interpretation as he offered a new and exciting take or spin on looking at things. I think it is a mistake to categorize a period of preparing for an interpretation, delivering it, and then considering the results. I think it is a mistake to claim that there are noninterpretive interventions versus real interpretations, or moments of meaning versus moments of non-meaning. Rather we would do better to realize that sometimes we get it, and sometimes we just do not. That last bit seems to be the problem.

Listen to how beautifully Philip Roth (1997) puts it in his book *American Pastoral*:

> You fight your superficiality, your shallowness, and so as to try to come at people without unreal expectations, without an overload of bias or hope or arrogance, as untanklike as you can be, sans cannon and machine guns and steel plating half a foot thick; you come at them unmenacingly on your own ten toes instead of tearing up the turf with your caterpillar treads, take them on with an open mind, as equals, man to man, as we used to say, and yet you never fail to get them wrong. You might as well have the brain of a tank. You get them wrong before you meet them, while you're anticipating meeting them; you get them wrong while you're with them; and then you go home to tell somebody else about the meeting and you get them all wrong again. Since the same generally goes for them with you, the whole thing is really a dazzling illusion empty of all perception, an astonishing farce of misperception. And yet what are we to do about this terribly significant business of other people, which gets bled of the significance we think it has and takes on a significance that is ludicrous, so ill-equipped are we all to envision one another's interior workings and invisible aims? [p. 35]

Roth goes on:

> The fact remains that getting people right is not what living is all about anyway. It's getting them wrong that is living, getting them wrong and wrong and wrong and then, on careful reconsideration, getting them wrong again. That's how we know we're alive: we're wrong. [p. 35]

One should not read that as a message of despair. It is one of encouragement. It recognizes our futile and silly efforts to be neutral and objective, it recognizes that equally unhelpful advice to approach each patient without memory or desire, and it alerts us to the often forgotten fact that our patients are as busy interpreting us as we are in doing the same to them.

If you are able to take hold of that idea of mutual, never-ending interpretation, then try to think of all of our so-called enactments as mere varieties of interpretation. It may at times seem a bit superficial, but you do interpret that smile or frown on another's face as carrying a meaning and you do respond accordingly, and that response is in turn interpreted. Just as our behavior does, so do our words become part of the ongoing circular process of our reading one another and trying to get it right. To say of enactments that they are "non-verbal, symbolic carriers of unconscious meaning" (Chused 1991, p. 615) fails in any manner to clearly distinguish what they are, since just about anything and everything can fill that bill. We live in a sea of words and gestures and behavioral routines that are never what they seem to be or, better put, are always more than what one may make of them. What psychoanalysis offers is a new and decidedly different decoding system.

Having accepted this surround of interpretation, it is a small step to recognize that "getting it" is equivalent to understanding and so to see that interpretation is the link and entrance to the understanding of others. How we accomplish such understanding and yet remain faithful to Freud and psychoanalysis involves the union of psychoanalytic interpretation and our connection to one another. It is the means by which we as analysts achieve an understanding in depth.

UNDERSTANDING AND MISUNDERSTANDING

I think we all would, at least for now, agree that merely knowing something about another person, anything from his date of birth to the contents of his unconscious mind, does not at all equate to our understanding of him. Lots of times many of us like to think that such knowledge does constitute understanding, but more often than not the result is that we are merely comforting ourselves that we are "getting it." Misunderstanding and its companion, anxiety, are terribly uncomfortable states, and so they are regularly combated by all sorts of devices we have devoted to convincing ourselves that we do indeed understand. We have earlier noted that some scholars (for example Heidegger) have claimed that understanding others is basic to human life; it is something these same scholars claim to be "primordial." It is true that there exists some very early feeling of kinship or fundamental connectedness to others that results in a feeling of safety and comfort, one that is to be regularly upset by our changing needs and the inevitable failings of others.

We have to be able to understand others in order to survive and, while this capacity has clearly evolved in humans, it is an ability that remains for many of us both central and ever in need of further development. In its simplest form, the gathering of information about others involves both a cognitive effort and a trial identification with another. The empathy that results is what most humans use to make their way in the world, from buying a pair of shoes to choosing a mate. Empathy joins the cognitive and the affective. Extending the effort of sustained empathy is the way most depth psychologists make their way in the world, through the constant conflicts over misunderstanding and understanding. We do not understand others the way we might make sense of a mathematical formula or the workings of the internal combustion engine. Rather we need somehow to see what it must be like to *be* that person. Empathy can be a very transitory experience, of the kind that occurs when we occasionally and automatically register the ill-will of, say, our newspaper vendor and proceed on our way, or it can be the primary work of our daily lives. Thus it goes hand in hand with interpretation as it, empathy, becomes the means by which we gather the data that is to be understood.

A noted philosopher (Davidson 1980), in an effort to comprehend how people get to understand one another, pointed out that the aim of interpretation is not agreement. This view is coherent with what we now know about being empathic with someone, which is not the same as agreeing with that person. This same philosopher urges us to listen to another person by means of a theory that is never fixed but is capable of modification and which, because of its goal of understanding, changes with each person. While the method he espouses is cognitive, the method of the psychoanalyst adds the emotional component of trial identification in an effort to capture both the knowing and the feeling. In this manner, we develop a theory of understanding and a way of interpreting each patient individually. Thus the interpretation of a smile for Patient X is not the same as for Patient Y, just as a gift from one patient need not have the same meaning as the same gift received from another, and the same can be said of a dream of (say) the Washington Monument for Patient X and Patient Y. It may be a bit more difficult to believe that this applies as well to a smile and everything else that may originate from the analyst in response to these different patients.

Over time, we learn about one another and settle into a pattern of what we take to be understanding. I believe this is where the problems begin, and they have to do with the manner in which a transient understanding may become a misunderstanding, as well as the complementary way a transient misunderstanding may allow for a new understanding that gets us back on track. For psychoanalysts, each of these moves results from transference, and so each of the countermoves offers us an opportunity for interpretation, but now it is an interpretation of a different sort.

CASE ILLUSTRATION—A BAG OF APPLES

One of my favorite examples from the literature is that of a patient who brings a bag of apples to her analyst (Akhtar 1999). Rather than interpret the act, the analyst explains to the patient why he cannot accept the apples—because it would break one of the rules of analysis. The patient listens, agrees, and then proceeds to associate to "apples" as per the analyst's suggestion. She comes to a point about apples and Adam and Eve that seems to please both herself and the analyst and she leaves happily with an equally contented analyst left behind. I offer this as an example of a mutual enactment that might well allow each participant to feel understood, but that could readily be seen by a dispassionate observer as a failure of the analyst to understand just why the patient brought the apples, just how she felt about the analyst's refusal of this gift, and moreover whether or not the Adam and Eve resolution was a perpetuation of this ongoing set of misperceptions.

There is no doubt that mutual exchanges of this kind occur in many psychoanalyses and might well constitute the bulk of some treatments. The interpretations that are offered are directed to an arena that is felt to be outside of the awareness of the analysand, such as her unconscious feelings about her analyst, and the analyst is able to point out the essence of these to the patient. As an aside, the very act of pointing out is worrisome, because it positions the analyst in something like a watchtower that is all-seeing and sitting high above the ground. Now consider for a moment an exchange that has to do with some unknown (to us) and unconscious (to the analyst) communication, one that goes to the patient from the analyst and indicates to her that he might well like a gift, or that he needs to be tested as to his willingness to accept a gift, or perhaps that he simply wishes to tell the patient more about analysis and its rules per se. Imagine the patient seeing this. To pursue this line one would need, at a minimum, to talk about the enactment as involving both parties, unwittingly or otherwise. We need not join with Hoffman (1993) in concentrating upon the patient's reading of the analyst's unconscious, nor with the intersubjectivists who urge us to see a jointly constructed intersubjective field (Stolorow and Atwood 1992) in order to primarily ally ourselves with Philip Roth, who beckons us to witness this "dazzling illusion" of two persons getting it wrong. Now all you need do is to recognize that the inexhaustibility of interpretation, the multidetermination of Freud, and the sliding signifiers of Saussure and Lacan all add up to this: one is never able to completely exhaust one's understanding.

The reason that psychoanalysis makes a claim to getting it right a bit more often is that it purports to be a depth psychology. This claim allows psychoanalysts to respond to ordinary interpretations, those that are part and parcel of folk psychology, as superficial, and also as often concealing something both secret and routinely inaccessible. Psychoanalysis makes a further claim to being involved in the business of a "talking cure." As such it combines these two features: having its interpretations framed by language, as well as acknowledging the unconscious and its supposed contents. It is probably safe to state that, as worthy or effective as they may be, therapeutic efforts that disclaim the unconscious and/or dismiss verbal reports essentially lie outside of psychoanalysis. They are not wrong, merely different.

LEVELS OF INTERPRETING

Let us try now to consider the activity of the analyst in the making of interpretations on three separate levels. The first level has to do with the observations that we make of the patient, his behavior, his character, his transferences. All of these we are able to point out to the patient much as the above-mentioned analyst observed the gift of apples and sensitively, but "from afar," told her it was not an option. We all do this some of the time, while some of us, with some patients, may do it practically all of the time. The second level includes another common (although different) kind of interpretation having to do with empathy and one's ability to feel what the patient is experiencing.

Although this level is less prominent in our synopsis of the apple incident, I think a reading of that article would convince anyone that this analyst was quite in tune with his patient. However, I would judge that a number of analyses are almost totally devoted to the singular enterprise of maintaining empathy with the patient and focusing upon its breaks and restitutions. When this is done to the exclusion of a consideration of the unconscious factors responsible for the ebb and flow of empathy, this second level falls short, much as does the first, the one "from afar." However, each of these levels is routinely and properly considered as interpretive, inasmuch as each fulfills the definition of revealing something to someone. Only the third level proposed here, that of verbally interpreting the particular transference configuration with its unconscious roots (a configuration that is comprehended by one's empathic connection to the patient), is the level of interpretation unique to psychoanalysis.

It is easy to view such a claim of uniqueness as a sort of elitist posture, but I want to buttress my position by a brief reference to the concept of the hermeneutic circle, a concept that enjoys the position of both being the proper foundation of the science of interpretation and being massively misunderstood by psychoanalysts. To attend to the second part first, we need to again emphasize that all science is hermeneutic, and that there is no division between pure science and interpretive science, since every scientist interprets, all the way from the numbers on the graph to the smirk on a stranger's face. The hermeneutic circle takes us a step further by allowing us to tease apart just how the act of interpretation is accomplished. In a nutshell, we come to perceive something with a preconceived idea that we then modify and alter in a feedback process of circularity (Heidegger 1946) as suggested by Davidson and others. Now the analyst has a preconception of the unconscious and he strives to get the patient to see things with that in mind. By combining the empathic connection with this preconception of unconscious contents, the analyst moves to the third level, the transference interpretation that discloses the nature of the relationship in depth. I think this is a crucial point, and it distinguishes this third level or step from other interpretive processes that remain on the level of understanding the patient and his or her unconscious—much as the apples in the aforementioned illustration—and so relies on the experience or the language as such to be helpful or even curative. Intense moments of affect need to be nailed down by words so that they do not become addictive, in an unending search to have the experience repeated once more. This level of verbal interpretation of the transference relationship is designed to accomplish the task of avoiding the addictive repetition by disrupting the ongoing understanding that has already been achieved. It is explanatory, and in the explaining it breaks the empathic connection. It is much like telling your dancing partner, in the middle of a romantic waltz, that he or she is stepping on your toes: the moment is destroyed. I would maintain that this particular and vital explanatory break in understanding is almost impossible without language, and so I would insist that experiential or nonverbal interpretations, no matter how important and meaningful they may be, cannot proceed to this point. Nor can pure language alone without empathy accomplish this much. We must first interpret to achieve understanding and then move to a deeper understanding by completing the hermeneutic circle. Of course one cannot deny that much can be accomplished without this deepened understanding, but that fact should not be used to conflate all levels of interpretation. The disclosure of unconscious content as such is insufficient unless and until it leads to competence, the empowerment of the patient, and the ensuing freedom that results from the combination of empathy and its verbal articulation.

THE SPACE OF INTERPRETATION

Think of interpretation as an expanding and contracting space. It expands with increased understanding and is diminished with misunderstanding. It has no clear-cut borders, but once outside of this space we are lost and bewildered, or else we are captured by the sirens of certainty and smugness. For a psychoanalyst to inhabit this space requires a method and a theory. For an analyst to live in this space, he requires a patient. This is so because psychoanalysis understands others, and it does so on the basis of its method and theory, although this is not to be equated with the full range of understanding that might, for example, belong to spiritual or romantic or cultural arenas. The recognition of this particular space of interpretation and its fluid but definable boundaries is the key to a proper definition of psychoanalysis. Although this is not the time or place to pursue that topic, I offer the suggestion that a concentration on the quality of this space will help to resolve such questions as why psychoanalysis is unable to develop a psychology of learning or to ever happily join with brain research. As true as it is that we are interpreting beings, the type of decoding done by psychoanalysis has important limitations. We all know how foolhardy it is for analysts to claim knowledge about arenas in which access to the unconscious is closed or absent. One of the great follies of our discipline has been to attempt to apply it in those areas where our expertise is on a par with the average truck driver. I remember some time ago watching an analyst presiding over ratings for motion pictures so as to indicate their suitability for different age groups. I thought that he was really good as well as quite convincing. But I could not help but wonder: Was he functioning as a psychoanalyst or just as a wise and intelligent person? We would all do well not to confuse and/or equate the two.

GETTING IT RIGHT

We are always getting it wrong with one another both because we read people erroneously, and because there is so very much to read. Psychoanalysis narrows the field. It does so by making an agreement to focus on certain issues like the Oedipus complex. When that periodically goes out of fashion, we can look at other items of mutual concern, such as selfobjects or intersubjective fields or even hate. I do not mean to equate these varied subjects in terms of significance, since the argument as to which one may be better or more effective is not relevant here. Rather, the mutual contract between analyst and patient, which aims to increase the patient's understanding, starts a process, one that ebbs and flows from misunderstanding to understanding. At each step of this self-correcting hermeneutic circle the patient (and perhaps the analyst) becomes more and more of a self-interpreting animal. As I have said before, I see no way that this can be readily accomplished without language, and I see no way that this process can be achieved outside of the transference to another person. The first requirement, that of the need for language, exists from infancy because we develop into people who are continually involved with inner speech and aspects of self-interpretation. Nonverbal communication is ultimately wrapped in words.

However, the second point, how we achieve self-understanding by way of another, is the most important. Essentially this involves the move from being understood by someone else to doing it oneself. Without entering into a discussion as to whether this process entails the building up of psychic structures, or modifying internal representations, or strengthening internal neuronal connections, the result is some sort of increased individual competence. It follows a sequence of understanding, misunderstanding, and understanding, or understanding plus explaining, or disruption and repair, or any other way we choose to talk about insight. But mainly it works by way of metacomment, that is, by one person saying to another, "Look at what just happened between the two of us." One becomes an observer of oneself and cannot help but see oneself differently. That is the essence of psychoanalytic interpretation. That is what I would have wished for the lady bearing the gift of apples: the analyst and she should have stepped to the side (figuratively) and commented on the entire transaction. (This must, of course, include the part the analyst played in the scene.) Such metacomment is strengthened by the consideration, in depth, of its unconscious links, and it is maintained the way any good maintenance work is, with constant vigilance and attention to ongoing repairs, something often called working through. Thus I become my imaginary helpmate who periodically stops and asks me to make sense of what I am doing. Of course this need happen only at points of feeling misunderstood, either by myself or by others, but the decoding mechanism is there when it is needed.

THE BEST INTERPRETATION

Interpretation is inexhaustible. One must take care *not* to take this to mean that therefore the meaning of any given dream or statement is indeterminate. Multideterminism does not mean indeterminism; and the fact that something has countless meanings should not lead one to say that it has no meaning. Nor should this suggest that one meaning is as good as the next. There are good ones, better ones, and even, at times, a best one. However, the qualification of "at times" forces one to acknowledge that the absolute best one on Tuesday may prove to be a flop on Wednesday. For example, the reason that we cannot assign certain psychological states to specific areas of the brain is that these states are multiply realized; that is, one set of neurons does the work on one occasion and another at another (Smolensky 1988). Similarly, the reason that one interpretation makes sense on one occasion and little or different sense on another is because different experiences can lead to the same interpretation; interpretations, too, are multiply realized. And a similar interpretation can also be totally irrelevant to what may appear to be a similar experience. Interestingly that is also true of certain neuronal configurations, which may yield different psychological states at different times. Therefore every interpretation must be considered in its total context. It could be perfectly correct but not very significant—good but not good enough.

There are times in every analysis and psychotherapy in which honest conviction of understanding is met with bland indifference or downright rejection. I think that Freud should not be too readily quoted in terms of the latter being a sign of a true interpretation. I think it best to occasionally embrace our misunderstanding. This is probably true not only of our patients but also of our particular theories and convictions. Not "getting it" is more of a blessing than a burden, and we all would do well to recognize that we are often quite in the wrong. I have vivid memories of being totally convinced of the rightness of my way of seeing things and the wrenching experience of trying on another perspective. The worst position for an analyst is that of complacency or comfort.

The inexact interpretation is the foundation of psychoanalysis. It carries the necessary emotional charge of discontent that fuels a good analysis. Somewhere between the pole of total bewilderment about a patient and complete comprehension of him is the space of interpretative activity. If the apple lady returned to her analyst with a mutual and implicit agreement that that enacted event was behind them, then they had settled upon a conspiracy of silence. Only if the event could be seen both as a consequence of something that was in need of interpretation *and* as a preamble to something else that would call for interpretation could it qualify as a part of the process of analysis. Psychoanalysts live and work in this space and are ever alert to slipping or falling outside of it. However, the most basic issue is the very simple one that we must remain in the space. Interpretation never ends; the conversation must go on.

At the end of that quote from Philip Roth, after he assures us that we are always wrong, he says: "Maybe the best thing would be to forget being right or wrong about people and just go along for the ride. But if you can do that—well, lucky you" (p. 35). I think it is safe to say that we are all not so lucky.

Interpretation is inexhaustible, but we are regularly lured into repeating the same ones over and over, or moving on to a list of those that are familiar and pleasing to us. The constraints that operate here come from the fact that interpretations are negotiated efforts that arise from a mutual undertaking. This is the aim of the next chapter, which points toward a new vision of the mind and focuses upon what psychoanalysts make of the mind.

8

An Inquiry into the Nature
of Psychoanalytic Data

INTRODUCTION

One of the ongoing debates and concerns of psychoanalysis has been that of constructing a definition of the very word "psychoanalysis," one that would satisfy the many students and practitioners of the enterprise. The results of such a pursuit have ranged from a rather narrow focus on the vicissitudes of the transference (Gill 1979) to a much broader one that allows one to define psychoanalysis by a sort of fiat, i.e., anyone may choose to term what he does as representative of analysis if he so wishes (Shane et al. 1997). There may be some gain in what has thus far been an unhappy resolution of the conundrum of definition if one steps back to see if a satisfactory agreement can be reached on the subsidiary subject of the nature of psychoanalytic data. Such an agreement might aid as a sort of launching pad to a broader definition of the field in its entirety. Relying on Webster's definition as a datum being that which is given from experiment or is assumed for a specific purpose, we can proceed to see if we can fashion a suitable case for the specifics of psychoanalytic data.

THE ADVANTAGES AND DISADVANTAGES
OF DATA RESTRICTION

All of the categories, and psychoanalysis is one such category, that are formed by an inquiry into a particular field are constructed by a combination of the instruments of data collection along with what seems to be the givens of the world. For instance, if we choose to examine a concept such as color or a discipline such as finance, we select what is available in the world along with how we shall observe whatever that selection offers to us. Inevitably, we regularly come up against the boundaries of our categories, all the while recognizing that other instruments and other selections may well offer new categorizations. If we stick to our eyes for seeing color, then we eliminate any other kind of electronic instrument, and so we avoid arguments about colorless objects "really" having color. That is true of concepts, and the same may be said of talk about disciplines such as finance.

This sort of data restriction applies to psychoanalysis in a very crucial way in that we regularly see the casual use of the word without a clear reference to the data being examined. Thus a statement about psychoanalyzing a society would demand some clarification about the nature of the data, that is, how it is obtained and what constitutes its boundaries. Of course, a rigid demand of this sort has the advantage of making one's efforts clear, along with the disadvantage of eliminating many such allied and well-meaning but essentially irrelevant efforts. One should be wary of any effort to legislate what is acceptable for the use of the term, but one should also be diligent about any failure to apply it correctly.

THINKING LIKE A PSYCHOANALYST

As a convenient thought experiment, one can compare the observations of scientists or professionals as they encounter what they may choose to circumscribe as a field of study, that is, the chemist studying chemical reactions, the economist examining economic trends, and so forth.

Imagine a designer entering a room and taking in the placement of furniture, the coordination of colors, and so forth. This person sees things in a very special way, one that the uneducated or untrained person may be unable either to grasp or to speak about. The designer, like a chemist or a psychoanalyst, clearly has at her disposal a working theory of design, one that may or may not be easily articulated but one that seems to immediately allow the possessor of such a theory to view the world and to make inferences from this viewpoint in a circumscribed manner. Probably no one would argue that many persons without such a theory might reasonably design a more pleasant or congenial placement of furniture and colors, but surely the first step to delineate what makes for the designation of a designer is this requirement of a world vision of sorts. However, a designer, more like a psychoanalyst and less like a chemist, might well confront a host of claimants to that very title, like many a person with a flair for color and coordination who would insist that his or her eye for effective design matches that of the so-called professional. That latter person, the professional designer, might argue that the field requires more than talent or an appreciation of aesthetics, that this naïve or even educated vision of beauty needs a theory that is also a map of what one must do in order to function as a designer.

To be sure, the mere vision of what one must make of things or act upon things is but a vision, a spectator view of the world. That sort of perspective is one that allows one to stand outside of the scene, to think about, and to entertain an explanation or a change without having an impact upon what is observed. When we nowadays speak of observation, we always (or usually) wonder about the effect of the observer upon the observed and so one should realize that it is only an imagined ideal that allows one to look at a room or a person and manipulate it in one's mind. The real change seems to reside in action, and the action of the psychoanalyst is to take certain steps and consider those as being decisive.

When Ernest Jones (1949) offered a psychoanalytic interpretation of *Hamlet*, he allowed us to see Hamlet in a different light and so he changed the reader's (or some readers') concept of Hamlet. Save for certain readings, Hamlet remained unchanged as a play and as a character. This is what we say for the most part about applied psychoanalysis.

The change resides only in the mind and imagination of the observer. This surely can be seen as data subject to psychoanalytic theory and explanation, but it may well fall short of what one may wish to consider as the data base of psychoanalysis. For that we must add a step that moves us from spectator to actor, that brings the observer into the field and that necessarily alters the field.

ACTING LIKE A PSYCHOANALYST

When one moves beyond the thought experiment to a field of action, the data seems to change. My designer friend tells me that she can envision a space and is able to walk through it in her mind. So, too, can a psychoanalyst read a novel or see a play or hear a case history and thereby construct a reasonable explanation of the story or narrative according to some preferred analytic theory. My designer begins to function as such when she chooses fabrics, selects furniture, aims for certain color combinations and, above all, works with her clients' wishes, limitations, and capacities. A psychoanalyst may well feel that he or she is functioning as such when, as with Jones, an interpretation is offered, and that may well be seen as what is fundamental to one's function as an analyst, that is, the very act of interpreting. When one begins to connect an analytic interpretation with its effect upon an object, then it appears to be necessary that a more complete encompassing of the role of the psychoanalyst includes the presence of a patient rather than a play or even an isolated dream. Of course no one can or should legislate a definition of what constitutes a psychoanalyst's activity, but it does seem fair to consider that it consists of the analyst–patient dyad.

In so considering this twosome we routinely include all of the niceties and rules of psychoanalysis in terms of frequency, the use of the couch, free association, and so forth. If we add to these the usual range of activities assigned to the analyst from suggestion to abreaction to manipulation to clarification on to interpretation, we usually see the last as the principle one with all others as subordinate (Bibring 1954). Any effort to delineate one or another of these therapeutic activities as unique to psychoanalysis is doomed to failure, yet there does seem to be some validity in considering interpretation as, at least, essential to psychoanalysis. Thus an effort to better detail the data of analysis must or should combine interpretation with what we consider as "given" for this purpose. What we interpret is thus the beginning outline of the database of analysis. It goes beyond what is observed to include what is acted upon, and the latter must now become central to the task at hand: "Exactly what about the patient is interpreted?"

The centrality of the transference usually seems the best answer to the above question. This sort of answer seems to eliminate any and all of the members of applied analysis without in any way diminishing the significance of using psychoanalytic theory to examine other forms of data. The crucial question that follows from our above best answer is one that asks what the analyst sees as the object of his interpretation and what he acts upon to effect a result of his action. Interpreting the transference surely narrows the subject of our inquiry and just as surely opens a plethora of questions and issues as to not only the particulars of the technique but, more cogently, what this, that is, the action, does to the data that we study.

Over the years we have learned that the psychoanalytic relationship is not comfortably seen as one of an analyst merely acting upon a patient but rather is best conceptualized as an open system of mutual activity—a reciprocal set of action and reaction, of transference and countertransference. Thus a simple act of interpretation always resets the system, changes the database, and alters the actors. The resultant change in the analyst requires yet another category of consideration in order to ascertain the data of psychoanalysis, inasmuch as the very definition of the database demands the participation of the one who gathers the data. Thus we must go beyond thinking and acting to properly categorize how an analyst gathers data in the role of one who is literally and actively participating in its formation. An essential quality of forming such a category requires that we dispense with the concept of bounded or defined entities that interact one upon the other and move to those that utilize ideas of openness, reciprocity, and fluidity. Of late, the idea of dynamical systems has been utilized to express the ideas of continual feedforward and feedback with the added feature of thinking in a nonlinear way. No doubt other or better ways of thinking about these dynamic interchanges will present themselves, and they should all be tested for their utility. Those theories of interchange or interaction need not alter the fundamental concept of the nature of the data that we collect. They only alert us to one of the factors that modifies the data, just as any experimenter must control for all of or most of the factors influencing the collection of data.

BEING A PSYCHOANALYST

Being engaged in the transference is surely not confined to psychoanalysis. Despite the many caveats and qualifications applied to the very idea of transference (Schachter 2002), one definition that usually seems to survive is that it is unreal, that is, transference as opposed to reality. Thus, in transference, one must live in a somewhat fictional world or, as some (Stern 2002) have said, the analysis is very much like theater—the actors join in a make-believe scenario that is primarily, but not exclusively, written by the patient. Consequently, the psychoanalyst's data is gathered by his or her living in the transference. This, however, requires a crucial step that distinguishes it from the host of transference situations that occur in everyday life, as well as in all of the therapies that wittingly or otherwise consider and utilize the transference. This essential step is that of the regular and parallel stepping outside of the world of the transference in order to objectify one's role. In this stepping out or objectification, the analyst is able to obtain or use or appreciate the data of involvement. The to-and-fro of living in the transference and then seeing it as such makes for the variations that we regularly use to differentiate one analyst from another. However, there is always a necessary "being in" and "moving outside" required of all analysts.

In order to be a psychoanalyst one must live for a while in the transference and then utilize one's theory to make sense of that life. A proper theory should be one that yields the highest amount of information from that transference experience and, over the years, has seen a wide variety of descriptions of what goes on in the act of being an analyst. Approaches to the best description should ideally confine themselves to the vocabulary and concepts of whatever psychoanalytic theory is employed and should avoid borrowing from other disciplines or using lay terms. The chemist does not explain a reaction by saying that she poured one test tube into another, but rather she names the reagents and the reactions. The designer does not say that he moved one piece forward and one to the side, but rather he needs to characterize the nature of the furniture. So, too, might we say that speaking of (say) persons as in one-person or two-person theories or interpersonal or any such resort to a nonpsychoanalytic term (i.e., person is ordinarily a term and concept of social interaction) is a fine example of our failure in gathering psychoanalytic data and employing social concepts to compensate for that lapse. Of course, the answer is to carefully resituate the word "person" within an analytic theory, all the while recognizing that what was once a borrowed word is now a member with a different meaning. Indeed it may be the case that many disagreements in psychoanalysis stem from the mixing of analytic data with nonanalytic data and the intermingling of words without clarifying their particular definition. One other popular example of this is that of the intrusion of neurologic data into an analytic discussion as a sort of explanation. Thus, when Reiser (1999) tells us that empathy has to do with shared nodes in the amygdala and hippocampus of patient and analyst, he is changing the subject under the guise of giving more information. For a psychoanalyst, that may be interesting but irrelevant. That is not to say that it is unimportant but rather to alert one not to be seduced into thinking it is a part of any psychoanalytic database. The hippocampus is simply not a member of any analytic explanatory effort.

THE VALIDATION OF DATA AS PSYCHOANALYTIC

The Gathering of Data in and outside of Psychoanalysis

It is not uncommon for a psychoanalyst to become involved in social settings that lend themselves to a feeling of uncertainty and even bewilderment as to one's role as an analyst if, for instance, a patient is also a part of that social setting. As a companion to this sort of confusion, we are all familiar with analytic situations in which the transference becomes real (as opposed to the above-noted bit of theater) and the participants act accordingly and even participate in boundary violations. Each of these problem areas is illustrative of a need for a clarification of just *when* and *what* should be considered psychoanalytic data that is taken as given.

Example I

I had occasion to visit a patient in analysis who was admitted to the hospital. Before I went, I mentioned my anticipated venture to a group of psychiatric residents who asked me if I was visiting as a regular visitor or friend or as a therapist. I answered that I had no idea as to just what I would be, and I privately thought that I would not know until I got there. My patient was quite familiar to me in an analytic setting, and, until that question from the residents, I was quite comfortable in saying that I knew him well. Of course, what I knew was what was revealed within the analytic setting and this ranged all the way from his regular clothing to his recurrent dreams. I automatically extrapolated this somewhat focused and confined, albeit deep, source of knowledge to the more general assumption of knowing what the person was like in every other sense. But I soon found that I was in error.

Perhaps much of the changed perception of my patient in the hospital could be attributed to my own feeling of disorientation, since I arrived on a weekend dressed in casual clothes and totally unprepared for everything from where I would sit (or stand) to the very topic of conversation. But beyond all the variations in setting and circumstances, I grew more and more convinced during the visit that I simply did not know an awful lot about my patient. To begin with, although he was quite ill, he clearly retained what I had considered his major transference configuration toward me. Theorists from different schools would probably call it by different names ranging from a paternal transference to an idealized selfobject. No matter. It seemed to fade into the background as we discussed his physical condition (something that may well happen in any analysis), but then this transference seemed to be lost to us both. He began to look like a different person to me. He was, of course, so much more than his transference.

I was introduced to his brother who, also predictably, did not fit my imagined picture of the brother and who spoke to me about my patient as if I were a member of the family. I could (and later did) manage to squeeze this brotherly communication into my already-formed psychological formulation of my patient, but that seemed more like what Ernest Jones did to Hamlet: interesting, but about somebody else. Nothing that I saw during my visit, a visit during which I was clearly identified as an analyst, seemed to belong to what the patient and I were doing in analysis.

I am sure some would argue that my visit could in no way qualify as an analytic experience, but it is not clear just why this is so. It certainly was therapeutic for the patient according to later reports from the family. It definitely retained the transference relationships that heretofore characterized the analysis. To the best of my memory I even made an interpretation about how and why the patient was so frightened, although it is not clear if that interpretation could not have also been offered by his cardiologist. This seems to be an ideal laboratory study for the topic inasmuch as it is filled with all of the questions needing to be answered. Perhaps one could readily make a claim that my visit was part and parcel of psychoanalysis; it could be readily adopted by both the narrow and the broad viewpoint, that is, it dealt with transference and it was done by an analyst and it helped. The difference lies with separating thinking from acting from being; a difference that is underscored by my own conviction that my data was different in the office and in the hospital.

Similar such differences are seen when one changes a patient from once-a-week psychotherapy to more frequent psychoanalysis, when one has occasion to analyze someone who had been either a student or colleague or friend, or when some form of these situations is reversed. We do not necessarily know them better, but we surely know them differently. It seems unwise to say that one is doing analysis or gathering analytic data merely when one is dealing with and interpreting the transference, and it seems untrue that we are free to call anything analysis if we so wish.

One of the great difficulties encountered by most analytic practitioners has to do with the ease or reluctance in their moving out of a lived-in transference experience. We can characterize this problem as one in which the transference is felt to be real. The shock of leaving a theatrical performance as one steps out into the street is akin to the act of wrenching oneself free of the drama being realized with the patient and perhaps allowing an interpretation to break the connection. The most striking examples of this issue are usually represented by analysts who seem to fall in love with their patients and/or become sexually involved with them, or even proceed to marry them with or without unfortunate results. These are striking and rare enough to claim the limelight but probably should take a back seat to a much more common and familiar one involving varieties of self-revelation on the part of the analyst.

Without now addressing the possible therapeutic benefits that might derive from the analyst's disclosure of personal thoughts and real features of his or her life, there does seem to be some need to determine the conditions under which such disclosures go beyond the acceptable parameters of an analysis (Holmquist et al. 2002).

Example II

A patient, of an analyst who had become ill and then died suddenly, came for a consultation and possible referral to a new analyst. She described her previous analyst in the most glowing of terms including tales of how he had shared with her the intimate details of his own life and his own children. The patient felt pleased and honored to be the recipient of such information and was convinced that the intense closeness of their relationship contributed both to her good feelings about her analysis and to her severe depression over her loss. She was open and honest in her need for a similar sort of closeness in her choice of a new analyst. It seemed well nigh impossible for her to consider seeing an analyst who would be less outgoing and more reserved, inasmuch as she was convinced that the sharing of personal feelings was the essence of her analysis. She certainly could give no credence to the suggestion that such sharing was more of benefit to the analyst than it was to her, and there seemed little doubt that the entirety of the analysis was felt as real to the both of them. Likewise it seemed that there was an obvious failure to distinguish transference from reality. That move from living out the transference to commenting about what had been (unwittingly) a mutual enactment seemed too painful an action for the two of them to risk. Interpretations that were given in that analysis were directed toward the patient's past and so served to enable them to avoid reflection on what was in the here and now. The so-called real relationship dominated the treatment, and they could do nothing else.

Of course this patient's experience with her now-deceased analyst is not meant to illustrate bad technique but rather to exemplify how the analyst was not operating from a psychoanalytic database. There are no doubt countless other examples of our recognition of the distinction between occasional transference-like incidents and a more wholesale immersion in the life of the transference. One need not be better or more therapeutic than the other, but the difference seems to be a fact.

Gathering the Data: An Activity

Interpretative activity takes place at the moment of disrupting the transference and entering what is seen as a separate realm of reality. In contrast to the view that one is empathic with and understanding a patient until that moment of disruption, it may be more felicitous to say that one is empathic in a different way or in a nontransferential sense when one makes an interpretation. Indeed, a correct interpretation seems to offer us another way to validate that the data are psychoanalytic, inasmuch as the analyst and patient should then enjoy a different form of shared experience. Ideally, they (analyst and patient) operate in two realms: that of transference and that of so-called reality. Each of these allows for a period of connection and each has characteristics that distinguish them from one another. I suspect that psychoanalytic data are confirmed by the existence of these parallel realms and much other forms of therapeutic activity do not have a similar set of concurrent experiences. Once again, this is not to say that there is necessarily an increased value to this set of experiences. Rather it may be fair to highlight the fact that many other therapeutic activities primarily live in a single mode of operation in contrast to psychoanalysis.

One illustrative example of material that might be ordinarily considered very much a part of psychoanalytic data gathering comes from a study of empathy, albeit in a nonpsychoanalytic pursuit (Preston and deWaal 2002). In this very extensive overview, Preston and deWaal confine their ideas and conclusions about empathy to work done on animals and infants, along with a brief extension to examining evidence from what they describe as "disorders of empathy," that is, autism and anorexia nervosa (p. 14). Theirs is a work primarily directed to the development of a model of empathy involving brain physiology and evolution. One cannot help but be struck by the omission of the sort of data that is gathered by way of empathy in a psychoanalysis. Utilizing the analyst as the instrument of data gathering starts one on the radical differentiation from that of the observer of animals who merely guesses or assumes what one animal feels for another. Analytic data seem to be more verifiable. More important than this one limitation is that of psychoanalysis recognizing that the capacity for empathy is rarely generalizable, since we have learned that, for example, some of us can work with pedophiles and some cannot. Different instruments record different data. But perhaps the most significant difference comes from the psychoanalytic distinction between the momentary understanding of another individual and the commitments to sustained empathy. Psychoanalysis gathers most, if not all, of its data from the latter stance of sustained empathy, and the dedication to that form of total immersion in another's psyche regularly yields information that is both different in content as well as in form from momentary observations, however accurate the latter may be. The form thereby usually becomes as, if not more, important than the content, since the analyst and patient develop a story line of cause and effect, of sequencing, and of goals, all of which is unavailable from most (and probably all) of the studies of rats, monkeys, and infants.

If we add to the different kind of empathic data available to psychoanalytic inquiry the parallel collection of both transference and more reality-bound information, we cannot help but be convinced that the database of psychoanalysis has a unique standing. Though no one would deny that empathy can and should be studied throughout the life cycle, that most disorders of empathy seem to be grounded in infancy and early childhood, that it may well be true that empathy has a clear and ultimately recognizable correlate in brain anatomy and physiology, it still remains important to remember that empathy is not a singular, momentary activity. Empathy as a centerpiece of psychoanalytic data gathering treats these above-mentioned facts as ancillary.

INTEGRATING THE DATA THAT IS GATHERED

Since our theories are our eyes, we can only start to talk about the data of psychoanalysis if we possess a theory that covers the data. We simply do not or should not allow theoretical terms borrowed from other viewpoints to have an equal standing in our work. For example, the self of sociology or of biology is certainly not exchangeable with the self of psychoanalysis. A different database prohibits (or should prohibit) our wandering too far afield in our speaking. Words like relation or relationship, infantile, maturity, love, and hate all tempt us to embrace what is now termed "folk psychology" and to equate a common parlance for what should be a more rigorous construction of terms. The task of appropriate definitions of terms is not an easy one, but surely we cannot progress to a proper study of "relationships" until we become clear as to just what they are or should be. To move the word into psychoanalysis changes its meaning.

Armed with a workable theory we proceed to the problem of the selection of data. The instrument of observation is the analyst, and that forms the support for the training and treatment of the analyst just as any science requires its instrumentation to be in order and regularly examined. The tendency to remain wedded to certain theoretical concepts and/or routine technical interventions may well be signs of a dulling of our instrumentation. So, too, may a thirst for a different form of data gathering such as seen in utilizing impersonal instruments from EEGs to PET scans that reflects a disuse or misuse of the primary analytic instrument.

The selected data is then to be arranged in a form that is congenial to both patient and analyst. This is most commonly presented as a narrative, but it remains to be seen if that particular construction is a product of the analytic work or if it itself directs the process. There is little doubt that some analysts and patients take comfort in writing and rewriting the story of a life, but it may be too glib to hold that effort responsible for the efficacy of analysis.

SUMMARY

Every scientific enterprise has to define and delimit its database, and every scientific theory selects from and expands upon its database. One may say that the theory determines the data, which in turn supports the theory. However, the data ultimately stretch the theory and allow us to say that all theory is underdetermined, that is, it cannot cover all of the data. Psychoanalysis is no different in its interplay between theory and data, and much of the confusion and argument about psychoanalysis as a science is a result of the failure to clearly distinguish itself from folk psychology (another different theory) and thereby to clarify the uniqueness of analytic data. Of course there is much to be said for folk psychology, but it is best not to have it compete with psychoanalysis. If we, for the sake of argument, restrict psychoanalytic data to that derived from analysis per se, then we may be better able to recognize the fact that the data of applied analysis, of group therapy, and of once- or twice-per-week therapy require different theories and alternative modes of explanation. To see any of them as different or lesser forms of psychoanalysis does them a disservice and misses the point. The point, once again, is to clarify the nature of the data, the givens, of what we do. The givens are never to be lifted away from the doing.

9

The Mutuality of Meaning

Psychoanalysts may or may not be surprised (or perhaps may or may not even be interested) in an ongoing debate among some philosophers as to whether meanings are in the head or else are best thought of as involving a wide system of environmental interactions (Pessen and Goldberg 1999, p. 150). As a rule, analysts are prone to thinking of the mind as the depository of meanings, and likewise that the mind somehow arises out of the brain (and necessarily is fairly well limited by and enclosed by the skull, with its accompanying anatomy). Psychoanalysts do allow for object relations of sorts, but some like to put all objects back into the head as representations that take on a rather active internal life, as in the creation of meaning. Daring or creative analysts focus upon relationships between people, but even some of those "interpersonalists" prefer to put everything back inside the head. This view is exemplified by those who claim that patients change because of the treatment, and that this change is then internalized and structuralized (Greenberg 1996, p. 36). So back into the head it goes. A more recent variation on the problem of the proper place for meanings is formulated by the "intersubjectivists" who would probably (I think) put meaning in the shared, co-constructed field created by those participating in its formation. This new place for meaning tends to leave the individual person, for the most part or even entirely, out of the picture. The claim that there are no isolated minds tends to make meaning somewhat more of a social phenomenon, and this conception is perhaps more compatible with the views of those philosophers who feel that meanings are communal or environmental products.

The philosophical quandary about situating meaning does have relevance for psychoanalysis. This is not so much in terms of a solution for our location question, but because it may be an opportunity to try out various models to see what might make the best sense for us. The one that I prefer to employ is the selfobject model, which does not confine the mind and its meanings to one individual but rather extends the mind or the self to include others who function as part of that individual and her mind. Self psychology is a one-person psychology in that it employs others as selfobjects, thereby allowing meaning to emerge from this wider concept of mind as well as of person. Therefore, not only are meanings not in the head but neither is the mind. In the self psychoanalytic model, a self extends beyond an individual's skin, and the mind extends beyond an individual's skull. In this model one must wrest the mind away from a supposed identity with the brain. Thus it may be helpful to think of mind more as a form of activity than primarily as a location. One immediate advantage that accrues from the suspension of concern with the place or location of the mind is the relief of no longer having to transpose all the furniture of the world from the outside to the inside. We can look at an apple or a person, think and feel what that percept means to us, and not have to miniaturize it and find a place for it in our heads. Our meanings do not demand a representation that we must contemplate but only an engagement with the things of the world that move us. Later we will investigate the changed view of the mind that this model entails.

The usual and ordinary conceptualization of meanings as being in the head consists in seeing the brain as a complex computer that operates on various internal representations or symbols in order to deliver new complex symbols. These symbolic printouts are the meanings. An alternate consideration of meaning sees it as lying in the web of activity or the interactions of persons in their environment. Here, one should not evaluate one theory or the other as being more truthful or more accurate, but rather question which one carries more usefulness and ease of explanation.

I should like to explore this open model of meaning-making in a presentation of clinical experience that I hope will to be better understood by way of the selfobject model. The central point about seeing the mind as composed of one's psychological life is that it allows us to see transference and countertransference as they are lived out in treatment, as opposed to viewing them as entities that are struggled with inside individual psyches. For example, any reader of Freud's Dora case can see the transference and countertransference issues, which are products of a continual and continuing feedback process that may be unknown only to the participants. The observer or reader is able to see what two persons mean to one another, and this is accomplished by a recognition of the enactments that occur between Freud and his patient. Meanings *move* us, and it seems but a small step to claim that these movements are the enactments of analysis. These are not confined to those of overt and striking behavior, but essentially cover the entire composition of an analysis. Everything that goes on between patient and analyst is an amalgam of conscious, preconscious, and unconscious meaning. That being the case, we may put aside any concern with the conflict-free sphere and direct our attention to assuming that the unconscious is ever-present. There is no dividing line between enactment and neutrality, inasmuch as silence and immobility carry as much meaning, or unconscious content, as sound and fury. It is all action, and so nothing is meaningless.

BACK TO THE DORA CASE

A careful reading of Freud and Dora (1905) allows one to employ or apply a variety of interpretations to the goings-on. Over the years, more and more attributions of meaning have been brought to the case. Nevertheless, one should be cautious in claiming that one particular meaning, for example what Dora meant for Freud, was residing in his mind or head at the time that he saw her. It would be better to say that we can *now* formulate new interpretations that give new meaning to that particular interaction. Thus a further step must be taken away from any static sense of meaning. Moreover, to the mix of what Freud and Dora meant to one another is added that which the reader or observer interprets as meaning. A process analogous to this is that of a patient telling her life story to the analyst, while the listening analyst changes the particular meanings of that life as it is told. And each telling of the story, in its own inexplicable way, seems to make for a different story. This is one outcome of an unrestricted concept of mind, in that each person incorporates his or her surround into the resulting psychological functioning of the participants. Thus our minds and our meanings can reach out to the world around us and become literally constituted by that world. Not only does it follow that the analyst cannot hide behind some shield of neutrality but also that he must ever be struggling to recognize how he impacts the patient as well as how the patient impacts him. Every such analytic or therapeutic relationship is therefore a mix of new and old.

This idea of mutuality is familiar to most of us although we may conceptualize it differently. However, because mutuality takes an unusual form in one group of patients whom we have studied, those who suffer from what we call behavior disorders, they therefore present us with an opportunity to explore our meaning-making models. For the sake of exposition, the patients discussed are divided into three subgroups, which a reader or listener may readily see as forms of countertransference. Hopefully each case will illustrate that the entire scenario, which is one of action, is best read as the working of the patient's mind as it operates in a particular context of treatment. Analyst and patient make meanings together.

THE BEHAVIOR DISORDERS

The first group consists of those patients who seem to silently, or perhaps implicitly, conspire with their analysts to become involved in an enactment that lives outside the immediacy of the treatment. In the Dora case it is generally agreed that Freud used Dora to illustrate the theory that he championed: the theory of the unconscious sexual content of dreams. The case reveals what some may call Freud's countertransference, seen in his rather clear exploitation of this young girl to further his theoretical claims (Ornstein 1993, p. 47). Yet one should be cautious in describing the encounter in terms of projection or internal representations or indeed of countertransference. Dora was an adolescent girl who felt exploited by her father and Herr K., and inexplicably revisited this exploitation with her newly assigned psychoanalyst. The reader of the Dora case may or may not choose to characterize this analytic encounter as that of a mutual enactment, but would we be allowed to make a claim that Dora somehow merely elicited an unconscious response from Freud appropriate to her particular pathology? It seems more felicitous to say that each character was living out very individual and meaningful scenarios with the other. Indeed, when one examines similar episodes of mutual action in analysis, one sees certain forms of behavior that can only be understood as split off from the main theme of engagement between patient and analyst, that is, behavior that is disavowed. The disavowal is not confined to a single individual but rather takes place in the interaction.

This silent conspiracy was noted earlier in the case of the celebrity in Chapter 4, where the patient had asked her analyst for permission to enter and leave his office by a side door so that she would not be seen by other patients in the waiting room. One can imagine all sorts of explanations for this state of affairs between that analyst and his patient, but at no time could it be said that the analyst was unable to be conscious of what he was doing and/or allowing. Rather, in Freud's classical sense, this reality was disavowed mutually. Moreover, even after acknowledging its possible negative effect on the treatment, the analyst in this case seemed unable to completely integrate this knowledge. Our first group of complex situations of this kind is composed of these split-off and mutual actions that either remain unexamined or are allowed to persist in spite of attention being called to them. The mutual and reciprocal behavior of analyst and patient is realized and persists in an arena of separate activity.

On a step further along the continuum are actions that become part of the analytic discourse and are thereby struggled over. These are unlike the meanings constructed in the first group, which exist without interference and live on in the split-off arena. The difference found in the second group is illustrated by the story of a patient, not one having a behavior disorder in this particular example, who usually came to his analytic hours a few minutes late. Although this was regularly brought up for discussion, it seemed to persist and, over time, the analyst found himself using these few minutes to replenish the coffee that he had poured earlier in the day. As the analytic work deepened, the work focused more and more on the transference and the patient announced one day that his late arrivals were efforts to allow the analyst the leisure of getting hot coffee. The analyst was upset. He felt that he was totally innocent in this scenario that had clearly been orchestrated by the patient. Yet there was no escape from the reality of his participation. When brought into the discussion and interpretation, the action was seen to represent the patient's effort to please (in this instance) his father at the expense of his own well-being and personal needs. Much like Dora, he had promoted a situation of exploitation with an accomplice who "went along" in a manner that combined transference and personal convenience. This was an example of a split-off arena that could be brought into the minds of both patient and analyst, but rather than remaining separate and isolated, it entered into the conversation.

Our study of behavior disorders has shown that even the most colorful and pathological sorts of behavior or misbehavior manage to become recreated in analysis with the cooperation of the analyst. Indeed, the successful treatment of such disorders seems to require the compliance or cooperation of the analyst, inasmuch as the meaning that comes alive in the treatment is a product of a union, an interaction. Once again we note the mutuality. It does not lie hidden in the depths of the patient's psyche waiting to meet the light of day so much as it presses for expression in behavior that commands a setting for its realization. The analyst becomes a ready catalyst in such a setting and only her awareness, not her prohibition, allows for a satisfactory interpretation.

Our third group of analytic characterizations of the action seen in behavior disorders goes beyond the disavowal that is unrecognized and remains split off, and beyond the disavowal that is interpreted and worked through, to reach the arena of the reactions of the analyst that can only be classified as rationalizations for the retention of a position of power. I say this about power because when the analytic position of knowing more is relinquished, and a relative detachment from the immediacy of the interaction is maintained, this allows both participants to enter into the mutual production of a meaningful experience. These are the ingredients necessary to achieve a proper analytic intervention. However, we regularly see how analysts are unable to relinquish this position. For example, one of our group agreed to sign disability waiv-ers for a patient who insisted upon this in order to continue in analy-sis. This analyst claimed that someone else would do it if he did not and used this rationalization to avoid investigating the meaning of that request. Others who engage in a variety of boundary violations that may or may not involve ethical or moral issues are able to give a variety of reasons for what they do or do not do, and thus avoid the pursuit of inquiry. Interestingly, some of the most resistant forms of rationaliza-tion are defended by an appeal to theoretical principles and convictions; here psychoanalytic sophistry is used in defense of behavior that remains split off from recognition.

As noted above in Chapter 6, as long as an analyst sees the issues in analysis as composed of contents that reside within the patient, she can conveniently explain away any and all reactions by one or another version of "the patient made me do it." So long as an analyst sees her-self and the patient as separate entities, the resulting behavior can be seen as lying outside both of them—either in the relationship or in an intersubjective field. My preference is to see both compliance and refusal as shared states of meaning within a partially shared mind. By ignoring one aspect, say the compliance, in favor of the other—the re-fusal—we split off or disavow part of our shared mind. Both patient and analyst utilize this split, *feeling* each aspect alternately. If as analysts we *comply* with the patient's request, we need to understand and interpret the results of that action; if we then move to *refusal*, that then must become the focus of our analytic work (see Chapter 5, Case I). Unless we are able to see this mutuality, we shall be forced to use one or an-other set of theoretical platitudes to rationalize our behavior.

Imagine that both patient and analyst share a set of feelings that involve the patient readily getting his schedule changed along with a parallel set that consists of his needing to conform to the analyst's schedule. There are thus parallel sets alive in both patient and analyst. To gratify one, say compliance, elicits feelings in both patient and ana-lyst, perhaps those of guilt for the patient and weakness for the analyst. To gratify the other could readily make the analyst feel guilty and the patient enraged. At some level, each recognizes the feelings aroused in the other. This complex mixture is the seat of meaning because it is active in the minds of both participants. Therefore, rather than claiming that the patient has penetrated your mind or that you have established something that is between the two of you, it might be profitable to examine what each of you means to the other, all the while recognizing that that "other" is now a functional part of you, that is, he is "in your mind" in the true sense of the term. Our minds do indeed include others.

It is not necessary for us to burden our explanation with other theoretical terms, but it may be necessary to underline how the analyst avoids recognizing the mutuality of meaning by the use of theoretical terms. Agreeing to schedule changes is really not inherently different from being rigid about schedule changes. Neither has a specific meaning until it is joined to and by the patient. For both participants, the response to the analyst's stance, whatever that stance may be, ranging all the way from the very liberal to the inflexible, makes for the emergence of meaning. My having a rigid schedule means something to me before I see my patient, and that meaning probably changes with each and every patient. That is especially true in psychoanalysis, because we engage our patients in depth and these connections necessarily resonate throughout our joined psyches. If I feel strongly about an inflexible schedule, I would do well to consider how that impacts upon a patient who feels the same as I do and then upon a patient who feels quite otherwise. Because we can regularly succeed in getting our patients to conform to our personal needs regarding times, fees, and the other minutiae of treatment, we can just as regularly fail to see how we sidestep an engagement that might facilitate an understanding of what all these issues mean to our patients. The patient who asks for schedule changes needs an analyst who herself can be torn, both about compliance and rigidity. Indeed there is no chance of a successful analysis if this request is seen as part of a "terrorist threat." Rather it must be seen as an invitation—an invitation to inquiry. From this inquiry comes a nascent meaning that achieves its life by way of engagement with another person who completes its form.

IMPLICATIONS

If meanings cannot be lifted out of a patient's head for examination, if meanings cannot penetrate into the analyst's head and thereby take possession of it, and if meanings cannot themselves form an intermediary field of co-construction, are they so elusive as to defy our comprehension and understanding? In our study of behavior disorders (Goldberg 2001) we dealt with patients who were involved in all sorts of aberrant behavior, ranging from addictions to perversions. Our aim in this study was to find out about the meaning of the behavior no matter how undesirable or obnoxious we felt it to be. The patient who requests a private entrance or who arrives a few moments late or requests a schedule change is hardly comparable to our collection of thieves and stalkers. Yet the comparison may still be a valid one, inasmuch as the study did allow us to concentrate upon the analyst's participation in the unfolding of meaning.

Although our study did not and could not involve a very large group of patients, we did seem able to reach some conclusions that we felt were generalizable both to behavior disorders and to the supposed trivial enactments noted above. The first of these patients demanded an analyst who was able to participate to some extent in the misbehavior, thus bringing out the mutuality of meaning. Simply put, a thief is best helped by an analyst with a bit of larceny in his own character. This, more often than not, manifests itself in some sort of action that may exist for a time outside of the treatment. For example, one of our patients had had a previous analysis without once mentioning to the analyst that he regularly stole books from his university bookstore. His second and successful analysis was with an analyst who seemed much more comfortable with this form of delinquency. To bring this misbehavior into the treatment, the analyst must himself struggle with its meaning and must himself experience this delinquency. Complete disapproval is of no help, while complete approval is folly. Thus another conclusion we reached—one that will surprise no one—is that the behavior must be understood as very necessary for the patient but as a bit less so for the analyst. Most of our patients resort to these behaviors to ward off intense depressive affect, and for an analyst to conceptualize these issues as only ethical and/or boundary problems is of little help except to the analyst.

To properly conceptualize the nature of shared meanings we need only consider the routine employment of empathy, the means by which we are able to take up residence in another person's mind. (I here use these spatial metaphors only as a convenience.) Our empathic connection with our patient, our reading of our patient, resonates with the patient's reciprocal reading of us. That, of course, defines the self-selfobject relationship. This union of empathy and the commonality of its inevitable struggle to all of our patients was a striking phenomenon in our misbehaving patients, who found themselves in us just as we could and did in them. An additional and often troubling phenomenon in behavior disorders is the disavowal that frequently accompanies those behavior aspects that could not be tolerated. Once we could recognize the disavowal, we could usually recognize our compliance in its status, whether outside the treatment or enacted in the treatment. Either way, the mutuality of meaning was brought home to us.

CONCLUSIONS

If we can divorce the concept of meaning from the notion that words or images are standing in for something significant, we can move on to consider meaning as an activity of a person, with all of its unconscious and preconscious elements. Thus an apple or a textbook or a mother has no meaning in the static sense of an internal representation, but rather its meaning lies in the active sense of how it moves us. That word "move" can range from silent contemplation to overt activity, but the apple or book or mother must impact the person in order to gain meaning. One of the peculiar and wonderful things about psychoanalysis is that it goes both ways. Analysts no longer "objectively observe" any more than they mirror or love their patients. Rather, their task is to interpret the meanings that capture and envelop each of the participants in this very unique conversation.

10

Representation in Psychoanalysis and the Place of the Mind

INTRODUCTION

It is now some forty years since the paper by Sandler and Rosenblatt (1962) on the concept of the representational world was published. Soon thereafter it began to serve as a template for students of analysis to use in considering the mind. In one form or another it offered a theory that focused upon the mind as formed by psychic representations. That latter word has since then become such a convenient vehicle for considering and expressing so many ideas that it probably needs a periodic reconsideration of its standing and definition. As with so many conveniences, we find it serving multiple purposes that, for some, seem to border on potential misuse. From the original definition offered by Sandler and Rosenblatt, that of a representation having a more or less enduring existence as an organization or schema that is constructed from a multitude of impressions (p. 153), we have moved to consider what would constitute effective treatment as gauged by these organizations. For example, Viderman (1995) describes one patient as moving from a representation as a damaged, unworthy, and vulnerable figure to one with strength and defined identity. Representations have come to be seen as the building blocks of the mind and have been made to serve as barometers of change as well.

The lure of the concept has likewise been enhanced by its use as dramatological simile to characterize the representational world. The characters on the stage represent the persons or objects as well as the self of the individual, who is the hero of the piece. While the ego does all the work of production, the self and object representations correspond to self and object images—that is, actors. This stage or TV screen is, of course, situated somewhere within the mind and is, inevitably, compared to the self and objects that exist somewhere out in the external world (p. 131). Although Sandler and Rosenblatt claim that the words external and internal were purely descriptive for Freud, they themselves go beyond him to claim that these references are to the internal and external environment. They were soon joined in this by Edith Jacobson (1964), who described a complex view of the mind as composed of this world of representations, which seemed to sit internally and apart from a sort of correlative world of honest-to-goodness objects. Indeed one could easily move on to the definition offered by Moore and Fine (1990) of a psychic representation as a "more or less consistent reproduction within the mind of a perception of a meaningful thing or object" (p. 166). A psychic representation thus is inside, is a copy, and is an enduring function.

It is but a small step from the structure of representations to relations, and Sandler (1990) continues the "two worlds" presentation as he differentiates the "real world" from the world of fantasy objects and speaks of how we are motivated to "bring the two worlds together . . . and to find ways of living simultaneously in both worlds" (p. 878). He speaks of finding objects in this real world onto which we can project external aspects of our internal objects. The representation(s) are now a sort of animated set of persons who have relations with one another inside that internal theater of otherness. Indeed we now seemingly live in two worlds and have relations in each of them.

In an update to the concept of representation, the Sandlers (1998) said: "It is important to add that the term 'representation' can itself be a source of confusion, in that it relates to subjective experience on the one hand and to what can be called non-experiential organization on the other. So, for example, self-representation can be a (conscious or unconscious) image, idea, or percept of oneself at a particular time, or a set of experiences sharing a common identity" (pp. 126–127). They go on to say that "image" need not be a visual experience but may also be applied to data from all sensory modalities, and that "representation" may refer to organizations or structures as well. They further state that a child gradually creates representations of self and others. Most importantly, they claim that an object relationship involves an interaction between conscious and unconscious phantasy representations of self and object (p. 127).

More recently, new aspects have appeared in the above-sketched theory of representations as contributions from cognitive science and computer science have extended the way the concept is now considered. These fields include stable representations and dynamic representations, as well as local representations and distributed ones. The field of neurology has also moved away from the static and frivolous notion of the "grandmother neuron" that claims a single site wherein my grandmother's image lies dormant but awaiting a call. Perhaps it is time for psychoanalysis to also move on from its notion of representations as stable or enduring organizations of impressions. Although psychoanalysis need not match its theory to other fields, it may well learn from them and certainly should be constrained by them and compatible with them. In fields other than psychoanalysis, ranging from philosophical interests to those of computer conceptualization, representation has a long and controversial history (Cummins 1989). One philosophical theory states that the mind contains the forms of perception; that is, a red ball produces a mental form or image or idea that somehow is of the same sort of stuff that the real ball appears to be. This is akin to the Moore and Fine (1990) definition in psychoanalysis. Of course the mental red ball exists only in mental space, but it can somehow be seen (or experienced) there. Though this may seem a bit outrageous at first, it does come quite close to how some analysts still tend to speak of representations. Another theory, credited to Hobbes by Haugeland (1985), claims that mental representations are language-like symbols. These symbols can be part and parcel of computations and are able to be manipulated. Of course, such symbols bear no similarity to the things that they represent and thus there can be no ease of introspection when one wishes to see what is said to be inside. A step away from *this* theory is one that insists that symbols themselves have no inherent meaning whatsoever, but rather emerge as epiphenomena from computations in connectionist systems, such as those where representation is distributed rather than localized and exists through the whole system. A further step leads one to seeing representations as being actual neurophysiology with no hint of resemblance or symbolic status. This view is similar to Sandler's nonexperiential category. Here, mental representation is a biological phenomenon with no grounding in psychology. The final blow to an understanding of representations may have come from Wittgenstein (1982) who said, "Indeed, I confess, nothing seems more possible to me than that people some day will come to the definite opinion that there is no copy in either the physiological or the nervous system which corresponds to a particular thought, or a particular idea, or memory" (p. 662).

Wittgenstein is confirmed by O'Regan and Noe (2001) who state: "There is no representation of the world inside the brain; the only pictorial or 3-D version required is the real outside version" (p. 946). They reject the "dogma" of "analytic isomorphism," the idea that "for every experience there will be a neural substrate whose activity is sufficient to produce that experience" and maintain that "no neural substrate will be sufficient to produce experience" (p. 967). "The fact that object attributes seem perceptually to be a part of a single object does not require them to be 'represented' in any unified kind of way or by a single process" (p. 967). One would be hard pressed to claim that much of the psychoanalytic theory of internal representation can withstand this sort of criticism.

This of course highlights one possible conclusion: that talk of representations may turn out to be hollow and empty of meaning. Thus the definition of a psychic representation as a pure reproduction is readily dismissed, and a reexamination of this concept seems necessary. Perhaps the most telling reason for such an inquiry comes from the implications of the concept. If one sees humans as subjects of representations, then the subject or self is primarily monological or disengaged. He is in contact with an "outside" world, including other persons and their bodies, but this contact is through the "representations" that he has within. The subject is first of all an "inner" space or "mind" capable of processing representations as would a computer. What "I" am, as a being capable of having such representations, is someone who thereby is a center of an individual psychology (Taylor 1989).

This disengagement from others is not an issue of isolation. What is underscored here is the individual as a separate albeit not isolated self, one who is personally responsible and self-reliant as opposed to one who is dialogical or engaged. In a sense, the disengaged self is one that is studied from afar while the dialogical one is always a participant in reaching understanding. If we review the way representations are utilized in psychoanalysis, we may get a better view of the division between engagement and separation.

The Place

The notion of "stored memory" is often associated with an idea of reaching back in time to recover something that is being held in storage. This filing cabinet picture of memory, whether these files be repressed or accessible, is at odds with newer theories about memory (Lenzinger-Bohleber and Pfeifer 2002, Target 1998). Experiments with animals show that different neuronal configurations can give rise to similar patterns of recognition, for example of such stimuli as odors, and so seem to lead one to conclude that what appears to be the same memory is usually and readily formed in many locations depending on the context (Freeman and Skorda 1990). Though this finding need not be crucial in altering psychoanalytic ideas about stored memories, it seems to suggest that memories are, more than likely, regularly constructed rather than merely released. The same would therefore be true of representations in that they seem distributed rather than local and so are formed in an ad hoc manner by varied neuronal connections as well as by varied psychological impressions. Representations are not fixed or stored or situated structures, but rather are active products. The stable organization that was once suggested for psychic representations may be better thought of as a dynamically created achievement of the moment. The definition offered by Moore and Fine (1990) is thus necessarily called into question, inasmuch as there is no place, no mental space for the representations to sit and await a call. The schema or organizations that the Sandlers (1998) refer to are, of course, products of activity rather than fixed entities.

Numerous authors have struggled with reconciling what Freud's ideas may have been about representations with those of more modern psychoanalysis. However, it may be that once again Freud has been misunderstood. In terms of where representation takes place, he said:

> But shall we not be making the same mistake in principle whether what we are trying to localize is a complicated concept, a whole mental activity, or a psychical element? Is it justifiable to take a nerve fiber, which for the whole length of its course has been a purely physiological structure and has been subject to purely physiological modifications, and to plunge its end into the sphere of the mind and to fit this end out with a presentation or a mnemonic image?" [Freud 1915, pp. 206–207]

As we move to reconceptualize our concept of representations, we need to keep in mind the many forms that localization theories have taken. Sometimes we employ language as the medium of storage, but non-language competitors include quasipictorial representation, holographic representation, all sorts of mental molds, and various sorts of connectionist representations (Stitch 1996, p. 14). From Piaget's contention that mental representations correspond to "internal imitations" of absent objects to Stern's (1997) introduction of RIGs as representations of interaction that have been generalized, we move from place to process, since place seems an incoherent concept. This movement culminates in a philosophical stance that insists that the entire idea of any intermediary between mind and world is a shadow with which we can dispense (Travis 2000).

The Process

Edith Jacobson (1964) said: "From the ever-increasing memory traces of pleasurable and unpleasurable experiences and of perceptions with which they become associated, body images as well as images of the love object emerge which, at first vague and variable, gradually expand and develop into consistent and more or less realistic endopsychic representations of the object world and of our own self" (p. 85). This sharp differentiation between inside and outside is carried on by Kernberg (1987), who writes: "In essence, patients may project a self-representation while they enact the object representation of a determined object relation activated in the transference, or vice versa, they may project an object representation while enacting the corresponding self-representation" (p. 216). Each author chooses to see the mind as somehow dealing with an internal world of representations and an outside real world. Yet as McIntosh (1993) so cogently warns us: "Patients are not informed and do not become aware, for example, that they have angry feelings toward the mental representations of their therapists (which they have hidden from themselves). Rather, they learn quite simply that they are angry at their therapists" (p. 706). With representations, we have introduced and interposed unnecessary intermediary shadows.

Although we have come to accept that there are no "grandmother neurons," we have often replaced that sort of explanation with one that describes a variety of forms of encoding. We now say that my grandmother is encoded or registered in some way in my brain and in my mind. We also know that codes need not be exact translations or replicas of things but often are directions for a process. The DNA for a limb contains no semblance of an arm but is rather a map for a series of directed steps or a program that, with the proper surround, will yield an arm. The surround or context is often the crucial ingredient in the determination of just what the programmed code will allow to unfold. Thus, rather than stay with the two-world idea, with an inner world of representations versus the real world, we might consider a move to a single world of multiple contributions to a representation, a world that need not be divided into inner and outer. From this perspective, how I feel about myself or my grandmother at any given moment depends on the context of my inquiry—the nature of the persons, places, and things that compose the larger environment of that question. Thus the process by which I call up or create a grandmother notion depends only partially upon the particular encoding of my grandmother. Different contexts yield different representations. So, rather than my projecting the qualities of my supposed internal objects upon those real external ones, it may be better to say that it is unwise to think that external reality goes on separately and unchanging any more than does this imagined internal world. Together they make up a unified view of my individual world. Only as an integrated whole can we determine the true meaning to me of my grandmother. If she is sitting across from me, she is as much a product of my registered code plus her perceived qualities as she is when she is far away. Usually those two products—here and away—are as variable as the context may be. We thus move to a position in which my perceptions are colored by my unconscious registrations, just as my memories are colored by the immediate situation of their recall. We do not therefore operate in two worlds so much as we live in one rather complex one. And so we are more likely "of the world" than we are a spectator observing it.

The Printout

The mysterious workings of a computer as it delivers a readable image on the screen are rarely of interest to the user. She knows that to push various keys or point at different icons is only to initiate a coded process. There are no words or pictures in the computer, just directions. What is finally printed out is, in the computer as in our minds, a recognizable image that we may choose to call a representation. It can be delivered visually or linguistically, and much of the final printout is a product that follows the requirements of representability first delineated by Freud in his discussion of dreams (Laplanche and Pontalis 1973, p. 389). Therefore, when Viderman (1994) characterizes a change in his patient's self-representation, he and we feel it may be a manner of speaking, an actual image of herself revealed in a dream or conscious fantasy, or a bona fide accessible registration residing somewhere in her head. Indeed representation as structure seems to straddle all three of these possibilities, but the most appealing of the three would be some tangible evidence that we could see or point to—some printout akin to the image in the computer screen or the developed arm that the DNA caused to form. If it is just a way of talking about patients, then it fails to qualify as a theory, and if it is meant as a guidepost to neurological entities, then it flirts with the reduction of psychology to biology. Thus we ordinarily claim representations to be structures of the psyche that have an existence that has an impact over time. However, this structure manifests itself in a variety of ways, and manifestations are like printouts of a computer program.

These printouts are, as noted, necessarily context-dependent and often become what they are as a result of the perceiver. We do thereupon read what we, in part, have asked the encoded message to deliver. And so, in analysis, part of the context that surrounds any so-called self or object representation is the presence of the analyst, who is also there to see what will be revealed. And that is perhaps the most compelling reason for us to reconsider the concept of representation, since everything from the recovery of repressed memories to the evaluation of a patient's progress (as noted earlier) is a necessarily collaborative effort. Just as the patient is embedded in the world, so too is the analyst a part of that world. This third consideration of the representation, which follows the place or site of the registration, is the process by which the registered is delivered to scrutiny. The final presentation of that registration should lead us to conclude that the usual psychoanalytic consideration of representation carries with it a number of dangers—those of an oversimplified story, of a seductive ease of description, and even of erroneous attributions as to the true contents of the mind. There are no representations of self and others waiting patiently to be lifted to scrutiny or acting as guides to changes in the self. That is much too simple. Rather there are potential capacities to deliver a complex print-out that is both a guide to the past and a coloring of the present. We do not re-present the world. We endlessly make it.

If we join these three ways of thinking about representation, we may be in a position to begin a more detailed investigation of the usefulness of that particular way of considering the mind. I offer this with the hope that such a reconsideration will have worthwhile effects upon our technique and possibly will assist us in better explaining the fact that much of today's psychoanalytic writing has to do less with what goes on within the mind of one person and more with what seems to go on between persons.

USING REPRESENTATIONS

For some analysts since Freud, the concept of representations has primarily been most useful in dealing with the disparity between psychic reality and external reality, which involves an activity of comparison; it also employs the unfortunate device of these two separate worlds.

Freud (1925) started it all when he established the primacy of psychic reality. He begins by telling us that the aim of reality testing is not to find an object in perception but to re-find it (pp. 237–238), and in doing so he creates the divide between inside and outside, that is, a perspective in which one searches for a match between the two realities.

For others, the concept seems focused on the state or organization of these representations, as seen in the following:

> Kernberg considers that the etiology of borderline personality organization is a core failure to have developed an integrated coherent self-concept, related to which is substantial impairment of differentiation of self- and object-representations and the persistence of a primitive "all good–all bad" orientation toward self and others; in turn these result from and secondarily reinforce primitive defenses centering on splitting maintained by an inordinate degree of regression. [Rinsley 1989, pp. 698–699]

Here the organization is a statement of pathology. Now these are not mutually exclusive perspectives, but for the most part psychoanalysis deals with the disparity between these two worlds of external and internal, of reality and hallucinatory wish fulfillment, of getting it right and getting it wrong. The use of the organization concept results in a description that has to do with a picture of an ideal internal system. The question is whether either usage is necessary.

From the perspective that classifies brains as computational because nervous systems represent and respond on the basis of the representations, it is a big step to one that states: "it no longer makes sense to talk of representations. The input flux provides a shifting constraint on the self-organizing process. . . . The outside is not re-presented inside but participates on the inside as but one constraint on a self-organizing process" (Globus 1995, p. 67). That step of openness removes the gap or divide, joins inside and outside, and allows memory and reality to come together. By contrast, the usual concept of representation introduces a duality between inner representations and external reality and has us standing apart from the world as spectators. The nonrepresentation concept has us knowing reality directly and immediately with nothing in between. This is one solution to the question of two levels. It requires a theory of the mind that *includes* the world rather than one that takes it in. It is what some have called a concept of the mental derived from participant models of development (Matusov 1998), in which boundaries are fuzzy and dynamic. It is an answer to an unnecessary division that has paralyzed psychoanalytic thinking.

Compare this form of participant model to one utilized by Paula Kernberg (1989), who presents a pictorial illustration of what is called normal self-esteem regulation in which an external object sits outside of a mind containing a collection of the ideal self, the ideal object, the actual self, and superego precursors. This mind model is employed to contrast this supposed normal state with that of pathological narcissism, in which the self-representation is fused with an ideal self-representation and an ideal object representation. These figurative portrayals are intended to be convenient ways to think of a patient's mental operations and organization and so to portray an imaginative snapshot of a mind. Indeed, one study (Glover 1988) aimed at delineating the precise attributes of object representations and self experiences in different groups of patients claimed to do just that job of taking a picture and seemed to take us a stop closer to confirming that these models had achieved the status of substantive entities capable of being just as real as certain physical (albeit theoretical) entities such as atoms and electrons. Some speak of moving representations during treatment and correlating such movement with clinical function, as if there were an internal monitor of progress. All of these views, which pit internal against external, lock us into dilemmas of our own making and encourage us to employ a model that inevitably leads us to a dead end.

The embrace of the actuality of these representations is also illustrated by a paper by Sandler (1993), in which he describes projective identification as

> an intrapsychic process of splitting off and projecting, or displacing, in unconscious (that is, preconscious) phantasy some unwanted aspect of the self representation into an object representation. The second step is the externalization of the object representation. . . . This externalization takes the form of actualization, a process in which the object is pushed, by a variety of subtle unconscious manoeuvers, both verbal and nonverbal, into playing a particular role for the patient. [1993, p. 1105]

The move is from the mind to the real world, from inside out. Sandler notes that for Melanie Klein that entire process was intrapsychic, and that it was extended by himself to be interpersonal. Later, Sandler (1996) says that these two broad frames of reference have a relationship, although it is not well worked out. In an effort to clarify the terminological confusion, Gill (1996) has proposed to substitute innate/intrapsychic and experiential/intrapsychic for internal and external, although he admits that present-day psychoanalytic writing does not reflect his position. Finally, he suggests that intersubjective concepts would overcome the subject–object dichotomy and would best express the dialectical interaction that he and Hoffman champion. One should keep in mind that the dichotomy that these authors struggle with and fail to resolve is a self-made dilemma that results from the model they have presented. It may not need a solution so much as a dismissal.

The same confusion over whether representations are real is evident in the fuzzy usage of the term: representations are sometimes regarded as real, sometimes as a convenient marker in clinical work, and sometimes are less than useful and even unnecessary. When Viderman (1994) says about a patient that "his self-representation shifted during the analysis . . . but there was no substantial change in the configuration of the major object representations of his early life" (p. 478), is he talking about an impression of his own or something that he feels is a tangible indicator? Or does it not matter? When an author states that a patient improved because he or she internalized the relationship with the therapist, is that meant as an explanation of cure or is it just a convenient way of speaking (Greenberg 1996, p. 36)? Just as one may say that one has learned the multiplication tables by memorizing them or internalizing them, we must recognize that this is really only a description. It may do the trick for some, or for a while, but it can also fool us into thinking that we have explained how learning takes place. The same may be said of many other theories that analysts employ in their descriptions, ranging from changing configurations of internal objects to a two-step process in which objects somehow push their way into minds. Of course there is no harm in the use of such fictions until they begin to inhibit progress. A reconsideration of the representational theory of the mind should not only call attention to the seductive allure of these mistaken versions of explanation, but should also open the possibility of a newer way of conceptualizing how a psychoanalyst may consider the mind. This is not to say that some descriptions may not be explanatory (Basch 1973), but for someone to explain how a sedative works by saying it contains a dormative substance is essentially a sleight-of-hand.

In discussing clinical material, if we agree that there has been a shift or change in both patient and analyst and that their relationship has been altered, such that some writers might claim that the corresponding representations have been modified, do we gain anything by speaking of representations? Isn't this little more than a redescription that cannot qualify as an explanation but might, in truth, detract us from searching for a more meaningful explanation? The present set of theories in psychoanalysis must themselves be held to account in order to make such explanations available to us in the arena of depth psychology, that is, in working with the transference and unconscious meanings.

Patients and analysts interact with one another according to an unconscious program (for the patient) coupled with analytic theory (for the analyst). The two connect and together participate in a dynamic interchange (Van Gelder 1998). One may prefer to see this as inter-subjective or interpersonal or any of a variety of descriptive connections, but one must keep in mind that these are no more than descriptions. My only point here is to understand this interaction as a real connection with no need for an intermediary replica of reality.

DISCUSSION

One view of psychic representations assumes that there is a ma-terial reality that differs from one's personal, inner, or psychic reality, owing to the latter being distorted or contaminated by individual dif-ferences. This dualism rests upon a convention found in much of science that knowledge is objective and true. The recognized goal of science is to approach and grasp the real world, but it is worth repeating that all of our perceptions of the world are mediated by signs or language, and that we never manage to grasp things in themselves no matter how much we may wish to believe otherwise. All of our knowledge must be interpreted or decoded and so all that we ever know is, in that simple sense, hermeneutic. Although we may wish to claim that biology is somehow more real than psychology, it is actually only more accessible to interpretation. We may see light as photons or see light as waves, but it is only by way of the fact that our interpretations change, that we see the world differently and, for the moment, feel that we have "got it right." Although we all live in the same world, we have different versions of it, and it is best not to assume that one version is eternally truer than another; however, one may work better than the other and so be true for that time. With this in mind we are all able to see reality with the proviso that we are not so much spectators of the world as inhabitants of it. Surely our realities differ, but that of the analyst need not have a higher claim to correctness over that of the patient: it is only different. Thus we work together with our versions of reality rather than becoming engaged in a process of helping the patient to get it right. Indeed the postmodern view of the world claims that we know reality directly and immediately, but in the way anything can be known. That is, we know it by interpreting the meaning, and all the way, from apples to democracy, everything passes through a sieve of interpretation (Globus 1995, p. 177). The hermeneutic view of the world is not something opposed to a real one—view or world—because psychic reality is what we all settle for. This position is part of an ongoing debate in both philosophy and psychoanalysis and connects directly with the debate about fixed or fluid representations. It should open the door for a more critical inquiry.

I think we can entertain the idea that the world is presented to us, and that we are not observing a re-presentation. This, of course, will require us to look as well at memory as construction rather than retrieval (Target 1998). It should also change our concepts of transference and the unconscious, although not in a manner that dispenses with them, which may be the danger in a concentration on the visible and overt relationship between persons. Rather we need a more up-to-date version that considers how a self-organizing system reacts to the input of the analyst. We need modifications that would lead directly to alterations in the concept of the representational theory of the mind, when this theory delivers a picture of an inner organization or world that is more or less fixed and often disordered in various forms of psychopathology. Such a mistaken and static picture comes from ideas about psychic development that are linear or sequential, and so assumes that the organization remains primarily unchanging. If we can see development as nonlinear and more chaotic or unpredictable than we may prefer, we may also see that those imaginary stages of development do us a disservice and that retaining them keeps us on a level of the dispassionate observer examining a fixed psychic product. Only a theory of the mind that allows for a dynamic interchange with the surround will ever enable us to be free of this erroneous view of a somehow frozen psyche.

CONCLUSION

The concept of mental representations has gone beyond being a stepchild of psychoanalysis (Linnell 1990), and representations, as fixed entities reflecting perceptions and misperceptions of an outside world, have come to dominate a theory of the mind (Cavell 1998). Perhaps it is time to recognize the limitations that our allegiance to such a theory places upon us. We need a theory of the mind that recognizes a view of the person as a self-organizing system in a dynamic exchange with the environment. However, we must also not lose our essential grounding in the concepts of the unconscious and transference. Such a theory is now evolving within the work that focuses on psychoanalysis as an activity of participation. If we can avoid the descriptive enticements of subpersonal neurology and interpersonal social psychology while recognizing and appreciating their accomplishments, we may achieve it sooner than we think.

PART FOUR

No Single Answer

11

Postmodern Psychoanalysis

INTRODUCTION

The principle of correctness permeates and envelopes psychoanalysis. From our worry over boundary transgressions to our hope for the correct interpretation, we struggle to be both honorable and helpful, to do the right thing. This rightness and propriety are nowhere more prominent than in the efforts to practice according to a prescribed method and eschew what is proscribed. All analysts thereby claim to honor and respect the psychoanalytic method, a collection of rules that if properly followed should lead, by a sort of internal logic, to a correct endpoint. Much to our initial surprise and eventually to our disappointment, those of us who adhere to this plan have learned that sometimes we cannot seem to manage to follow the rules, while at other times a seemingly faithful following may result in unhappy results, and on some occasions a complete disregard of the rules turns out to be the most felicitous route to an agreeable resolution. The analyst can only wonder, then, if he or she did indeed follow the method correctly or if, perhaps, our rules are misguided—or even if, peculiarly, psychoanalysis and correctness do not easily line up together in a comfortable union.

The practice of psychoanalysis or the application of the method entails, as does every procedure that lays claim to a method, a commitment to following the rules. Everyone who wishes to learn analysis has a group of books that explain how one is to act, a supervisory experience that allows for the study and adjustment of errors, and a professional life with patients. All of these are designed to sharpen one's skills and, like it or not, permit one to gather together one's own set of rules, which regularly are seen to conform to books, supervisors, and patient success or failure.

There can be little doubt that psychoanalysis has of late witnessed a variety of changes in method, changes that some say result from a relaxation of the rules. Others insist that these changes are a modification of the rules. Still others dismiss all change as a disregard of the rules punishable at times by banishment from membership in the psychoanalytic community. Not only do these changes affect the frequency of appointments—as witnessed in an erosion from five to four to three to even once-per-week analysis—but they extend to rules that one once would have felt were sacrosanct. Some analysts dispense with the couch. Some describe analysis by telephone. Many analysts encourage revealing personal feelings about themselves to their patients, even to the point of asking patients if they are interested in what would otherwise be private information (Aron 1996). Of course, at the point where one is encouraged to share positive, loving feelings toward a patient, there often is heard a sharp outburst proclaiming that this is no longer qualified to be called analysis. One could consider drumming out the disbelievers to maintain some semblance of conformity, but one wonders if and how one could possibly circumscribe all of the changes in the rules and the method. Perhaps we may begin with a different goal, one concerned less with the issue of correctness and more with an inquiry as to the source of all of this present-day "wild analysis."

BACKGROUND

A search for the source of psychoanalytic method and the rules that are to be followed (or ignored) today finds itself not on that road

Freud laid out and with which all analysts are familiar, but rather one that runs unsteadily between two quotes. The first is attributed to the analyst Wilfred Bion, who said: "It is difficult to stick to the rules. For one thing, I do not know what the rules of psychoanalysis are" (Bion 1990, p. 139). The second is derived from the philosopher who has championed postmodernism, Jean-François Lyotard, who both tells us that the postmodern is "incredulity towards metanarratives" and claims that all of science legitimates itself with reference to a metanarrative, which is a set of rules of the game (Lyotard 1984, p. xxiv). Thus Bion says he is ignorant of the rules while Lyotard is untrusting of them. And although Bion was perhaps practicing a certain sort of playful elusiveness, he was also communicating a deeper truth that may join with that of Lyotard. Each of these men voices a skepticism and wariness about the adoption of rules that lead to a method that may, by virtue of its insistence on correctness, serve less to direct than to constrain and even to distort.

The postmodern outlook in its most general sense speaks for a multiplicity of approaches that cannot be linked together in a grand narrative or an overarching theory. It allows for many languages, and the resulting Tower of Babel in turn has led many of its critics to condemn it as a view that says "anything goes." It thus is unsettling and frightening, and threatens to undermine the solidity of any rule-governed enterprise. I think this is an unfair and naive comprehension of postmodernism, whose actuality is best illustrated in Lyotard's statement that each self lives in a fabric of relations that is more complex and mobile than ever (p. 15). Seeing the mind from within this sense of its complexity allows us to recognize that such complex and open systems are neither predictable nor determined. Indeed, in an extension of Freud's concept of overdetermination, one can list a series of differences by which rule-based systems differ from complex networks or interconnected systems. These range from self-organization (compared to preprogrammed options that are defined a priori) to a multiplicity of final solutions (compared to a specific endpoint) (Cilliers 1998, p. 91). In brief, the postmodern approach moves from a general theory or metanarrative, which aims to explain everything, to particular examples that depend upon the set of local conditions—that is, the context.

If one grants such a step toward flexibility and the existence of uncertain borders that complex systems call for, then a corresponding

move can be made toward considering many of our rules (and the subsequent method) as devices that need have little or no overall validity.
Rather, they all must be recast into particular moments of applicability; that is, the rules are local rather than general. The caution that must
of course be a constant companion here is one that is unfortunately
regularly disregarded; for example, just because a rule may be altered
in one set of circumstances does not therefore mean it must be changed
in another set. We are unable to generalize with ease. We are not so much
in an arena of "anything goes" as in one of "everything matters." This
then calls for a persistent activity of framing, of "meta"-examination of
all that transpires—yet, again, only within its particular context. We no
longer can take anything for granted.

Clinical Notes—Apples Again

A rather innocent yet strikingly illustrative anecdote in our literature (described in Chapter 7) tells of an analyst (Akhtar 1999) refusing a patient's gift of fruit while tactfully explaining the rules (the
reasons) for this refusal. The explanation seemed to be offered primarily in terms of the analyst's need to frustrate the patient's instinctual
drives, and the patient complied with this explanation. This *could* be
seen as an example of our method gone astray, its very generalization
of the rule revealing that an overall metanarrative is in place. The application of this or any rule that is imposed upon the analysis by a general theory may indeed be necessary or even innocent, but it regularly
falls outside of the analytic process of inquiry. The anecdote thus illustrates the following of a rule rather than understanding it. That particular patient could have been one who needed to give a gift for some
reason quite different from the analyst's preconditions, but, again, that
can only be determined in the context of the moment. For the analyst
to apply a rule can (or perhaps must) remove him, with his own presence, from the dynamics of the situation because the rule comes from
elsewhere. All of our usual and necessary concerns with such questions
as what does this dream or fantasy or enactment mean, to both patient
and analyst, are sidetracked when the issue of correctness or the excuse
of proceeding according to the rule is introduced. I believe that one can
honestly attribute that principle of nongenerality to Bion who, by saying that he was ignorant of the rules, may have meant that rules can

have no bearing outside of what is going on with a particular patient at a particular time, and that one is therefore best served by a not-knowing beforehand.

RULES AND METHODS—CLINICAL RELEVANCE

Let us return to that group of patients whom we could conveniently classify as not living by the rules (Goldberg 1999), who are usually considered as having behavior disorders, and who run the gamut of misbehavior from lying to stealing and from sexual eccentricities to unlawful perversions. They are also people who are ordinarily not considered for psychoanalysis, either because of the severity of their pathology or because of their inability to conform to the rules of analysis. The study of these patients (Goldberg 2001) allowed us to turn a searchlight on analytic rules and method, inasmuch as we became forced to develop rules in an ad hoc manner in our therapeutic efforts, or, as Lyotard would say, rules with local validity and applicability. Our patients routinely could not fit into our individual methods of analysis, and each of them required some sort of individualized method. Perhaps this is also true of many, if not all, of our patients in some more subtle manner.

Case Example—Conrad

Conrad was a lawyer involved in client litigation who developed sudden acute anxiety when arguing in courtroom trials and so was forced to suspend all such public appearances. He felt himself extremely fortunate to have earlier purchased a disability insurance policy that paid him handsomely as long as he was unable to pursue his normal occupation, which for Conrad was appearing in court. Under the terms of this policy it did not matter that Conrad could pursue other forms of legal activity, and he quickly chose to be disabled and to collect on his insurance. Not surprisingly, the policy demanded that a regular validation of Conrad's condition be submitted by a psychiatrist; that is, Conrad needed to be seen by someone who would agree to such a contract. Initially this was no problem for Conrad, but his first analyst, a psychiatrist, balked after a bit, inasmuch as Conrad's need for such a disability certification seemed to be interfering with the treatment.

Conrad went shopping. A few analysts agreed to treat him but all insisted on staying clear of this insurance requirement. Finally Conrad found an analyst who agreed to see him *and* to regularly certify him as disabled.

At this point many analysts would no doubt claim that a bona fide analysis was impossible, since the rules of analysis were not being adhered to, and rather than a therapeutic alliance, this arrangement might more properly be termed a financial negotiation. This extreme example of a deviation from the analytic method is offered not as an instance of an ethical deviation, which is a separate subject, but rather as an opening to an inquiry into whether rule changes are feasible and so can themselves be subject to analysis. In brief, this analysis was felt to be workable for some time until, despite the patient's improvement, the analyst recognized that a termination seemed difficult if not impossible. The analyst presented this case to a group and was roundly criticized for being corrupt and having colluded with this patient. The protest of the analyst began with his insistence that "if I did not do it, someone else would." However, the group was unrelenting in its blame, and shortly thereafter a chastised and depressed analyst sought supervision for his conduct of the case. He discovered much about his own greed and dishonesty and subsequently saw it confirmed in the material that had emerged in the analysis. After some time he was able to revisit the analysis with new insight, and soon thereafter the patient decided independently to discontinue his disability benefits and to terminate his analysis. The case was then again presented to the group, which remained critical but also less certain. Was this indeed a case of an analysis that simply could not follow the rules? Without resorting to the familiar "this is not analysis," is it possible for some analyses to live outside of the usual rules as long as these exceptions ultimately become themselves scrutinized? Perhaps, most intriguingly, one may ask: Does one need to share some similar pathology in order to be able to work with some patients?

THE ANALYST AND THE RULES

What our group (Goldberg 2001) did learn from a study of a number of such rule-breaking patients was that almost all of the analysts had what might best be called a corresponding, albeit often unconscious, inability to stick to their own pre-set rules. Indeed we soon came to believe that *only* a rule-breaking analyst could hope to be effective with our misbehaving patients. Conrad's analyst was able to examine his own preoccupation with money, and he thus later claimed that his own movement from financial chicanery to professional honesty was a mark of this movement and its later effectiveness.

If we could allow the truth of that position, we might be able ourselves to make a parallel claim that all of our rules derive from our personal and individual needs, which become sanctioned by membership in groups that are like-minded. Once again we must remind ourselves that this does not and cannot lead to license. It also raises a more fundamental question as to just what can be said about the analytic method that does not devolve to the level of such niceties of the ritual such as gifts, couch, and frequency? To put it another way, What enables an analyst to function as an analyst? How can one understand rather than conform to a rule?

THE PATIENT AND THE RULES

One lesson learned by our group as we discussed each of these cases was that not everyone could do what was required of him by each patient. Whereas one analyst might help a thief but not a cross-dresser, another could easily reverse his or her predilections. The most outstanding conclusion that we reached was one that identified a rather persistent and significant blindness that accompanied our preferences and convictions. Just as Conrad's analyst seemed to disavow his own obvious (to others) dishonesty, so too could we see similar defensive positions operating in all of our behaviors. Out of these combinations of personal rationalizations and denials, there seemed to emerge a collection of procedures that we tried to apply to all of our patients. If we could free ourselves from these preconceptions, we might better explain the variability of success and failure with patients. In a nutshell, the inevitable conclusion is that some patients require certain rules while having no problem with others. Thus one cannot operate according to a fixed set of rules and an expected analytic method, anymore than one can operate with a totally flexible set of rules and an equally unpredictable method.

The question of what enables someone to function as an analyst is similarly applicable to an individual and his or her comparable ability to be a patient. The task of any analysis is to determine the requirements of a given patient as these differ from those of others, and to then see if these requirements articulate with the capabilities of the analyst. It makes no sense to assign qualities such as optimism, openness, or even neutrality to analysts, since each of these rather admirable qualities may not serve any particular patient well and may not be natural features of any single analyst. Nor does it make sense to insist that patients should not read analytic books, or should not marry, or should not bring gifts, since each of these injunctions may or may not be in the best interests of the analysis. We need to take a step back to grasp what is essential about the analytic method and its applications.

DISCUSSION

Psychoanalysis is grounded in understanding. This is not the casual understanding seen in relationships that prosper according to such an achievement, but an in-depth understanding that is conditioned by the complexities of the transference and the unconscious. It is a form of understanding that puts comfort and agreement into a secondary position. There is no doubt that Freud felt that he achieved this form of understanding through the technique and conditions that he employed, or, to put it differently, by the method he felt was most likely to allow the development of the state of transference that was desirable. Freud (1912) said, "I must however make it clear that what I am asserting is that this technique is the only one suited to my individuality" (p. 111). Many analysts have felt the same, and one cannot possibly discard the knowledge that derives from that tradition. However, it is also possible that other analysts might achieve that understanding under different conditions. If the method of such understanding requires a sustained empathy on the part of the analyst, then one needs to attend to the conditions that enable both patient and analyst to make that possible. If one feels that other forms of data gathering are required, then that too becomes a mutual undertaking by both patient and analyst. Since people are different both in personality and pathology, it seems foolhardy to insist that Freud's tradition applies to all. Yet it seems equally foolhardy to claim that nothing whatsoever need apply to all. Thus we do not aim for some intersubjective state of agreement, but for a one that allows an optimum inquiry of one person by another. Put simply, one is doing the right thing as long as one understands what one is doing. But that requires a situation in which everything is bracketed as a local narrative with local rules, and thus allowing everything to be scrutinized. And *nothing* is free from being the object of such sought-for understanding.

12

Me and Max:
A Misalliance of Goals

One of the burned-in memories of my lengthy life as an analytic candidate took place in a case conference chaired by Dr. Maxwell Gitelson. Dr. Gitelson was a crotchety and imposing man who was fairly humorless and could easily and honestly be characterized as opinionated. This particular moment of meaning of mine occurred when, to the best of my memory, a student said something or other about either his and/or the patient's hope (and goal) that the patient would soon feel better. Gitelson proclaimed (rather than offered) his opinion that psychoanalysis was not meant to make people feel better or to relieve symptoms; the goal of psychoanalysis was to allow patients to better understand themselves. Relief of symptoms might be a chance by-product of such understanding, but it was definitely *not* the goal of analysis. Nor should any psychoanalyst pursue that essentially secondary effort. My silent reaction to Gitelson's "Bah, humbug" appraisal of symptom relief was my own "Bah, humbug," since I was convinced that almost everyone I knew in analysis wanted to feel better. If self-understanding was what had to be swallowed, then that medicine could and would be endured, but it was hardly the goal that I personally would rank as number one. It seemed clear that one person's goal was just not properly or necessarily made for another. Rather than one size fitting all, it seemed that the goals of the patients and the goals of the analysts and the goals of the field of psychoanalysis might well be areas of separate concern. They need not be in opposition, but they surely are not and cannot be reduced to identical significance and importance.

The combination of my desire to be a good student plus my near-total intimidation by Dr. Gitelson allowed me over time to adopt his singular goal as mine. I periodically and often surprisingly found myself saying and even believing that the goal of psychoanalysis was self-understanding, especially when my patients would point out that I was not helping much with their psychic distress. I could readily recognize the comfort that this adopted stance offered to me, inasmuch as it allowed me to cast myself as someone in pursuit of this more noble effort of seeking a variation of "truth" rather than settling for the lesser mettle of mere comfort and relief. Also, one's ability to observe symptom relief as a happy though accidental companion of psychoanalysis enables one to achieve a feeling of personal pleasure without the encumbrance of satisfying someone else's (the patient's) wishes. In this way I found myself allied with what I imagined were the more lofty aims of the field rather than joined with those of the individual patient: selfish but safe.

Sooner or later one surely must realize that a worry over the proper goals for what one achieves or what discipline one espouses is basically a moral question. The pursuit of doing well all too readily collapses into doing the right thing, and so a conflict occurs, at times, between making the patient feel better versus (say) satisfying Freud's axiom of "where id was, there shall ego be." Unless the satisfaction of the axiom yields an equal degree of contentment for the patient, one cannot reduce the latter to a byproduct of the former. From this moral stance, the relief of symptoms and the happiness of the patient become the goals, with the goal of self-understanding trotting alongside. One could, of course, eliminate the problem if these two or three goals always emerged and then merged together, but we are regularly haunted by analyzed patients who claim that they feel no better, alongside happy ones who seem quite psychologically opaque. My loyalty to Dr. Gitelson was severely tried.

My next memory, a bit less severely etched, comes from another teacher, Dr. Charles Kligerman, who was anything but crotchety but probably equally opinionated. He would regularly say that analyzed people were just different from nonanalyzed ones. He would also pronounce this with a certain sense of the former belonging to a very exclusive club and with the secondary message that one would do well to limit one's acquaintances, friends, and certainly spouses to that membership. Putting aside this seductive elitism, Dr. Kligerman's position made it clear that psychoanalysis did something that was lasting and that it was more than just making one free of psychic pain, since having that last quality alone would never be sufficient to gain one admittance to this exclusive club. Therefore the goal of psychoanalysis involved some significant alteration in the patient, one that went beyond symptom relief and perhaps even beyond that ephemeral state of understanding. It made one a different person and, at least to some, a better one as well. Somehow the goals were beginning to become better demarcated, although perhaps not in the way Max and I might have wished for. They were not singular in that they had to satisfy a multiplicity of needs. Yet perhaps the most striking alteration or addition to this original and somewhat encapsulated version of goals offered by my mentor was that the change was not limited to the patient but seemed to extend to the analyst as well. That is, the practitioners of psychoanalysis were different both because of their personal psychoanalysis and because they were practicing the somewhat noble enterprise of turning out special people. To combine the views of my two mentors, I thought, might well lead to being overwhelmed by the elitism as well as the altitude of this rarified atmosphere.

The challenge that presented itself to me was that of somehow reconciling or unifying what seemed to be a set of three goals: self-understanding, relief of discomfort, and a lasting or relatively permanent change or enhancement of value. All three seemed essential and each seemed connected to the others. Thus any focus upon one or another should contain some element that would lead to the others. Without in any way denying the multitude of subsidiary benefits of treatment, which might range from a happier marriage to a more fulfilling sex life, these three endpoints should be all-encompassing. So let us now examine them each in turn.

SELF-UNDERSTANDING

The dominance of the ego and the accumulation of insight into one's unconscious are together assumed to lead to a body of knowledge that enables one to comprehend one's self differently. This difference may take the form of a narrative of one's history or, on other occasions, might narrow in on a retelling of a more focused event such as a particular moment of trauma. Patients surely differ in the manner in which they reflect back upon their psychoanalyses. No matter how much one insists upon psychoanalysis being an activity in which the participants engage in narration (Schafer 1992) or one of the recovery of memory (Fonagy 1999) these are more properly seen as one or another *form* of the procedure than as its fundamental goal. There can be little doubt that some patients prefer telling their life story, some wish to concentrate on the here and now with little reference to their personal history, and some seem peculiarly devoted to elaborate Proustian reminiscence. That these personal preferences regularly match the preference of the analyst alerts us to the likelihood that the search for this particular aspect of the goal may sometimes lie outside of the essence of the process.

Consider the following patient. A young professional man entered into psychoanalysis with the clearly defined and stated aim of getting married. He claimed to have had a host of involvements with marriageable women but had never done much more than live with one or another for a few months. That particular experience was characterized by emotions ranging from discontent to disgust, with not a hint of a wish for the couple of roommates to remain together. Yet he insisted that he longed for marriage to the right woman, and he hoped that an analysis would make that a realized possibility.

I shall not detail the conduct of this analysis save to say that somewhere along the line he did marry, but that occurred long after he had dropped that issue as crucial to his life as an analysand. What memories that he did recover seemed minimal, and as Alexander (1940, p. 146) long ago suggested, these were more confirmatory than revealing. I believe that he and I would be hard pressed to recount a detailed new version of his life as well. Indeed most of his analysis had to do with his father, and concentrated not surprisingly on the minutiae of the transference reflective of this. Toward the end of his analysis there was no doubt that he saw himself differently, and thereafter almost everything problematic in his life, from a telephone call to his mother to a loss of money on a promising stock, became subjected to self-scrutiny. His psychic life could be said to have two parts: the first was characterized by a relative ease in events and relationships with others, while the second showed an intense self-reflection upon anything that represented conflict or difficulty. It should not be necessary to underscore that such a division is not true of everyone, inasmuch as many of us are regularly carefree while others seem never free of concern and worry. My patient regularly reviewed and reflected upon the puzzle of everyday life, and he did so in a manner and with a method that clearly was a miniaturized version of his analytic experience.

I think it safe to conclude that the self-understanding that was facilitated in this analysis was a product of the personalities of both of us and that it could be characterized by using a variety of theoretical lexicons. That I spoke a certain language that my patient over time made his own should not be seen as mere brainwashing. His way of thinking about himself during the analysis often would begin with his announcing: "I know that you would say . . ." I took this both as a form of identification as well as of differentiation. Indeed one might well say that my patient began by understanding me, and then moved on to an understanding of himself. I take this feature as essential, in that I think the gradual dissolution of the transference should over time reveal the analyst to the patient. The greatest obstacle to this hoped-for sequence is often the unwitting or unnecessary self-revelation of the analyst. The discovery of what the world, any world, is like may follow the guidelines or map of another but it is not to be equated with a carbon copy of the other. This analysis ended with each of us changing and yet remaining quite different persons. The outstanding feature for him was his newfound capacity to puzzle over his life's ups and downs—his personal form of self-reflection.

RELIEF OF SYMPTOMS

Another patient reported to me after a year of analysis that she felt much better, at least in comparison to how she felt a year earlier, but could in no way say just what her analysis had accomplished. This feature of feeling better is a happy companion to psychotherapy, psychopharmacology, and even the ordinary occurrences of everyday life. Everything from a good night's sleep to winning the lottery is capable of bringing about reports of this kind of contentment, but only a few persons seem able to sustain this desired endpoint. No doubt a certain amount of ongoing maintenance in the form of the above-mentioned self-analytic or self-reflective work is essential for the sustaining of this feeling of being better, but it seems not to be the whole story. Just as I now might give credit to one or more of my teachers who studied and wrote about post-termination self-analysis (Robbins and Schlessinger 1983), I can state I owe my debt about the more lasting effect of analytic improvement to Heinz Kohut.

Kohut was often at odds with those analysts who emphasized the role of self-analysis following one's work in a therapeutic analysis. He felt that the establishment of meaningful selfobject relationships or the opening of empathic connections between persons was the foundation of an analytic cure (Kohut 1984), and thus that one need not be concerned with self-analytic work save for moments where disruptive breaks occurred in these empathic connections. For him, the availability and deployment of selfobjects were the essentials for navigating through life, and psychic health was equivalent to this dual capacity. Thus Kohut looked upon self-analysis more as evidence of an incomplete analysis than as a process of ongoing maintenance. If one had established a firm and lasting sense of self-cohesion, then there need be few occasions for the self-reflective work needed to repair an empathic disruption. Or so the story goes. My own ecumenical bent was to join the two issues, inasmuch as I remained ever short of perfection, and most if not all of my patients were wedded to regular self-reflection. No one had achieved the sought-for ideal state of persistent selfobject sustenance alone. Although this was a desirable point of personal achievement, it was often just as elusive. For some patients it was overwhelmingly elusive, while for others self-reflection was a rarity. Once again the mix of the goals was a reflection of the complexity of the interaction between two complex entities—the patient and the analyst—along with these two elements of supposed cure. The patient who reported feeling better after a year of therapy had no doubt made the necessary connection to allow for a firm sense of self-solidity with her selfobjects. But would it last?

THE LASTING VALUE

The lasting value of feeling better is a product of an underlying change that is attributable to something called psychic structure. Although this change may be described and developed in a variety of ways, its value underscores a way of talking about one's stability over time. This stability may be thought of as something enabling both self-reflection and the relief of symptoms. Although it may seem intangible and even tautological, it is the theoretical convention that we employ to characterize the improvement associated with analytic goals. This gain or growth of psychic structure is often claimed to be equivalent to the ordinary processes of normal development. It may, however, more properly be thought of as analogous to development. Normal persons are not analyzed persons. Achieving a solid sense of connection with one's selfobjects, as well as gaining insight into the contents of one's unconscious, cannot be readily equated with the process of a normal child's development. However, for the first, that of enduring connections, one can see an ease of selfobject relationships in normal development that is rarely the case in adult analyzed persons, who are at best able to only cautiously and carefully choose those others to whom they connect. For the second, that of gaining insight into one's unconscious, it is otherwise. Only a failure of repression reveals the unconscious to an unanalyzed adult who is generally most successful if his or her drives are neutralized or sublimated. Such non-neurotics cannot claim insight. Of course, any psychoanalytic theory can be used to distinguish and describe the analyzed person as different from the unanalyzed but non-neurotic one, yet all of them ultimately point to a crucial distinction of some sort. In a nutshell, analysis *adds* something to the person who is analyzed, and this addition, no matter how one speaks of it, becomes a lasting and distinguishing characteristic. Psychic structure is the catchword for what is added. It is by way of this concept that one is able to consider the significance of the time axis in the achievements of analysis. Change that lasts, or enduring improvement in function, reflects this under-lying something that offers stability and sustenance. Now, perhaps we are able to weld together and join the three measures of analytic accomplishment.

ALWAYS ANALYZING

My now-married patient, who is presently gripped by the sheer curiosity of living, once complained to me that he was jealous of those friends and acquaintances who seemed to be happy—or even un-happy—but who had no concern as to the origins of their psychic status. Indeed they seemed to move through life without really thinking about it. In a way, he was envious of their unconcern, and he often wished that more things did *not* matter so much to him. It was not that he worried, although he would readily admit to that, but rather that he was ever curious. And he was convinced that his psychoanalysis had given him this affliction of persistent puzzling. As glad as he might be about his ability to better see himself, it was also very much as if a chronic illness had been bestowed upon him. What a burden to have— as if life were some sort of continuing mystery story whose clues were endless. Nevertheless, as any lover of mysteries will tell you, it is a lovely addiction.

To borrow a phrase from a work by the eminent French philoso-pher Paul Ricoeur (1992): one is able to (and should) see "oneself as another." This quality of perception, which takes place as we step to one side of where we are habitually situated, is usually distorted by all our subjective prejudices and preconceptions. We may, however, gain a modicum of objectivity with the aid of psychoanalysis. We do so not by a sharing of another's (the analyst's) subjectivity, because, although it is to be valued in part, it is possibly merely another man's opinion. That would ignore the whole point of psychoanalysis, which lies in the fact that it is a body of knowledge based upon some fundamental prin-ciples and ideas about transference and the unconscious. So my patient must see himself through this lens regardless of whether he is more or less successful as an autobiographer. The point is that, since this auto-biography is coauthored, its credibility rests upon a faithfulness to psy-choanalysis rather than to some personal clarity or concealment. My patient explains himself to himself by way of psychoanalytic understanding while perhaps failing, more or less, as a writer of fiction. Fiction might be more interesting and/or fascinating, but perhaps less worthy of faith. Rather, the rote quality of analytic lore may make for a dullness of revelation, inasmuch as one's self-scrutiny, faithful to our theory, returns again and again to the situations highlighted in the treatment.

IMMUNIZATION

The return of a patient who has completed a course of psychoanalysis, with either a concomitant return of symptoms and problems or a whole new set of difficulties, is an event that happens often enough so that it appears to be inevitabile in the life of every psychoanalyst. With this return there is often an implicit registering of a complaint, one that suggests a disappointment that the analysis did not quite work, did not protect the patient from further difficulties, or did not confer a sort of lifelong immunity. It is as if one were to say that all future troubles are essentially a return of the old ones, either in the same or in a different form, so that, at heart, the expected solution turned out to be but a Band-Aid. This implicit complaint seeks a voice despite the fact that time has passed, circumstances have changed, events that no one could have foreseen have occurred, and, quite likely, self-scrutiny has diminished and faded.

While we may embrace the concept of structural change as underlying psychoanalytic effectiveness, we may struggle to account for the continued frailty of our discharged patients. We rationalize our limitations with portentous statements about the limits of analytic treatment, citing the problems inherent in libidinal stickiness, or making irrelevant references to biological givens, all the while aiming to remove ourselves and the psychoanalytic method from the equation. Perhaps it is our own sales pitch, the one about the very special status of psychoanalysis offered to me by one of my teachers, that has led us to this illusion of a perfect psychic paradise. Psychoanalytic treatment, like politics, is local. It can make no claim to permanently insulate a person from the unexpected, innumerable vicissitudes of life because, as much as one would hope otherwise, the neuroses of childhood are not complete explanations for the trials of adulthood. The two-part explanation discussed above for the successful ending of an analysis, involving self-analysis and open empathic connections, leads us into a better picture of why the theory of infantile neurosis is incomplete and of the resulting continued possible problems of analyzed patients.

FORM VERSUS CONTENT REVISITED

Freud's axiom about making the unconscious conscious, stated above, implied that psychic health was inextricably tied to insight, that knowledge was empowering, and that this new power was curative. Put simply, this is a "content cure" wherein the exposure of the contents of the unconscious enabled a change that, although later elaborated with various forms of energic variations, was fundamentally based upon knowing. The reexperiencing of the conflicts of infancy and childhood, classically thought of as the infantile neurosis, should allow one as an adult to see things differently. To be sure, this reexperience required the full affective charge to qualify as a valid one, but the fundamental idea was that of revisiting an earlier trauma, but now with *adult* competence. The transparency of the analyst, even in its present guise of a neutral position (Baker 2000), insists that an earlier situation is and must be reenacted in treatment and that this can only be effected by allowing history to repeat itself within the analysis. Such repetition also calls for the analyst not to interfere with the emergence of the unconscious material, since this material remains the root cause of the neurosis.

This is certainly not the explanation when one is dealing with "form" rather than the content. Here it is not the "what" that is the problem but the "how." For such a patient we shift our explanation from conflict over unfortunate events to one of deficits resulting from faulty development. To be sure, one can readily see that every conflict somehow implies some sort of a deficit, either in repression or neutralization of drives, or ego weakness, or any variant of alternative theoretical explanations. No matter the theory, one may still comprehend a difference between the patient who needs insight and the one who needs more, no matter how one chooses to characterize or pathologize the latter. This second patient is the one who seems to gain relief from the regularity of the visits, the listening of the analyst, and the feeling of being understood—all those ingredients that are lumped together under the unhappy wastebasket term "the relationship." This is the patient who may, upon recalling her analysis, speak of the analyst's tone of voice, the feelings aroused upon entering the room, the long and difficult termination punctuated by an occasional re-visit, and the very expected Christmas card exchange. Often this is also the patient about whom we may be a bit guilty or embarrassed, the one for whom some administrative boundary had been breached. Our aim is to turn that form into content so that now the patient knows what she most needs.

The thesis that I wish to offer flows from my earlier conviction that one size does not fit all, that analysis means and does different things for and to different people, and that the straitjacket of our rules leads to a rigidity in the determination of our goals. Every patient has an individual mix of self-reflection coupled with empathic connections, and one is not to be prized over the other. Indeed this variability of needs carries over to different patients at different times, and is also certainly true of one patient with different analysts. So it is only in the most general sense that we can meld together the activity of self-reflection and meaningful connections with others to fashion an endpoint applicable to any single patient. However, it is well to keep in mind that we can never divide up an analysis into the convenient categories that we may sketch. It is not true that we can determine that now we are dealing with transference configurations and now with new development, or that now we have a real relationship and now a visitor from the past. We are never so lucky.

DISCUSSION

If one were to ask an internist or a college teacher or an auto mechanic what the goals of their occupations were, they would probably all preface their response with an "it all depends." In a way those dreaded and dreadful words only hide the fact that the respondents first require some input from you in order to shape and determine the answer. Yet it is different with the plumber called in to unplug your sink, or the teacher of first-year French, or the internist treating a specific patient with pneumonia. The easy answers correspond to focused efforts at fixing a specific problem; the hard ones deal with general aims of amelioration. Psychoanalysis does not enjoy such focused fixes. As much as we would like it to be otherwise, we are haunted by vagueness. Yet this atmosphere of uncertainty makes analysis the rich field that it is, so that if every patient has an oedipal problem then we know we are too much the plumber. "Never knowing for sure" is the proper place for our own "it all depends" and our own insistence on the individual patient finding his own goal.

For example, the supposed grammatical error of my title for this chapter comes from a linguistic choice. It is meant to state itself in the accusative case, that is, as the object of a verb. It is meant to say what the goals of psychoanalysis mean to me and to Max, since Max and I continue to think quite differently, just as I continue to live with uncertainty. The vibrancy of psychoanalysis derives both from its fundamental thesis of transference and the unconscious, coupled with the indeterminate shape of each of these fundamentals. To combine the two—fundamentals plus change—results in our being able to state the goals of psychoanalysis with the addition of some phrase like "as of now" or "for the time being" alongside of "for this particular person." In this way we can and should embrace the vagueness of our work. Max was a great teacher because he was so sure of himself and paradoxically could deliver a student who could live happily with a multitude of opinions.

This multitude is the fundamental underpinning for the inexhaustibility of interpretation and the many roads to understanding. The sequence of misunderstanding leading to understanding subsumes them all and gives us the freedom to be open to the endless possibilities available to us.

13

A World of Possibilities:
Two Philosophic Approaches
to Psychoanalysis

Usually the introduction of a philosophical perspective on scientific issues is feared, in that it may draw one away from the particulars of the scientific inquiry to a rather distant point that allows for generalizations or global perspectives—those that give little promise for a solution of any one particular quandary. Yet it is sometimes possible to demonstrate that certain seemingly unresolved problems are really problems of misapplied conceptual thinking or issues in logic that need clarification, and that they can be solved as a result of such an inquiry. Here, I would like to look at some contemporary struggles in the theory and practice of psychoanalysis from the vantage point of philosophical conceptualizations in order to make an effort in the direction of clarification, with the hope of possibly even removing some of the heat and acrimony that percolate among us because of this perceptual fogginess.

I shall start with an idea borrowed from a prominent American philosopher, Hubert Dreyfus, but I will offer so many elaborations and conditions to the loan that my benefactor may disown me. Dreyfus (1989) presents two fundamentally opposed views of the mind. Others have made similar divisions, but we shall follow Dreyfus. The first he calls the epistemological approach, which he attributes to Freud. The second he terms the ontological approach, which he assigns to Merleau-Ponty. He describes the epistemological approach as one in which the mind contains ideas that correspond or fail to correspond with what is out there in the world. The mind represents the world. Freud is said to have embraced this approach although he added his fundamental contribution about the lack of immediate access to certain parts of the mind, namely, the unconscious, that are concealed. For Freud, knowing was primary.

The ontological approach is different. We should begin with the definition of ontology, which is the search for the meaning of things, often said to be the study of being. Philosophers who pursue the ontological approach to the mind are concerned with how one lives in the world and how one relates to the world. Although there are a number of ways to describe and discuss ontology, it often can be reduced to the question: "What is it like to be a _____?" It is a study of existing or being-in-the-world and thus it does not set off or situate a subject as apart from and looking out at the world but rather presents an image of a person experiencing, or living in, the world. Thus the division: thoughts versus experience.

That Freud conceived of the mind as partitioned into conscious and preconscious areas split apart from an unconscious one is a cornerstone of psychoanalytic theory. The basic concept underlying his technique of psychoanalysis had to do with allowing the unconscious to become conscious so allowing the patient to "know" what had until then remained unknown to him. The ultimate goal of treatment was "insight," and this was in keeping with an approach aptly termed epistemological, which is an adjective applied to knowledge. Of course Freud (1910) also cautioned us not to reduce this approach to the mere acquisition of knowledge when he warned

It is a long superseded idea, and one derived from superficial appearances, that the patient suffers from a sort of ignorance, and that if one removes the ignorance by giving him information (about the causal connection of his illness with his life, about his experiences in childhood, and so on) he is bound to recover. The pathological factor is not his ignorance in itself, but the root of his ignorance is his inner resistance; it was they that first called this ignorance into being, and they still maintain it now. [p. 225]

It is this caution that still allows us to claim that the goal of treatment is ultimately to see things more clearly, and today's consideration of symptoms as compromise formations directs one to proceed by an unpacking technique that yields a result similar to Freud's plan for recovery. We should ideally end up by knowing what was unknown. As Freud (1909) so clearly announced in his account of the Rat Man, "At this point I told him that he had now produced the answer we were waiting for" (p. 182). We look for answers and we anticipate their emergence as a solution.

With the many qualifications applicable to the study of psychoanalysis as a purely cognitive exercise, we still manage to conclude with some complex set of answers, some sort of knowing. The starkest contrast to this lies in an approach that makes such knowing secondary and even unnecessary (Fonagy 1999). It would seem that a crucial limitation of this latter thesis would have to be that it is another sort of knowing, or else how in the world would one ever know just what was effective, let alone curative, in a therapeutic effort? Psychoanalysis, as a rule, does have some cognitive as well as emotional criteria with which to approach an answer to this particular question, inasmuch as the transference is talked about and its resolution is said to be examinable (Reed 1994), and thereby is an object of study. However, the arena of experiencing or being, though available as a subject of inquiry, is still said not to depend solely, if at all, upon what is known. There is no doubt that casting these two approaches as opposite extremes may highlight their interdependence, but occasionally one does come across clinical material that seems to make these approaches appear to be a world apart. Here is one example that, although it is an exercise in psychotherapy, presents one part of the two sides. It is a treatment effort that presents itself as being all experience, and it even calls into question the entire definition of treatment.

First Case Illustration

Dr. T. is a psychiatric resident wishing to learn more about psychotherapy, both how to do it and just what constitutes it. He is surrounded by teachers and practitioners of psychopharmacology and, indeed, one of the first patients that he inherits from a graduating resident is a young man who is being treated and has been treated with a variety of medications for depression and panic attacks. Dr. T. arranges an appointment with his prospective patient who arrives dutifully but so late as to leave little time except for a reconsideration by Dr. T. of the present medications and the issuing of a new prescription. However, Dr. T. is intrigued with this potential patient and arranges another appointment in a week, this in order to take a detailed history and perhaps to launch a psychotherapy. Alas, it turns out that this patient can never accommodate the planned agenda of Dr. T., who reluctantly retreats to a more modest wish to see the patient merely in order to better monitor the medications. A whole series of missed appointments, telephone calls and letters follows, all of which are characterized by the efforts of Dr. T. to snare the patient who remains both elusive and yet peculiarly available. When Dr. T. renews the prescriptions but only for a week's worth of medication, the patient calls after two weeks for a new supply. When Dr. T. reaches the patient on the phone he hears the exasperation in the voice of the patient who has unwittingly been trapped into talking with his doctor.

Dr. T. talks to his colleagues and supervisors about his slippery subject, and almost all of them insist that he has no patient, that this man must be disconnected from a charade of psychiatric care. Dr. T. then dutifully but reluctantly writes a letter to his non-patient stating that the care (such as it is) will be discontinued if the patient does not call and arrange a meeting before a certain date. The date passes, Dr. T. feels unburdened, and soon thereafter the patient calls. They talk briefly on the phone, arrange an appointment, and the patient arrives on time. Dr. T. is excited and lays out a choice for the patient of psychotherapy, cognitive behavioral therapy, or medical management of the psychopharmacologic treatment. The patient chooses the first and sets up a weekly hour of psychotherapy. Dr. T. is able to ascertain that the patient's life has been one of rebellion, defiance, and the championing of unwelcome causes. Now when the case is presented to colleagues and supervisors, Dr. T. is told that he and the patient were acting out a transference configuration, that the patient was and is quite involved with Dr. T., and certainly qualifies as a patient, albeit one who could not readily submit to the control and authority of anyone else. It even began to seem that the patient, who regularly insisted that none of his medications did much for him, had improved a bit by way of this peculiar set of actions with Dr. T., none of which seemed understandable at the time.

However, Dr. T. was befuddled. At one point in his involvement in the selling of psychotherapy to his patient, as well as to himself, he had loaned a book on psychotherapy to the patient, one that Dr. T. himself had read. Nowhere in the book did it seem that what had happened and was happening with this patient would qualify as therapy. The problem, one that was emphasized by the author of this book, was that many beneficial (as well as deleterious) things happen in treatment that are never talked about. This seemed to Dr. T. to open the door to a treatment that worked without talking. However, how was he to understand what was happening to and with his patient if they could not discuss it? Perhaps more important was an even more fundamental question: Was anything happening? However, Dr. T. seemed to feel that surely all this smoke and heat had to mean something. When he did manage to sit across from his patient in their newly arranged psychotherapy session, there was a long moment of silence that seemed to Dr. T. to stretch on and on. Finally the patient broke the impasse, looked at Dr. T., and said, "This isn't working." Though taken aback and even stunned, Dr. T. was able to think to himself and then to say: "No, I think it is." For Dr. T. this was another version of the struggle that had characterized the treatment from the very start. Neither he nor his patient were of a mind to end this mutual experience, since it was clear that the patient was improving and that the doctor was beginning to be able to make sense of what was happening.

No, this is not meant to be a presentation of a well-conducted case, but it is one that consisted almost entirely of experience. Although one might say that no analytic or therapeutic response can be swept clean of experience, and Gill (1979) may insist that no interpretation has any chance of being effective without it being experienced immediately in the transference, we next take a further step toward seeing some of the discourse that some say remains as an essential ingredient.

Second Case Illustration

In contrast to the case of Dr. T., let us look at a case in which talking and knowing was central. This is the case noted previously in

Chapter 7, in which the analyst is discussing the analysand's "need to know." The analyst states that the frustration of the patient's defensive and projected need for causality is essential if the world of inner objects is to be called forth. He illustrates this with an example in which it was felt to be helpful to explain something to a patient. This vignette consisted of a female patient bringing Dr. A. a bag of apples that the doctor refused to accept. Dr. A. then attempted tactfully to explain his reason for doing so to the patient. Then he asked this patient to associate to apples. "She answered, 'Adam's apple . . . Adam and Eve . . . forbidden fruit'" (Ahktar 1999, p. 138). She smiled, blushed, and left shaking her head, saying, "I understand, I understand." The author clearly intends this as illustrative of his patient seeing and now knowing something that might otherwise remain concealed. He also clearly offers this exchange with an open affirmation of the "seeing" as crucial.

In contrast to a therapy which seems to consist primarily of a mutual set of enactments by both patient and therapist, this scene of the gift of apples presents action as a prelude to knowing. Dr. T. did begin to see patterns of behavior between himself and his patient, and so he did start to make some sense of it. Dr. A. seemed to consider action as something to be minimized, as in his refusal of the apples, or something to be lifted away to see what was underneath by way of the patient's associations, or something to be explained in terms of the analysand's need to know. Thus far these do seem to illustrate rather antithetical approaches: one that is ontological or consisting primarily of a living out of something, the other epistemological and so directed to allowing the patient and the doctor to see and to know something. Some of us may possess a bias toward either experience per se or insight, and it is often the case that having a bias seems to direct the treatment along such a favored line.

THE WHEN AND HOW OF THE TWO APPROACHES

Dreyfus (1989), no psychoanalyst, offers the idea that the epistemological approach is suited for neurotic symptoms while the ontological best serves to explain and deal with ways of living. The psychoanalyst Shane and colleagues (1997) claim that patients sometimes need their old patterns to be unearthed and interpreted while at other times they require new experiences between patient and analyst. In what appears to be an extension of this explanation, Fonagy (1999) champions a view that claims that experience is central, and bases this position on alterations in a category of memory called procedural memory. Without now going further into the validity or credibility of these presentations, it does seem to be true that present-day theories or opinions tend to pull apart the two approaches and even to make claims for some kind of neurobiological underpinnings. Much of this is supported in studies of attachment behavior (Bowlby 1988) and/or can be seen in clinically presented cases that give priority to what is called relational therapy (Aron 1996). Indeed, as more and more literature comes to our attention, the further apart it seems to drive these two approaches. Thus we see presentations that separate interpretive work from what is said to be the essential curative factor, the "something more" of therapy (Stern et al. 1998). This nicely culminates in the statement, "New ideas, by themselves, cannot sustain change" (Fonagy 1999, p. 220), as if the phenomenon of a new idea living alone or by itself were indeed a possibility. All the way from those who insist on a different brain site for ideas versus those crucial emotional experiences, to those who speak for the supposed fact of "working only with the part that is verbalized" (Joseph 1985, p. 448), what began as a wedge between epistemology and ontology has grown to a gap that separates therapeutic approaches, to the point where they are now appear almost fully in opposition.

Even the many studies and post hoc interpretations of Freud and his work appear to support such an opposition, as evidenced in certain writers who compare the case of the Rat Man with the notes on the case (Freud 1909) and see two different Freuds. However, in his study of character and in his conceptualization of normality as being one in which the person is able to love and to work, there is little doubt that Freud's primary concern was that of living, of being-in-the-world. The oft-told story of Freud having Helene Deutsch sit up after an analytic hour of hers in order for him to explain to her just what he had done may be seen either as an opposition of knowing to doing, or else as an artificial construction of a difference. So, too, can his feeding the Rat Man be considered a deviation or part of a larger process. A reading of Freud as someone devoted to the simple unearthing of repressed material does not live happily with his arranging for loans for the Wolf Man. The effort by those who claim to have discovered "something new" in psychoanalysis to pigeonhole Freud may have only set up an artificial opposition.

It seems to me that Dreyfus is wrong not only about Freud but also about Merleau-Ponty.

Merleau-Ponty, a French philosopher regularly characterized as a phenomenologist, focused upon the living body and its presence in the world. For Merleau-Ponty each person has his or her own embodied understanding of what counts as real in a shared public world. Although it is often felt that ontology deals with phenomena or experience while epistemology deals with the intellectual or truth of something, Merleau-Ponty is also said to be a philosopher who insisted that constructed dualities, such as facts versus meanings, are in error. He felt that there was no contradiction between the two (Dillon 1997, p. 57). Merleau-Ponty concluded that one could not perceive something without both adding something of oneself to the perception and missing something that might be seen. In a rather colorful quote he said, "Each aspect of a thing which falls under our perception is still only an invitation to perceive beyond it, still only a momentary halt in the perceptual process. If the thing itself were reached, from that moment it would be arrayed before [us] and stripped of its mystery. It would cease to exist as a thing at the very moment when we thought to possess it" (Dillon 1997, p. 265). This particular point of Merleau-Ponty's underscores the fact that the one who sees is really a participant in an experience; one never "knows" anything without input from the observer.

This very brief rebuttal to the effort to divide knowing from being, Freud from Merleau-Ponty, and the enterprise of interpretation from that of experience has a modern-day corollary in those who prefer one or the other, and who do so by arguing for a dualism that may not exist. In contrast, Susan Hurley (1998), in a careful and detailed review of both the neuropsychologic and philosophic literature on perception and action, tells us that the two are so interdependent and co-constituted that they are essentially part of a complex dynamic feedback system that does not allow for any separation of seeing and doing. She sees the duality as a unity. The idea that we obtain inputs from the world and then react to them in some manner is no longer tenable, since what we take in is determined by our behavior (p. 421). We must be seen as living in the world (ontological) and thus knowing it (epistemological). The primary reason that "new ideas by themselves do not sustain change" is that there can be no such thing as a new idea "by itself." We know that every idea or percept or bit of knowledge involves the entire person in action. We also know that every bit of new behavior alters our repertoire of ideas. Equally important is the fact that psychoanalysis has always operated with this dynamic feedback system in mind, whether or not this is clearly understood by most theories.

Dynamic systems theory is a study of complexity. Complex systems do not follow rules that allow for a linear sequence but rather are networks that are both unpredictable and self-organizing. One can never be certain if any single intervention will lead to any single reaction, inasmuch as the system is in a continual organizing effort. The mind is such a system, and thus the study of one mind by another in itself leads to a host of unpredictable results. So, too, does the action of one mind upon another create a new complexity. But psychoanalysis insists that overdetermination is operant in all inquiry as well as in all action and, if inquiry and action are co-constituted, it is not possible to claim that now one operates and now another. Rather it can be only a matter of convenience to claim a concentration on the one rather than the other. This convenience is essentially an economy of effort, as for instance when the analyst chooses to consider one facet of the transference rather than another. No analyst, however, would be foolhardy enough to claim that a singular focus is sufficient, and thus no analyst can claim that either knowing or experiencing can exist alone. Such a division is a convenience that has gotten out of hand. The next task is one of explaining how and why this unruly and unwarranted division is so alive in psychoanalysis and whether a proper resolution is possible.

A LIFE IN SEARCH OF ITS OWN HISTORY

As Paul Ricoeur (1991) has remarked, "Life can be understood only through the stories that we tell about it, [so] then an examined life, in the sense of the word as we have borrowed it from Socrates, is a life recounted" (back cover).

If one learns a skill such as mastering a musical instrument or riding a bicycle, that skill becomes a part of one's self. There is no doubt that there is always a significant neurological component that can be termed a subpersonal one, that is, it resides in the nervous tissue and makes no claim to exist as separate from the individual. There may also be an interpersonal component of playing or riding as part of a group ensemble or in an adventure. Here, the person joins with other persons in a more or less social setting. Each and every activity of the person may change that individual and all become a part of that person's life. That life, the life that psychoanalysis studies, is one that is in search of its own history (Ricoeur 1991, p. 181). The skills that a person learns, although they may be said to form a category of procedural memory, and may be retained in spite of some unfortunate amnesiac experiences such as Alzheimer's disease, are still a part of that person's history. The relationships that are formed, which may involve yet another category of memory, are also a part of that person's history. Indeed that person is a complex system that cannot be easily lifted out of whatever context he or she is a part of, but it is a complexity that psychoanalysis studies as the self, or perhaps better said, as the mind that joins the brain and the world.

The examination of the self is always, for psychoanalysts, one that utilizes a time dimension and is organized in the form of an autobiography. So, too, does the treatment offered by psychoanalysis involve a participation that exists both over time and in the present. Such an examination and treatment is recounted, and in the recounting this life becomes understood. Much else happens in the treatment that is not understood, just as much happens in life that is not recounted. Playing an instrument need never be talked about and yet can be an essential part of that person's life. Many experiences are left outside of our discourse and many things are understood without being a part of our discourse. However, there may come a moment when we do need to contemplate and study the self, and that event almost always involves language and, in psychoanalysis, always involves a dialogue with another. Certainly at times learning how to play (say) a cello involves a good deal of conversation and may well lead to a feeling of solidity and emotional growth. Certainly at times the process of therapy or analysis involves a good deal of unspoken experiences that may well lead to an amelioration of discomfort. It is important that we do not collapse these two occasions into the same sort of event. We are not educators or trainers or coaches.

If we agree that psychoanalytic therapy based upon a depth psychology differs from mastering a new skill, we do not diminish the common elements of the two nor do we insist upon a total uniqueness. The same applies to a wide variety of social relationships that likewise become compared to and ultimately collapse into analytic treatment. The practice of psychoanalysis is that of a reconfiguration of a person's life: a reconfiguration based upon whatever analytic theory that makes for a new picture of the self through time. It necessarily involves material that was unavailable or unconscious to the person just as it involves material and events that are lived in the moment. Although one may see elements of education, striking affective moments, or new ideas and concepts, they are all subsumed in this new configuration. Only the examination and recounting of this configuration qualifies as psychoanalysis for most of its practitioners. However, this last definition is regularly augmented with provisions that insist upon external features such as frequency of visits, as well as internal ones that include the niceties of the employed theory such as the Oedipus complex.

In an elegant review of hermeneutic psychoanalysis, Elyn Saks (1999) lists the criteria for a therapy qualifying as psychoanalysis. A therapy is psychoanalysis only if

1. It purports to work via beliefs
2. The beliefs include propositions about what kind of a person one is
3. The beliefs include propositions about one's conscious and unconscious mental states
4. The beliefs include propositions about mental states that play a causal role in one's behavior.

I shall not pursue the question as to the exact definition of belief except to say again that it is clearly a form of knowledge as well as a way of life. The way we talk about what we believe and the way we form the propositions about our unconscious mental states takes the linguistic form that is offered by psychoanalysis. That is to say, we enter a particular culture that speaks a special language; or, as Wittgenstein (1963) said, we participate in a language game that spontaneously emerges in a *Lebensform* (form of life) (p. 225). We can sidestep the problem of whether or not these beliefs are true or real by recognizing that these truths are also determined by the forms of life that make up our world. Thus we summarize the work of psychoanalysis as one of examining the history of a person in and with another who joins in this construction of an autobiography.

REPRISE

It is not unusual for clinicians to see the two cases mentioned above as points on a continuum, with that of Dr. T. as representative of one end encompassing a maximum of experience, and the case of Dr. A. as devoted primarily to knowing. The next, not unexpected, step would be to assert that one of these endpoints was more qualified to exemplify psychoanalytic therapy while the other was almost beyond membership in any category of psychotherapy. If one were to adopt a more or less radical position of there being no real differences between these two save that dictated by the patients and the therapists, this would flirt with the danger of giving no credit to training and competence. This possible debate is one that goes on in our field, although there is no good hope for a resolution aside from what is usually no more than one opinion being claimed with more volume than the other.

To say that psychoanalysis is "the active construction of a new way of experiencing self with other" (Fonagy 1999) not only privileges experience but also subtly eliminates knowing. To claim some ever-present separation for a category of memory called procedural isolates experience from the contents of interpretation, something that surely is a procedure. But rather than bemoan the sad existence of such a need to divide, a more productive psychoanalytic effort would be one of questioning the origin of this need to ever misunderstand Freud. To attribute a more or less pure epistemologic approach to Freud is an error that continues on in those who insist upon it as a license for action. Whatever their individual reasons, which may range from inexperience to personal unconscious issues, there is little doubt that analysts who do privilege experience find it (in some form or other) effective with some patients. However, there is also a wealth of evidence that insight per se is the crucial ingredient for other patients. We routinely, regularly, and sadly seem to forget. Not only do all patients need both to be understood and to experience that state, but they also need to have such understanding explained to them. However, some patients demand long periods of understanding, and so may seduce us into thinking that

that is sufficient. Some other patients take easily and quickly to interpretations that explain and so may seduce us into thinking that knowing was all that was needed. Our task is to better understand and delineate which patients do best with what, as well as to see what differs in a single patient, rather than to generalize a single element as responsible for cure. We must remember that it is not the case that "something more" is added, since that something was always there. The wide variation in patient populations plus the personal predilection of analysts has suggested a division that Freud never meant to be. Thus our naive resident may have lived at one end of a continuum with our seasoned analyst at the other, but it would be folly to build a wall between the two of them.

Divisions of all sorts seem to plague psychoanalysis. We began with that of the mind and the brain and the many efforts to reduce the one to the other and so to eliminate that divide. The next division in search of unity was between understanding and explaining, and here we noted the futile effort to pit one against the other and to insist that psychoanalysis could thereby become an acceptable entrant in the field of science. Within psychoanalysis there has always been the duality of action versus words, and our long history of privileging the latter over the former can blind us to the interpretive status of enactments. So too did we see that form and content are so interwoven that concentration on one of these can lead to a dismissal of the totality needed for understanding. Perhaps no more enticing and deleterious duality has plagued analysis than that of a long-standing commitment to the two-world hypothesis: one that insists on an inner copy of an outer world with one being "real" while the other is merely "psychological." An unfortunate result of our preoccupation with the external versus the internal world has been that some analysts have focused more on the so-called external world, and in doing so flirting with a psychology that becomes a social one rather than a depth psychology. The final and perhaps most deleterious division, and one that connects to that of brain studies, has involved an effort to separate knowing from experiencing, even to the point of claiming some patients benefit more from the one than the other, and to our even being able to design and prescribe more of one than the other.

Essentially our study of these divisions, along with our effort to unify them, is really another hidden yearning for simplicity. Unfortunately that goal will always elude us, since interpretation is infinite and understanding is its companion.

There is surely a certain innocence to the myriad efforts that are directed toward the reduction of the complexity of psychoanalysis in favor of the simplicity of one or another brain mechanism or form of interaction between patient and analyst. Without denying the existence and efficacy of these explanatory efforts, they regularly miss the relevant point. Psychoanalytic therapy is admittedly at one and the same time so complex as to defy our fully encompassing it and yet appears so simple that it easily can be said to be "no more than _____." We must live in the space between the impossible and the obvious, while recognizing that we may have only begun to explore all that psychoanalysis has to offer. Dr. T.'s work is a groping toward understanding a patient, and many could say that it was unsatisfactory and unsuccessful. But some would say that Dr. A missed the point of what his own acts of refusal meant to the patient. The joining of approaches—one that concentrates on knowing with one that emphasizes experience—results in a union of possibilities. Rather than attempt a reduction of psychoanalysis to a single or focal form of effort and inquiry, it is much more profitable to see it as an opening to a world of possibilities. The cases presented offer to us (as well as to the patients) a range of criticisms, comments, and opportunities to change our minds. That should be the proper philosophical approach to our field, that is, one that offers not an ease of seeing or being, but rather a balanced participation in a truly impossible profession. We do ourselves a disservice to settle for less.

Appendix

An Odd Couple:
Martin Heidegger and Heinz Kohut

INTRODUCTION

My personal imaginary marriage of these two unlikely partners is all the more fanciful because each member of this supposed union probably never heard of the other. Well, perhaps Kohut did know of Heidegger because of his stature as a philosopher, but it is a sure bet that Heidegger had no knowledge of or interest in this psychologist. For the philosopher, psychology missed the point (Heidegger 1927). For the psychologist, his personal view of psychoanalysis came from the consulting room and not from the armchair, and therefore was grounded in experience. These differences are starkly apparent in the works of each man. Heidegger's magnum opus, *Being and Time*, was first published in 1927, went through seven German editions, and was first translated into English in 1962. Kohut's ground-breaking volume, *The Analysis of the Self*, reached the English-reading public in 1971 and was published in German in 1974. One may be fairly confident that both the philosopher and the psychoanalyst knew of and read Freud, but also that this common experience would be as likely to separate as to unite them. Although they were both German-speaking, they seemed to speak a different language.

So why the coupling? The marriage may provide a better understanding of each man's belief system. As a start, it does take a little work to bring two people together in any project, be it a romance or the mutual commitment to a religion. This project is made more difficult since both of these individuals, throughout their lifetime, insisted upon their own powerful need to be different from everyone who had gone before them. Or perhaps this very yearning for uniqueness gives us the commonality that is needed to launch our inquiry.

THE BACKGROUND

Although I may be immodestly overqualified to present a discussion of the work of Heinz Kohut, I am woefully underequipped to dare to talk about Martin Heidegger. However, the similarities in their respective ideas became clear to me over time and seem to cry out for public presentation. Unfortunately, few of my psychoanalyst colleagues are familiar with Heidegger, while fewer philosophers, even those who are interested in psychoanalysis, have more than a cursory acquaintance with or knowledge of self psychology. And, certainly, not many of either group seem concerned about this deficiency or its remedy, by way of a joining of these interests. There does, however, seem to be a quality that leaps out in any discussion among the relatively uninformed (as opposed to the unabashedly clueless), and that is one of hostility, which regularly takes the form of dismissal. I personally became inured to the regular lambasting of Kohut by my "classical" friends, but have never quite grasped the antagonism and/or dismissal of Heidegger by many professional philosophers. The likelihood that their thought presents a potential threat to entrenched positions seems the most obvious explanation, inasmuch as one could not easily assimilate the work of either man with that of their predecessors. Yet, over time, each of these men would gain acceptance through an insistence by their reluctant readers on their unoriginality. Heidegger got his ideas from John Dewey and Kohut got his from Ferenczi and Winnicott. Somehow this makes them easier to swallow. Nevertheless, this is the beginning of their unlikely unity: my personal curiosity.

THE MEN

There is now an outstanding biography for each of these men (Safranski 1998, Strozier 2004); therefore my aim here is not an historical one. Each of my respective heroes had a classical education and became outstanding in his specialized field, both as a teacher and as an original thinker. They each developed faithful adherents, as well as equally critical dissidents. One could not easily be matter-of-fact or casual about either Kohut or Heidegger, and cottage industries devoted to the debunking of each of them developed alongside their popularity. For the most part, Kohut got a much better press than did Heidegger, who had an association with Nazism that permanently tarred his reputation. Yet Kohut's own inability to embrace his personal tradition of Jewishness was felt by many to be an equally striking character flaw. Each man remains unforgiven by many scholars to the present day.

Although both men lectured and wrote widely, for each the linchpin of his work was a single book. *Being and Time* became the bible of Heideggerian thinking, while *The Analysis of the Self* was itself an analytic phenomenon. Countless other books and interpretations of these seminal works followed, usually from lesser writers who aimed to make the ideas more palatable and digestible, but whose efforts often had the effect of losing the ideas in the process. Thus this project of the marriage of ideas runs the real risk of oversimplifying each man's theories to a similarly disappointing point—their disappearance. So my effort here is not intended to offer anything approaching a full survey and explanation; rather it is to entice the reader who is familiar with the one to perhaps be intrigued by the other. Kohutians should get a glimpse of some philosophical underpinnings to self psychology. Heideggerians ideally should become interested in a psychoanalysis that is not Freudian yet remains a depth psychology.

HEIDEGGER AND DASEIN

The heart of Heidegger's work is the concept of Being. He says that the question of Being is prior to all other areas of philosophy although it is a question that is regularly forgotten. Rather than define Being as such, Heidegger presents the one who asks the question as Dasein. This can be a troublesome word, with all sorts of interpretations, but essentially Dasein is a human who inquires about his existence, who is aware of his being. Dasein is you and I when we care about our existence and our lives.

The next fundamental point is that Heidegger analyzes Dasein in a manner quite different from other philosophers such as Descartes. Heidegger insists that Dasein is not a separate subject distinct from the external world but rather is essentially Being-in-the-world or "being contextualized in equipment contexts, in a culture and in history" (Guignon 1983, p. 106). Dasein is not a distinct, individual mind or person or self but is one engaged in activity, connected with others and living along an axis of time. Dasein cannot be a worldless subject who takes in or internalizes the world but is always a part of the world in which the person exists. Thus Heidegger starts out with a fundamental erasure or dismissal of the subject–object dichotomy. One—the subject—does not stand apart and look at the world; rather one is in the world.

KOHUT AND THE SELF

The heart of Kohut's work is the concept of the *selfobject*. The selfobject revolutionized classical psychoanalytic thinking, which up to that point had considered the self as the individual person seeking gratification from others seen as objects separate from the self. For Kohut these others serve as part of the functional architecture of the self; they become a necessary part of the self. The other person is thus contextualized and no longer stands apart from others and/or in opposition to others. Indeed the very word "person" becomes problematic.

Kohut's concept of selfobjects was and is for some just as troublesome as Dasein. His students were unsure whether one grew out of and away from such an arrangement and were even uncertain about what qualified as a selfobject. Kohut made it clear that the selfobject is of lifelong duration and serves to connect a person to others. Thus he eliminated the idea of the primacy of psychological independence, save in a social sense, as in the person standing alone. However, the person without emotional connection to others could not be long tolerated psychologically. Separation-individuation was *not* a basic developmental step in self psychology.

With this fundamental thesis of connection to others, Kohut went on to explain the kinds of connections—that is, the meanings of self-objects seen as mirroring, idealizing, and twinning. Essentially this filled out the why and wherefore of the self as constituted by others. He gave an added dimension to the concept of connection by describing just which connections accomplish cohesion and community.

HEIDEGGER AND CONNECTING

For Heidegger, Dasein is Being-in-the-world by way of action and participation. In the now-famous discussion of his use of a hammer, he spoke of its functional role as opposed to its standing alone as an object. The world is encountered and discovered in terms of the usability and/or handiness of things. So, too, are other persons seen essentially as giving meaning to one's situation in a given culture or society. Others are, for Heidegger, what they do (1927, p. 118). Thus there is a lessening of concern for the private subjective domain of the mind and an increase in emphasis on the web of relationships that the self or person has vis-à-vis others. Of course, one can conclude that Heidegger provides no place for the unconscious in this conceptualization; however, that need not be seen as indicating his opposition to the concept so much as his considering it temporarily irrelevant to the major point of the person as part of a network of relationships. Lifting a person out of his or her historical and cultural context made that person what Heidegger called "inauthentic."

KOHUT AND CONNECTING

Indeed, just as Heidegger did, Kohut saw others as connecting by virtue of their usefulness. Kohut's second fundamental thesis, one that is part and parcel of the selfobject concept, has to do with empathy as the vehicle that operates in connecting the self to its selfobjects. Selfobjects, by way of empathy, become a part of one's self and so give purpose and meaning to the self. Whereas Heidegger (1927, p. 117) downplayed empathy as a secondary phenomenon, he essentially stressed that empathy was only possible on the basis of our being with others.

What Kohut did was to flesh out the mechanism of this connection, the manner in which we feel ourselves into another person's life. Thus, Heidegger, in a simple quote, sounds much like Kohut when he says: "The relation of being to others becomes a projection of one's own being toward oneself into an other. . . . The other is a double of the self." In his discussion of the nature of the relationship with others Heidegger says, "The world of Dasein is a with-world. Being-in is being-with others" (p. 112). Ultimately, however, the implications of empathic connection with another become foundational for psychoanalytic inquiry; empathy becomes the vehicle that goes beyond the mere gathering of data to encompass the more basic relationship, that of understanding.

HEIDEGGER AND KOHUT AND UNDERSTANDING

It is in and around the concept of understanding that one may best see the common ground of these two thinkers. And, not surprisingly, it is here that we also gain a better conceptualization of misunderstanding. Heidegger felt that understanding was the essence of our being, a form of grounding ourselves in a feeling of kinship with others. For the philosopher, understanding is the sine qua non of life. Existence is maintained by the feeling of understanding or oneness with others, while misunderstanding creates disconnection.

As a psychoanalyst, Kohut felt that the work of analysis begins with understanding, which is achieved by way of an empathic connection; when one has managed to understand someone else, then a number of possibilities present themselves. A mutuality of connection now exists, and the feeling of being understood resonates with understanding another. Indeed this is the heart of a two-way empathy, as opposed to a one-way empathy that focuses on understanding someone else while oneself remaining opaque.

For Heidegger, understanding is the fundamental way of existing in a world in which Dasein is able to be open to the myriad of possibilities of being. He says that that is what "being" is all about—that is, to be freed for your own possibilities. Kohut says that understanding is what makes one feel whole, that is, connected with other selfobjects and so able to feel fulfilled. At this point it is important to distinguish what may appear to be two types of understanding. The first is associated with kinship or the feeling of being at one with others, something that Heidegger offered as the essence of life and that Kohut seemed to assign to an early stage of mirroring or twinship. The second or later employment of empathy occurs in its deployment as a data-gathering operation, in order to learn more about, to understand, and to become connected with another person. It is this latter step, one aimed at achieving understanding, that Heidegger prefers to call interpretation. It is, of course, not assigned quite the same meaning as it is for most psychoanalysts, yet it launches Heidegger on an extensive discussion of the nature of interpretation or hermeneutics and the hermeneutic circle. Kohut's ideas about interpretation, although in the same spirit as those of Heidegger, focus upon the role of interpretation in the treatment process and thus give it a much different emphasis. But once again, these two thinkers seem to be on a very similar road of inquiry.

HEIDEGGER AND KOHUT AND INTERPRETATION

Because understanding for Heidegger is the essence of Being-in-the-world, both its development and its relevance belong to the category of interpretation. Understanding is said to be realized in interpretation, meaning that it is *inherent* in interpretation. The constituents of this interpretive activity or hermeneutic activity are members of a threefold process and are called (1) fore-having, (2) fore-sight, and (3) fore-conception. This is the hermeneutic circle, which involves (1) a tentative knowing of what is to be uncovered or disclosed, followed by (2) an approach that makes things comprehensible, and then (3) a grounding in a definite conception. These are the steps of the circle, and this circle is the structure of meaning. Something becomes intelligible or has meaning when interpreted and understood.

Because for Kohut understanding has to do with the establishment and maintenance of empathic connections, the interpretive process occurs when there are breaks in the self-selfobjects union. These breaks follow the pattern familiar to most psychoanalysts in that they are representative of a particular transference configuration in the patient–therapist relationship. Of course, the act of interpretation does conform to the hermeneutic circle described above, inasmuch as the analyst does tentatively (1) know what is to be disclosed on the basis of his or her overall conceptualization of the unconscious, (2) sees the material that is uncovered or disclosed, and then (3) formulates it within a particular concept. For both Kohut and Heidegger, this sharing of understanding makes for a new way of judging oneself, resulting in a more cohesive self and a greater range of possibilities in which to "be" in the world.

IMPLICATIONS

The parallels and/or similarities of thought between Kohut and Heidegger are readily dismissed as interesting but not of much import unless these likenesses have some utility. A student of philosophy might wonder if some of the vagueness or murkiness of Heidegger's writing might be clarified with a substitution of language and/or an approach from a different direction. A psychoanalyst may see that Kohut's ideas are or are not an expansion of classical psychoanalysis and so may demand a more radical vision of these theoretical offerings. It may be worthwhile to examine a few more concepts to test these possibilities.

REPRESENTATIONS

The computer model of the mind is one in which the operation of a program upon certain symbols is considered to lead to more complex and different symbols. These symbols are spoken of as internal representations that stand in for the objects or persons in one's real or external life. This model is, once again, derived from Descartes, who claimed that one could stand aside and contemplate the world and so "represent" it to one's mind. Such a model necessitates a division into a "real" world of honest-to-goodness persons, places, and things, and an "inner" world of reproductions or copies that may be fantasied, or influenced or contaminated by fantasy. Heidegger asks that we dispense with this model inasmuch as the only world is the world that we experience; there need be no facsimile of it in an imaginary inner theater. We do not live in two worlds simultaneously (Sandler 1990, p. 878), since that view assumes that we could somehow tear ourselves away from our always being in *the* world. Heidegger (1927) says that, in this older model, perception is interpreted as "a process of returning with one's booty to the 'cabinet' of consciousness after one has gone out and grasped it" (p. 62). This describes an isolated subject with a hookup to the world at hand (p. 200). However, we are unable to drive a wedge between an "I" and the world to which it is related. Thus Heidegger goes on to say: "Self and world are not two entities, like 'subject' and 'object,' or 'I' and 'Thou,' rather self and world are the basic determinations of Dasein itself in the unity of the structure of Being-in-the-world . . . Dasein is its world in existing" (p. 364).

The concept of one's inextractability from the world also serves to differentiate Kohut's self psychology from classical analysis, with its complex internal world of self and object representations; from interpersonal psychology, with its picture of separate individuals relating to one another in the pursuit of changes to be internalized (Greenberg 1996, pp. 25–38); and from intersubjective theory, which posits a shared intersubjective field formed by two separate subjects (Stolorow and Atwood 1992). One can surely see how the effort to move away from Descartes and an internal world filled with representations may succeed by embracing social phenomena, but will thereby lose the essence of selfhood. There is but one person for Kohut and that is Dasein-with-others or the self and its selfobjects. There is no space in between.

INSIGHT AND AUTHENTICITY

The present state of psychoanalytic thinking, one that is something of a departure from Freudian theory, often involves a debate between knowing and experiencing, between insight and relating to others. Where Freud claimed, "Where id was, there shall ego be," he appeared to mean that the unconscious contents of the id would be made available by way of analysis to the conscious scrutiny of the ego. This would allow one to see and so to know what had previously been hidden. In contrast to this claim is one made by a host of others (Fonagy 1999), who state that it is the lived experience, which is placed in a category of procedures and procedural memory, has the true beneficial effect, and so need not have any particular knowledge attached to it.

Heidegger characterized two ways of living: the authentic and the inauthentic. The first is a matter of understanding oneself, of clearing away all of the concealments and obscurities that block one's access to a genuine comprehension of oneself, allowing one to have some idea of the truth of life. The second has to do with the everyday manner in which we live, with many of our motives concealed from us, and with no overview of the significance of the project of living. Heidegger thought that both ways were genuine, but considered that an authentic life is not mundane, inasmuch as it has a sense of its history and its possibilities. However, most of us live in an everyday, inauthentic way because the self-reflection that is demanded of the authentic life is often unpleasant and sometimes frightening.

Kohut spoke and wrote of a two-phase sequence of treatment that begins with understanding and then moves to explanation. The latter gives one a capacity to perceive oneself and to reflect on and construct a concept of the self in continuity in time and space. Some patients require long periods of understanding in order to tolerate explanation and some therapists (and patients) seem content to remain in the understanding phases. These therapists champion the emphasis on the experience of understanding by utilizing various theories, which range from the above-mentioned nonverbal procedural category to an invocation of the need for new relationships that need not be interpreted as products of the past (Shane et al. 1997).

In his reflections upon self-analysis, Kohut seemed to eschew self-reflection and even explanation. In this regard, he and Heidegger may have held similar views. Kohut insisted that a truly successful analysis would result in one's being connected with supportive selfobjects and thus able to live out a program of fulfillment *without* a need for self-scrutiny. It is only at points of disruption that a self-analytic exercise is necessary in order to overcome the misunderstanding. Ideally this would be a rare occurrence, the underlying assumption being that mental health is equivalent to feeling understood. Without the disjuncture caused by misunderstanding, there is no need to reflect on or analyze anything. Kohut does, in this special circumstance, seem to echo Heidegger, who says that authenticity is not so much knowledge as it is "living correctly"; and that word seems to connote a capacity to fulfill all of one's possibilities. Here one must recognize that the ideal states of "living correctly" and of being in the presence of optimal selfobject relations are more hopeful than probable.

TIME

One concept that was of great interest to Heidegger was the complex issue of time. Psychoanalysis has always considered the passage of time as being part of the study of development and, over the years, has described successive stages as a sequential way of presenting man's movement from primitive to mature. When Kohut spoke of the self, he emphasized its continuity in time and space, and he deemphasized the concept of epochs or stages. He underlined the fact that in one sense he was, at age 60, the same little boy that he was at age 4. This view was also in keeping with psychoanalytic theory in terms of the omnipresence of the past, but not in the form of preserved memory—rather in that of ongoing existence. Heidegger (1927) said that Dasein is its past (p. 17) and that Dasein occurs out of its future. For him we are an amalgam of our history, both our present and our future expectations, and we can never step out from them. Heidegger also said that we should not conceal our history from ourselves. Here the affinity with psychoanalysis is evident and warrants further consideration.

TWO VIEWS OF MAN: GUILTY AND TRAGIC

The dual perspective of man presented by Kohut was an alternative to the classical psychoanalytic view that described the psyche as the center of instinctual drives with all their accompanying prohibitions and inhibitions. The arena of conflict became the struggle over the expression and gratification of the drives, and the affective components of this struggle were anxiety and guilt. The pleasure gained by way of instinctual gratification was paid for by and resulted in the feeling of guilt. This view of man as being guilty about his desires, conscious or unconscious, is dominant in Freudian thought. Kohut's view of man is concerned with self-development and self-fulfillment rather than with drives being gratified. Thus, in contrast to guilty man or man struggling with desire, there is tragic man or man struggling to achieve worthwhile goals. Kohut never meant to claim that one should or could replace the other, or that one could choose between guilt and tragedy. Rather he suggested that some psychological issues could be better understood by one perspective than the other.

Although Heidegger did not use the word tragic, he clearly differentiated two forms of guilt: one that he called the "vulgar" interpretation of conscience, and one that he labeled the "existential." The vulgar, or ordinary, guilt is always specific and determinate, such as that which follows running a red light (Hoffman 1993, p. 211). Existential guilt is general and unconditional. According to Heidegger, one needs to see oneself as having a fate and a destiny as well as having heroes to model oneself after (Hoffman 1993, p. 213). There is an uncanny parallel here to Kohut's developmental line of the self, in that one cannot have a static picture either of Dasein or the self.

Some psychiatrists, such as Medard Boss and Ludwig Binswanger, were influenced by Heidegger and were called existential therapists. They openly rejected Freud's notion of guilt and claimed that it concealed the deeper phenomenon of "existential guilt." They elaborated the latter as man's failure to fulfill all of his possibilities (Guignon 1993, p. 222). The importance of personal fulfillment and the tragedy of being unable to achieve goals is, of course, a major concern of philosophers from Aristotle on. These existential psychiatrists thought that the nature of the psychological discomfort could differentiate guilty man from tragic man. It may be an error to claim the exclusive operation of one or the other, but it is worthwhile to contemplate that different states of dysphoria may result from *either* conflict over guilt or failure to achieve one's goals.

ALIENATION

Perhaps the best example of the common ground found between Heidegger and Kohut is seen in their focus upon and discussion of what psychoanalysts would call a feeling of estrangement or alienation. Heidegger said that the recognition of our own mortality makes us feel homeless and therefore always in search of others who offer a homecoming (Dallmayer 1993, pp. 149–180). He wrote about estrangement, nothingness, and the feeling of wandering and searching, all in a manner that can be elliptical and difficult to understand. Similarly, Kohut made alienation and empty depression the cornerstones of his psychopathology. Without others we feel disconnected and without purpose. Others, experienced as selfobjects, give us vitality and goals.

Interestingly both men were critical of technology, seeing it as fostering alienation. Heidegger insisted that while the use of technology was not harmful, the technological way of thinking was the problem. At issue was "the saving of man's essential nature" (Dreyfus 1993, p. 309). Kohut once described his waking from surgery surrounded by intravenous tubes and mechanical apparatus. He recounted his feeling of terror and despair at somehow feeling part of the machinery that literally gave him life; he could not tolerate the feeling of being isolated from other human beings *because* of the technology. Once again, what was fundamental to him was empathic connection. Unbridgeable isolation leads to emptiness and isolation.

CRITICS

There is intense controversy about the contributions of each of these men. Heidegger is roundly condemned as being either unreadable or incomprehensible because of his idiosyncratic use of language. Yet he is also said to be one of the greatest philosophers of the twentieth century (Guignon 1993). He does seem to elicit either dismissal by those who cannot understand him or else devotion by those who do. Kohut enjoys a similar bifurcation of response in that, although arguably less murky a writer than Heidegger, he is either easily brushed aside or else adored and idealized. Furthermore, Kohut is also routinely chastised for his betrayal of classical psychoanalysis as well as the gratifying and coddling of his patients. Behind the criticisms of these two men, there does seem to be that undercurrent or theme of betrayal. The source of this may be their own need to distance themselves from their predecessors. A possible rapprochement with these predecessors is then achieved when the angry reader settles on the claim of a lack of originality. It is interesting that both of these men who concerned themselves with estrangement and alienation seemed determined to distance themselves from other thinkers while simultaneously constructing a vision of the world that demanded active involvement with others. Perhaps this is the way of most creative efforts, but not all elicit such heat and antagonism as did the contributions of Kohut and Heidegger.

COMMON GROUND

It is tempting to explain the content of the theories of Heidegger and Kohut as products of their personal psychologies, but one runs the risk of diminishing their significance by so doing. Such a pursuit is of limited value since there is no doubt that scores of persons with similar backgrounds produce little of comparable worth. However, one can never fully escape the personalities of these complex men. What is interesting is the difference in their sources of data. Heinz Kohut insisted that he discovered his ideas by observing the transference and counter-transference phenomena in his patients. Ultimately he learned what he came to know by learning more about himself. Heidegger never made any such claim but returned over and over to the Greeks and to poetry. However, each man held in common the importance of a personal struggle against isolation, manifested for one in the concept of Being-in-the-world and for the other, the self-selfobjects relationship. They are clearly joined in the voice of the outsider who needs to find a place within the world but cannot seem to wholly succeed in doing so.

Another common thread that joins these two men and differentiates them from so many others is the missionary zeal that drove them. They had an absolutarian view of their positions. Their ideas were all-encompassing; perhaps necessary for mankind's salvation, and in need of wide dissemination. This zeal bordered on the religious and, indeed, many theologians have been taken by the work of both Kohut and Heidegger. So their ideas transcended their data, or, perhaps better put, allowed them entrance into new areas of scholarship.

CONCLUSION

For those of us raised in the tradition of linear thinking, of insisting on a scientific and objective scrutiny of the unknown, it is a wrenching experience to try on another kind of thought process. We prefer to think of ourselves as having a purity of vision and as being effectively insulated from the minds of others. Moving into contextual thinking robs us of our individuality. The embrace of neurophysiology is often seen as an antidote to the fuzzy subjectivity of psychology, a return to the safety of supposed objectivity. Heidegger is the philosopher who demonstrated to us that our presence is always in-the-world and urged us to forever forsake the subject–object dichotomy. Kohut is the psychologist who saw that we could see the person in depth rather than in the social sense, and that this person is always functionally connected to others. Together these two men offered a new vision of living in and with others, in and with the world. Separately they do not fare as well: Heidegger without Kohut has no psychological depth, and Kohut without Heidegger can never be emancipated from the dichotomy insisted upon in object relations theories. Kohut will continue to be misunderstood by those who insist that the self-selfobject relationship involves two persons, a truth only within a social view of persons. So my fantasied union is a justified one, inasmuch as these masters of connection clearly need each other for the mutual enrichment of their ideas. Each one is in the world, and each mirrors the other.

References

Akhtar, S. (1999). Distinguishing needs from wishes. *Journal of the American Psychoanalytic Association* 47:113–151.

Alexander, F. (1940). Psychoanalysis revised. In *The Scope of Psychoanalysis*, pp. 137–164. New York: Basic Books, 1964.

Anderson, M. K. (1999). The pressure toward enactment and the hatred of reality. *Journal of the American Psychoanalytic Association* 47:503–518.

Aron, L. (1996). *A Meeting of Minds: Mutuality in Psychoanalysis*. Hillsdale, NJ: Analytic Press.

Bacal, H. (1985). Optimal responsiveness and the therapeutic process. In *Progress in Self Psychology*, Vol. 1, ed. A. Goldberg, pp. 202–227. Hillsdale, NJ: Analytic Press.

Baker, R. (2000). Finding the neutral position. *Journal of the American Psychoanalytic Association* 48:129–153.

Basch, M. F. (1973). Psychoanalysis and theory formation. *The Annual of Psychoanalysis* 1:39–52.

Bibring, E. (1954). Psychoanalysis and the dynamic psychotherapies. *Journal of the American Psychoanalytic Association* 2:745–770.

Bion, W. P. (1990). *Brazilian Lectures*. London: Karnac.

Bouveresse, J. (1995). *Wittgenstein Reads Freud: The Myth of the Unconscious. New Fresh Thought*. Princeton, NJ: Princeton University Press.

Bowlby, J. (1988). *A Secure Base: Clinical Applications of Attachment Theory*. London: Routledge.

Cavell, M. (1998). Triangulation: one's own mind, and objectivity. *International Journal of Psychoanalysis* 79:449–468.

Chalmers, P. J. (1996). *The Conscious Mind*. New York: Oxford University Press.

Changeux, J.-P., and Ricoeur, P. (2000). *What Makes Us Think?* Princeton, NJ: Princeton University Press.

Churchland, P. S. (1986). *Neurophilosophy*. Cambridge, MA: MIT Press.

Chused, J. (1991). The evocative power of enactments. *Journal of the American Psychoanalytic Association* 39:615–640.

Cilliers, P. (1998). *Complexity and Postmodernism*. London and New York: Routledge.

Cioffi, F. (1998). *Freud and the Question of Pseudo-Science*. Chicago: Open Court.

Crews, F. (1995). Unauthorized Freud: doubters confront a legend. *New York Review of Books*.

Cummins, R. (1989). *Meaning and Mental Representation*. Cambridge, MA, and London: MIT Press.

Dallmayer, F. (1993). *The Other Heidegger*. Ithaca, NY: Cornell University Press.

Davidson, D. (1980a). *Essays on Actions, Reasons, and Causes*. Oxford, UK: Oxford University Press.

——— (1980b). *Inquiries into Truth & Interpretation*. Oxford, UK: Oxford University Press.

Dennett, D. (1987). *The Intentional Stance*. Cambridge, MA: MIT Press.

Depue, R. A., and Collins, P. T. (1999). Neurobiology of the structure of personality: dopamine, facilitation of incentive motivation and extroversion. *Behavioral and Brain Science* 22:491–569.

deSaussure, F. (1916). *Course in General Linguistics*, trans. W. Baker. New York: McGraw-Hill, 1959.

Descartes, R. (1993). *Discourse on Method and Mediations on First Philosophy*, 3rd ed., trans. D. A. Cress. Indianapolis, IN: Hackett.

Dillon, M. C. (1997). *Merleau-Ponty's Ontology*, 2nd ed. Evanston, IL: Northwestern University Press.

Dreyfus, H. L. (1989). Alternative philosophical conceptualizations of psychopathology. In *Phenomenology and Beyond: The Self and Its Language*, ed. H. A. Durfee and D. F. Rodier, pp. 1–182. Boston: Klewer Academic Publishers.

———— (1993). Heidegger on the connection between nihilism, art, technology, and politics. In *The Cambridge Companion to Heidegger*, pp. 289–316. Cambridge, UK: Cambridge University Press.

Edelman, G. M. (1992). *Bright Air, Brilliant Fire: On the Matter of Mind*. New York: Basic Books.

Fisher, P. (1999). *Wonder, the Rainbow, and the Aesthetics of Rare Experience*. Cambridge, MA: Harvard University Press.

Flanagan, O. (2000). *Dreaming Soul*. Oxford, UK: Oxford University Press.

Fonagy, P. (1999). Memory and therapeutic action. *International Journal of Psychoanalysis* 80:215–223, 614–616.

———— (2000). The mechanism of action of psychoanalysis: panel report. *Journal of the American Psychoanalytic Association* 48:919–927.

Frank, K. (1999). *Psychoanalytic Participation: Action, Interaction and Integration*. Hillsdale, NJ: Analytic Press.

Freeman, W. J., and Skorda, C. A. (1990). Representations: Who needs them? In *Brain Organization and Memory Cells, Systems, and Circuits*, ed. J. L. McGaugh, J. L. Weinberger, and G. Lynch. New York: Guilford.

Freud, S. (1905). Fragments from the analysis of a case of hysteria. *Standard Edition* 7:3–122.

———— (1909). Notes upon a case of obsessional neuroses: some obsessional ideas and their explanation. *Standard Edition* 10:151–318.

———— (1910). "Wild" psychoanalysis. *Standard Edition* 11:221–227.

———— (1912). Recommendations to physicians practicing psychoanalysis. *Standard Edition* 12:109–120.

———— (1915). The unconscious. *Standard Edition* 14:206–207.

———— (1918). From the history of an infantile neurosis. *Standard Edition* 17:3–127.

———— (1925). Negation. *Standard Edition* 19:235–239.

Gadamer, H.-G. (1962). *On the Problem of Self-Understanding in Philosophical Hermeneutics*, ed. D. E. Linzi. Berkeley: University of California Press.

———— (1989). *Truth and Method*, 2nd rev. ed., trans. J. Weinsheimer and D. Marshall. New York: Crossroad.

———— (1994). *Heidegger's Ways*, trans. J. W. Stanley. Albany, NY: State University of New York Press.

Gardner, S. (1999). Psychoanalytic explanation. In *A Companion to the Philosophy of Mind*, ed. S. Guttenplen. Oxford, UK: Blackwell.

Gazzaniga, M. S. (1998). *The Mind's Past*. Berkeley: University of California Press.

Gedo, J. (1997). Reflections on metapsychology, theoretical coherence, hermeneutics and biology. *Journal of the American Psychoanalytic Association* 45:779–806.

Giddens, A. (1976). *New Rules of Sociological Method*. New York: Basic Books.

Gill, M. (1979). The analysis of transference. *Journal of the American Psychoanalytic Association* 27 (Supplement):263–288.

———— (1996). Discussion: Interaction III in interaction. *Psychoanalytic Inquiry*, vol. 16. Hillsdale NJ: Analytic Press.

Glenn, J. (1980). Notes on psychoanalytic concept and style in Freud's case histories. In *Freud and His Patients*, ed. M. Kanzer and J. Glenn. New York: Jason Aronson.

Globus, G. (1995). *The Postmodern Brain*. Amsterdam and Philadelphia: John Benjamin.

Glover, L. (1988). A study of intrapsychic structure and processes in three groups of patients: one schizophrenic, one borderline and one neurotic. In *Borderline and Narcissistic Patients in Therapy*, ed. N. Slavinsky-Holy, p. 174. Madison, CT: International Universities Press.

Goldberg, A. (1996). It is all interaction. *Psychoanalytic Inquiry* 16:96–106.

———— (1999). *Being of Two Minds*. Hillsdale, NJ: Analytic Press.

———— (2001). *Errant Selves*. Hillsdale, NJ: Analytic Press.

Greenberg, J. (1996). Psychoanalytic intervention. *Psychoanalytic Inquiry* 10:25–51.

Grossman, L. (1966). Psychic reality and reality testing in the analysis of perverse defenses. *International Journal of Psychoanalysis* 77:509–517.

Grossman, W. J., and Simon, B. (1969). Anthropomorphism: motive, meaning, and causality in psychoanalytic theory. *Psychoanalytic Study of the Child* 24:78–111. New York: International Universities Press.

Grünbaum, A. (1984). *The Foundations of Psychoanalysis.* Berkeley: University of California Press.

Guignon, C. (1983). *Heidegger and the Problem of Knowledge.* Indianapolis, IN: Hackett.

——— (1993). Authenticity, moral values, and psychotherapy. In *The Cambridge Companion to Heidegger*, ed. C. Guignon, pp. 215–239. Cambridge, UK: Cambridge University Press.

Habermas, J. (1971). *Knowledge and Human Interest.* Boston: Beacon.

Hanig, M. R., and Stark, H. E. (2001). Epistemic unification. *Journal of Mind and Behavior* 23(1):1–22.

Hartmann, H. (1927). Understanding and explanation. In *Essays on Ego Psychology*, pp. 364–403. New York: International Universities Press, 1953.

——— (1950). Comments on the psychoanalytic theory of the ego. *Psychoanalytic Study of the Child* 5:74–96. New York: International Universities Press.

——— (1953). *Essays on Ego Psychology.* New York: International Universities Press.

Haugeland, J. (1985). *Having Thought: Essays in the Metaphysics of Mind.* Cambridge, MA, and London: Harvard University Press.

Heidegger, M. (1927). *Being and Time*, trans. J. Stambaugh. Albany, NY: State University of New York Press, 1946.

Hesse, M. (1980). *Revolution and Reconstructs in the Philosophy of Science.* Brighton, UK: Harvester.

Hoffman, I. Z. (1983). The patient as interpreter of the analyst's experience. *Journal of the American Psychoanalytic Association* 19:389–428.

Hoffman, P. (1993). Death, time, history: Division II of *Being and Time*. In *The Cambridge Companion to Heidegger*, ed. Charles Guignon. Cambridge, UK: Cambridge University Press, 195–214.

Holmquist, R., Hansjons-Gustafson, U., and Gustafson, J. (2002). Patients' relationship episodes and therapists' feelings. *Psychology and Psychotherapy. Theory, Research, and Practice* 75(4):393–409.

Hoy, D. (1993). Heidegger and the hermeneutic way. In *The Cambridge*

Companion to Heidegger, ed. C. Guigon, pp. 176–194. Cambridge, UK: Cambridge University Press.

Hurley, S. L. (1998). *Consciousness in Action*. Cambridge, MA: Harvard University Press.

Jacob, T. (1986). On countertransference enactments. *Journal of the American Psychoanalytic Association* 34:289–308.

Jacobson, E. (1964). *The Self and the Object World*. New York: International Universities Press.

Jones, E. (1959). *Hamlet and Oedipus*. New York: Norton.

Joseph, B. (1985). Transference: the total situation. *International Journal of Psychoanalysis* 66:447–454.

Kant, I. (1965). *Critique of Pure Reason*, trans. N. K. Smith. New York: St. Martin's Press.

Keller, J. (1999). Untitled article. *Chicago Tribune*. December 28, p. 18.

Kernberg, P. (1989). Narcissistic personality disorders in childhood. In *Narcissistic Personality Disorders*, ed. O. Kernberg and W. J. Saunders. Philadelphia: Harcourt Brace Jovanovich.

Kohut, H. (1971). *The Analysis of the Self*. New York: International Universities Press.

——— (1984). *How Does Analysis Cure?*, ed. A. Goldberg. Chicago: University of Chicago Press.

Laplanche, J., and Pontalis, J.-B. (1973). *The Language of Psychoanalysis*. London: Hogarth.

Lear, J. (1998). *Open-Minded: Working Out the Logic of the Soul*. Cambridge, MA: Harvard University Press.

Lenzinger-Bohleber, M., and Pfeifer, R. (2002). Remembering a depressive primary object. *International Journal of Psychoanalysis* 83:3–34.

Linnell, Z. M. (1990). What is mental representation? A study of its elements and how they lead to language. *Journal of the American Psychoanalytic Association* 38:131–166.

Lyotard, J.-F. (1984). *The Postmodern Condition: A Report on Knowledge, Theory, and History of Literature*, vol. 10. Minneapolis, MN: University of Minnesota Press.

Matusov, E. (1998). When solo activity is not privileged: participant internalization models of development. *Human Development* 41(5–6):326–346.

McDowell, J. (1994). Aristotle's Necomachean ethics. In *Mind and World*, p. 83. Cambridge, MA: Harvard University Press.

McIntosh, D. (1993). Cathexes and their objects in the thought of Sigmund Freud. *Journal of the American Psychoanalytic Association* 41(3):679–711.

McLaughlin, J. (1991). Clinical and theoretical aspects of enactment. *Journal of the American Psychoanalytic Association* 39:595–614.

Meissner, W. W. (2000). Reflections on psychic reality. *International Journal of Psychoanalysis* 81:1117–1138.

Michels, R. (1995). Psychoanalysis as science. Commentary. *Journal of the American Psychoanalytic Association* 43:963–1023.

Miller, R. W. (1987). *Fact and Method: Explanations, Confirmation, and Reality in the Natural and the Social Sciences*. Princeton, NJ: Princeton University Press.

Mitchell, S. A. (1988). *Relational Concepts in Psychoanalysis: An Integration*. Cambridge, MA: Harvard University Press.

Moore, B., and Fine, B. (1990). *Psychoanalytic Terms and Concepts*. Washington, DC: American Psychoanalytic Association.

Munz, P. (1985). *Our Knowledge of the Growth of Knowledge*. London: Routledge & Kegan Paul.

——— (1999). *Critique of Impure Reason*. New York: Praeger.

Ogden, T. H. (1997). Analyzing forms of aliveness and deadness. In *Reverie and Interpretation: Sensing Something Human*, pp. 21–63. Northvale, NJ: Jason Aronson.

Okrent, M. (1988). *Heidegger's Pragmatism*. Ithaca, NY: Cornell University Press.

Opatow, B. (1999). On the scientific standing of psychoanalysis. *Journal of the American Psychoanalytic Association* 47:1107–1124.

O'Regan, J., and Noe, A. (2001). A sensorimotor account of vision and visual consciousness. *Behavioral and Brain Sciences* 24:939–1031.

Ornstein, P. (1993). Did Freud understand Dora? In *Freud's Case Studies: Self Psychological Perspectives*, ed. B. Magid. Hillsdale, NJ: Analytic Press.

Pessen, A., and Goldberg, S. (1999). *The Twin Earth Chronicles*. Armonk, NY, and London: M. E. Sharpe.

Plato (1892). Meno. In *The Dialogues of Plato*, trans. B. Jowett. New York: Random House.

Preston, S., and deWaal, F. (2002). Empathy: its ultimate and proximate bases. *Behavioral and Brain Sciences* 25(1):1–71.

Putnam, H. (1987). *The Many Faces of Realism.* La Salle, IL: Open Court.

Quartz, S., and Synowski, T. (2000). Constraining construction. *Brain and Behavioral Sciences* 23.

Raine, A., Lencz, T., and Behrle, S. (2000). Reduced prefrontal gray matter and reduced autonomic activity in antisocial personality disorder. *Archives of General Psychiatry* February:119–127.

Reed, G. (1994). *Transference Neurosis and Psychoanalytic Experience Perspectives on Contemporary Clinical Practice.* New Haven, CT: Yale University Press.

Reiser, M. F. (1999). Memory, empathy, interaction. *Journal of the American Psychoanalytic Association* 47:485–501.

Ricoeur, P. (1991). *On Paul Ricoeur: Narrative and Interpretation,* ed. D. Wood. New York and London: Routledge.

——— (1992). *Oneself as Another.* Chicago: University of Chicago Press.

Rinsley, D. B. (1989). Notes on the developmental pathogenesis of narcissistic personality disorders. In *Narcissistic Personality Disorders,* ed. O. Kernberg and W. J. Saunders. Philadelphia: Harcourt Brace Jovanovich.

Robbins, F., and Schlessinger, N. (1983). *Developmental View of the Psychoanalytic Process: Follow-up Studies and Their Consequences.* New York: International Universities Press.

Roth, M. S. (1998). *Freud, Conflict and Culture.* New York: Knopf.

Roth, P. (1997). *American Pastoral.* New York: Random House.

Rychlak, J. (1997). *In Defense of Human Consciousness.* Washington, DC: American Psychological Association.

Sachdev, P. (1999). Is reduction of mental phenomena an attainable goal? *Journal of Neuropsychiatry, Clinical Neuroscience* 11:274–279.

Safranski, R. (1998). *Martin Heidegger: Between Good and Evil,* trans. E. Osers. Cambridge, MA: Harvard University Press.

Saks, E. R. (1999). *Interpreting Interpretation: The Limits of Hermeneutic Psychoanalysis.* New Haven, CT: Yale University Press.

Sandler, J. (1990). On internal object relations. *Journal of the American Psychoanalytic Association* 58:859–880.

——— (1993). On communication from patient to analyst: not everything is projective identification. *International Journal of Psychoanalysis* 74:1097–1108.

———— (1996). Comments on the psychodynamics of interaction. *Psychoanalytic Inquiry* No. 16. Hillsdale NJ: Analytic Press.

Sandler, J., and Rosenblatt, D. (1962). The concept of the representational world. *Psychoanalytic Study of the Child* 17:128–148. New York: International Universities Press.

Sandler, J., and Sandler, A.-M. (1998). *Internal Objects Revisited*. Madison, CT: International Universities Press.

Schachter, J. (2002). *Transference: Shibboleth or Albatross*. Hillsdale, NJ: Analytic Press.

Schafer, R. (1992). *Retelling a Life: Narration and Dialogue in Psychoanalysis*. New York: Basic Books.

Searle, J. R. (1992). *The Rediscovery of the Mind*. Cambridge, MA: MIT Press.

Shane, M., Shane, E., and Gales, M. (1997). *Intimate Attachments: Toward a New Self Psychology*. New York: Guilford.

Shevrin, H. (1995). Psychoanalysis as science. *Journal of the American Psychoanalytic Association* 43:1023–1026.

Smolensky, P. (1988). On the proper treatment of connectionism. *Behavior and Brain Sciences* 11:1–23.

Stern, D. (1997). *Unformulated Experience. From Dissociation to Imagination*. Hillsdale: NJ: Analytic Press.

Stern, D., et al. (1998). Non-interpretive mechanisms in psychoanalytic therapy: the "something more" than interpretation. *International Journal of Psychoanalysis* 79:903–921.

Stern, J. (1990). Unpublished manuscript.

Steward, H. (1997). The ontology of mind. *Oxford Philosophical Monographs*. New York and Oxford, UK: Oxford University Press.

Stich, S. (1983). *From Folk Psychology to Cognitive Science: The Case Against Relief*. Cambridge, MA: MIT Press.

Stolorow, R., and Atwood, G. (1992). *Contexts of Being: The Intersubjective Foundations of Psychoanalytic Life*. Hillsdale, NJ: Analytic Press.

Stroll, A. (2000). *Twentieth-Century Analytic Philosophy*. New York: Columbia University Press.

Strozier, C. (2004). *Heinz Kohut: The Making of a Psychoanalyst*. New York: Other Press.

Sulloway, F. J. (1979). *Freud: Biologist of the Mind*. New York: Basic Books.

Target, M. (1998). The recovered memories controversy. Book review essay. *International Journal of Psychoanalysis* 79:1015–1028.

Taylor, C. (1989). *Sources of the Self: The Making of the Modern Identity*. Cambridge, MA: Harvard University Press.

Travis, C. (2000). *Unshadowed Thought Representation in Thought and Language*. Cambridge, MA: Harvard University Press.

Tulving, E. (1983). Elements of episodic memory. *Oxford Psychology Series No. 2*. New York: Oxford University Press.

Uttal, W. R. (1998). *Toward a New Behaviorism: The Case Against Perceptual Reductionism*. Mahwah, NJ, and London: Lawrence Erlbaum.

Van Gelder, T. (1998). The dynamical hypothesis in cognitive science. *Behavioral and Brain Science* 21:615–665.

Viderman, M. (1994). Uses of the past and the family romance. *Journal of the American Psychoanalytic Association* 42:469–489.

——— (1995). The reconstruction of a repressed sexual molestation fifty years later. *Journal of the American Psychoanalytic Association* 43(4):1169–1195.

Wittgenstein, L. (1963). *Philosophical Investigations*, trans. G. E. M. Anscombe. Oxford, UK: Basil Blackwell.

——— (1978). *Culture and Value*, ed. G. H. von Wright, trans. P. Winch. Oxford, UK: Basil Blackwell.

——— (1982). *Last Writings in the Philosophy of Psychology*, Vol. 1. Chicago: Chicago University Press.

Index

Action. *See also* enactment(s)
  as prelude to knowing, 111, 188
Affirmation. *See* understanding
Aggression, case material on, 96.
  See also cases, Bernard
Akhtar, S., 111, 164, 188
Alexander, F., 174
Alienation and estrangement, 210–212
Analyst(s)
  acting like an, 122–124
  authoritarian, 100
  being an, 124–125
  compliance *vs.* refusal of patient's demands, 137–141

death of, 128
impact on patient and analytic relationship, 12
position of, 98–101
rationalizations for retention of position of power, 138–139
role of and patient's need for, 32–33
and the rules of technique, 166–167
thinking like an, 120–122
Analytic relationship, 180–181
Anderson, M., 72, 76
Anthropomorphism, 14–15, 19
Antisocial personality disorder, neurological deficits in, 65